The Conference of the Tongues

Theo Hermans

St. Jerome Publishing
Manchester, UK & Kinderhook (NY), USA

Published by
St. Jerome Publishing
2 Maple Road West, Brooklands
Manchester, M23 9HH, United Kingdom
Telephone +44 (0)161 973 9856
Fax +44 (0)161 905 3498
stjerome@compuserve.com
http://www.stjerome.co.uk

InTrans Publications
P. O. Box 467
Kinderhook, NY 12106, USA
Telephone (518) 758-1755
Fax (518) 758-6702

ISBN (pbk) 978-1905763-05-4
© Theo Hermans 2007

Printed and bound in Great Britain by
T. J. Internatinal Ltd, Cornwall, UK

Typeset by
Delta Typesetters, Cairo, Egypt
Email: hilali1945@yahoo.co.uk

British Library Cataloguing in Publication Data
A catalogue record of this book is available from the British Library

Library of Congress Cataloging-in-Publication Data
Hermans, Theo.
  The conference of the tongues / Theo Hermans.
     p. cm.
  Includes bibliographical references and index.
  ISBN 978-1-905763-05-4 (pbk. : alk. paper)
1. Translating and interpreting. 2. Intertextuality. I. Title.

P306.H43 2007
418'.02--dc22

                              2007024329

The Conference of the Tongues

THEO HERMANS

The Conference of the Tongues offers a series of startling reflections on fundamental questions of translation. It throws new light on familiar problems and opens up some radically different avenues of thought. It engages with value conflicts in translation and the social accountability of translators, and turns the old issue of equivalence inside out. Drawing on a wealth of contemporary and historical examples, the book teases out the translator's subject-position in translations, makes notions of intertextuality and irony serviceable for translation studies, tries to think translation without calling on the idea of transformation, and uses a controversial sociological model to cast a cold eye on the entire world of translating.

This is a highly interdisciplinary study that remains aware of the importance of theoretical paradigms as it brings concepts from international law, social systems theory and even theology to bear on translation. Self-reference is a recurrent theme. The book invites us to read translations for what they can tell us about translating and about translators' own perceptions of their role. The argument throughout is for more self-reflexive translation studies.

Theo Hermans is Professor of Dutch and Comparative Literature and Director of the Centre for Intercultural Studies at University College London. A founding member of the Translation Research Summer School and the International Association for Translation and Intercultural Studies, he also edits the series Translation Theories Explored for St Jerome Publishing. He is the author of several books, including *Translation in Systems* and *The Structure of Modernist Poetry*, and editor of *Translating Others*, *Crosscultural Transgressions* and *The Manipulation of Literature*.

Contents

Preface

This is a book of translation theory. It has a double focus. It seeks to gain insight into translation by exploiting slightly unusual perspectives based on such things as the concept of authentication, the doctrine of the Real Presence and social systems theory. It also tries to tease out the way in which translators position themselves in their work and translations can be read as speaking about themselves.

Chapter One reads equivalence as equality in status and concludes that translations can never be equivalent to their originals. This is a good thing, because it creates room for translation to reflect on itself, which is the topic of Chapter Two. A practical consequence of the translator occupying a subject position in a translation is explored in Chapter Three, which offers a model to analyse translators' attitudes to what they translate. Chapters Four and Five are more exploratory. One sketches an approach to translation that does not invoke the notion of transformation. The other proposes a sociology of translation based on Niklas Luhmann's social systems theory, which would deny translators a place in the translation system. The final chapter engages with the cross-cultural study of translation and argues that the discipline needs to be thick to do the job well.

Very few of the ideas in this book are my own. Most have emerged, in one form or another, from reading, listening and talking, or even in the course of writing. All were initially aired in the form of lectures, seminars or papers delivered in a variety of locations and to different constituencies. I am grateful to all the audiences who endured half-baked expositions and helped to improve them with their critical responses. I want to thank in particular Martha Cheung, Alexandra Lianeri, Ubaldo Stecconi, Harish Trivedi and Maria Tymoczko for some inspiring conversations, and Robert Hodgson for checking the theology of Chapter Four.

The title of the book derives from the sixteenth-century scholar Pedro Simón Abril, who suggested, in the preface to a Latin and Spanish translation of Aesop's fables, that learning a foreign language consisted less in piling up precepts than in 'the conference of the tongues' (*la conferencia de las lenguas*) and imitation of good practice. At the time, *lengua* also meant 'interpreter'.

Earlier versions of several chapters appeared in journals and conference proceedings. All have been reworked for the present book.

Acknowledgements

Thanks for permissions are due to the following:

UCL Library's Special Collections, for permission to use the illustration from John Gould, *A Monograph of the Ramphastidae: or Family of Toucans* (London: Published by the author, 1834) for the book's cover;

Statens Museum for Kunst in Copenhagen, for permission to reproduce the *Board Partition with a Still Life of Two Dead Birds Hanging on a Wall* and *The Reverse of a Framed Painting* by Cornelius Gijsbrechts;

Soprintendenza per il Patrimonio Storico Artistico ed Etnoantropologico delle Marche at the Palazzo Ducale, Urbino, for permission to reproduce Paolo Uccello's *La Profanazione dell'Ostia*;

The Random House Group Ltd, for permission to reproduce the map from the 1939 American translation of Adolf Hitler's *Mein Kampf*;

Bayerisches Staatsministerium der Finanzen, Munich, for permission to reproduce the cover of Adolf Hitler's *Mein Kampf* of 1925-6 and its Dutch translation of 1939.

1. The End

Let us begin with a series of remarkable events. They unfolded in a place called Palmyra, in a far corner of New York State, just south of Lake Ontario. There, on the evening of 21 September 1823, a quiet Sunday, a young man named Joseph Smith, a farmhand then aged just eighteen, received an unexpected visitor. Joseph Smith had never met this person before. The stranger, a tall, bearded man, wore a long white robe, and his presence filled the room with light. Looking more closely, Joseph noticed that the visitor's bare feet floated approximately twelve inches above the ground. Joseph had experienced the occasional vision before, but he had never seen this. The visitor was an angel. Speaking the universal angelic tongue, the angel introduced himself in English as Moroni and engaged the young farmhand in conversation. He informed him of the existence of an ancient book written on gold plates, and of 'seers' prepared by God for its translation. The book, he declared, contained "the fullness of the everlasting Gospel" and "an account of the former inhabitants of this continent" (Hill 1977: 57). On departing, Moroni assured his host that he would return in due course to direct him to the gold plates, which he said were buried in a nearby hill.

Moroni paid Joseph Smith several more visits in the next few years, each time bringing the same message. Then one day he announced the time had come. In the early morning of 22 September 1827, following the angel's directions, Joseph Smith dug up and carted home a pile of gold plates that had been stowed in a stone box in a hill called Cumorah (in Manchester, New York). The plates were made of thin gold leaf and could be rifled like the pages of a book. They were later estimated to have weighed around sixty pounds. They were embossed with text in a hitherto unknown script which bore a passing resemblance to both Hebrew signs and Egyptian hieroglyphs. At this time, the late 1820s, Egyptian hieroglyphs had not yet been properly deciphered. In France, Jean-François Champollion, the founding father of Egyptology, had made his first breakthrough in 1824 working on the recently discovered Rosetta Stone. He was appointed professor of Egyptology at the Collège de France in Paris in 1826 and would spend the rest of his short life (he died in 1832, aged forty-one) compiling his great Egyptian grammar and dictionary.

Joseph Smith was luckier. As the angel had predicted, he found two stones buried together with the gold plates. They were small, transparent, three-cornered diamond-like stone disks mounted in loops of metal wire. These were the 'seer stones' or 'interpreters' Moroni had spoken of and even given names, Urim and Thummim, terms which also occur several times in the Old Testament

(Exodus 28, 30; Deuteronomy 33, 8; Ezra 2, 63 and another four places). By placing the transparent stone disks on his nose like a pair of glasses (or, as some accounts have it, under his hat), Smith would be able, to his own amazement, to read the script on the gold plates, and therefore to translate it.

Having brought the plates home, Smith kept them hidden, as Moroni had instructed him to do. He began to translate late in December 1827. Speaking from behind a screen to shield the plates from his companions' gaze, he initially dictated to his wife Emma, then to two friends and followers, Martin Harris and Oliver Cowdery. Some time in the spring of 1828 Harris took 116 translated pages away to show his sceptical family, who promptly lost or possibly destroyed them. The angel severely rebuked Smith and instructed him not to retranslate the lost pages.

Two years later the translation of the book, a weighty tome, was ready. By then Joseph Smith had gathered round him a number of disciples. In June 1829 the most faithful among them witnessed two more apparitions of the angel Moroni, during which they were allowed to see and touch the gold plates for the first and last time. Afterwards all signed statements confirming what they had witnessed. They also confirmed that during Moroni's visitation a voice descended from heaven assuring them that the book was true and the translation accurate (Brodie 1945: 77-9; Bushman 1984: 107; Hill 1977: 91-2). The volume appeared in print in Palmyra in March 1830. The title page mentioned Joseph Smith as "Author and Proprietor", but this was probably for copyright reasons; the designation was later changed to "Translator". Smith's loyal friend and disciple Martin Harris first mortgaged and then sold his farm to cover the costs of printing five thousand copies.

Together with the Christian Bible the book became the foundational text of the Church of Jesus Christ of Latter-Day Saints, also known as the Mormon Church after the *Book of Mormon* as translated into English by Joseph Smith. Mormon, the main prophet whose life and work is chronicled in the *Book of Mormon*, was also the father of Moroni, who appeared to Smith in the guise of an angel. The Mormon Church grew rapidly in the 1830s, despite hostility from local people. Joseph Smith was murdered in Carthage, Illinois, in June 1844. Some years later his successor, Brigham Young, led the growing Mormon community to Salt Lake City, Utah. Today the Church of Jesus Christ of Latter-Day Saints, with its headquarters still in Salt Lake City, numbers approximately twelve million worldwide and runs a vast business empire as well as the world's largest genealogical archive. The *Book of Mormon* is available online for all to read.[1]

---

[1] http://scriptures.lds.org/bm/contents

Words from above

The Museum of Mormon Church History in Salt Lake City has a manuscript page from Joseph Smith's English version of the *Book of Mormon* on permanent display. I have seen this page. It is written in a rather elegant longhand and, remarkably for a translation, shows not a single deletion or correction. As I pored over this unusual artefact and wondered about its pristine state, a helpful museum attendant came up to me ("Are you interested, sir?") and explained that Smith dictated his translation virtually without hesitation, guided as he was by "the gift and the power of God", as indeed the title page of the *Book of Mormon* has it, and also by Urim and Thummim, the two 'seer' or 'interpreter' stones which enabled him to read, understand and render into fluent English the otherwise incomprehensible signs on the gold plates.

The fate of the gold plates is also of interest. It is directly connected with the pronouncement that determined the status of Joseph Smith's translation. During the two final visitations of the angel Moroni in 1829, when Smith's earliest disciples were granted sight of the gold plates, a voice from on high announced that the book was true and the translation accurate. In the words of one witness, David Whitmer: "While we were viewing [the plates] the voice of God spoke out of heaven saying that the Book was true and the translation correct" (Hill 1977: 91). The divine utterance authorised the translation to serve in place of the original. This is what subsequently happened. At the end of the session the angel Moroni took the plates under his wing and vanished with them. They have not been seen since. However, their disappearance need not worry us. We know that we possess a wholly adequate translation, equivalent to the original. As a result, we no longer need recourse to the original. The translation has replaced it, totally.

The heavenly pronouncement only confirmed what the miraculous nature of the translation's creation already intimated. A version helped along by "the gift and the power of God" must be correct. In this respect the story of the *Book of Mormon* shows similarities with that other remarkable tale, that of the origin of the Septuagint.

The Septuagint is the Greek version of the Hebrew Old Testament produced in the third century BCE on the orders of the Egyptian king Ptolemy Philadelphus for the Greek-speaking Jewish community in Alexandria. Accounts of the creation of the Septuagint differ to some extent. They agree that seventy-two translators completed the task of translating the Jewish Bible in seventy-two days. According to the oldest account, the so-called 'Letter of Aristeas' (probably written around 130 or 100 BCE), the translators took great care to compare notes and consult among themselves as they composed their

Greek text. When the version was complete and found to be accurate in every respect, it was ordained that no-one should presume to alter it in any way. Indeed the king, upon being presented with the scrolls, recalled that several individuals who had earlier translated parts of the Holy Book too rashly, had been punished by God with bodily afflictions.

According to the most influential account of the Septuagint, that recorded by Philo of Alexandria (also known as Philo Judaeus) around the beginning of the Christian era, the translators worked independently of each other, in separate cells. After seventy-two days they emerged with identical Greek texts (Schwarz 1955: 17-44). This astonishing feat, seventy-two identical translations of a long and complex original, could only be explained as the product of divine inspiration. God's spirit had presided over the interpreters and breathed the one correct rendering into each translator's ear. Philo is emphatic that under divine guidance the translators "arrived at a wording which corresponded with the matter [of the original], and alone, or better than any other, would bring out clearly what was meant" (Schwarz 1955: 23).

Saint Augustine, like most of the early Christian theologians except Jerome, appears to have accepted the supernatural origin of the Septuagint. In *On Christian Doctrine* (*De doctrina Christiana*, probably written *ca.* 416-19 CE) he still allowed for the possibility that the translators consulted among themselves, but his major work, *The City of God* (*De civitate Dei*, written 410-28), favoured the more miraculous account. Here Augustine argued that "in truth there was the one Spirit at work in them all" and that "the same one Spirit was manifestly present in the scholars when without collaboration they still translated the whole in every detail as if with one mouth (1972: 820, 822). He also perceived a reason for this divine intervention: "this was the purpose of their receiving such a marvellous gift of God; that in this way the authority of those Scriptures should be emphasized, as being not human but divine" (*ibid.*). As a result, the Septuagint translators were freed of "the servile labour of a human bond-servant of words" (Augustine 1972: 821; Schwarz 1955: 41).

The accounts of the creation of the Septuagint and the *Book of Mormon* oblige us to assume that in each case the relation between translation and original is one of full equivalence. In each of these texts the translator and the originary speaker speak with the same voice, intent, force and authenticity. As a result, no dissonance or interpretive difference opens up between original and translation, and the translator, as the producer of the secondary discourse, nowhere utters a thought or occupies a subject-position that is not wholly consonant and indeed identical with that of the first speaker. The first three witnesses who were present during the angel Moroni's visitation in June 1829 stated that they heard the heavenly voice declare: "These plates have been revealed by the power of God, and they have been translated by the power of God" (Bushman 1984: 106). Augustine wrote likewise in *The City of God* that the Septuagint had been achieved "by the power of God," and "the very same Spirit that was present in the prophets when they uttered their messages was at work also in the seventy scholars when they translated them" (1972: 821; Schwarz 1955: 41). The translation, that is, can speak for the original. It can effectively replace the original.

On this point the *Book of Mormon* is rather more emphatic than the Septuagint. The *Book of Mormon*'s gold-plated original has literally disappeared without trace. We also have an explicit statement, a revelation straight from heaven, affirming the translation's unique quality and complete adequacy, granting it full authority to speak for and even in lieu of its original. This makes the *Book of Mormon* the most dramatic example I know of a translation which is not only promoted to fully equivalent rank with its original but has so totally occupied the latter's place as to hide it from view once and for all. Joseph Smith's version has pushed Mormon's scriptures into irretrievable obscurity, overwriting them wholesale.

There are two aspects of these stories which need elaborating. The first bears on the notion of equivalence. The accounts of the origins of the *Book of Mormon* and the Septuagint suggest that equivalence, understood as equality in value between a translation and its original, comes about as a result of verbal statements concerning the relation between the texts involved. The statements, as speech acts, possess performative force. Both in the case of the *Book of Mormon* and of the Septuagint the initial assumption is that a translation, as a text seeking to echo a pre-existing text, is not automatically put on equal terms with the original to which it refers. Putting both texts on the same footing, lifting one up to the other's level of authority by means of a verbal utterance, constitutes a performative speech act. In the case of the *Book of Mormon* the intervention takes the form of words falling from the sky: the book is true and the translation correct. The statement instigates the equivalence between Joseph Smith's translation and the encrypted gold plates. This equivalence is total, as the disappearance of the gold plates demonstrates. Because the two versions can each stand for the other, one can also render the other redundant, and has in fact done so. The story of the Septuagint lacks the apodictic enunciation and subsequent disappearing act that make the *Book of Mormon* so spectacular, but it, too, relies on a divinely inspired origin to lever itself up to a state of equivalence with the Hebrew Bible. Philo of Alexandria speaks of the Greek and Hebrew versions as "sisters, or rather as one and the same, both in matter and words" (Schwarz 1955: 23). Augustine implored Jerome to use as the source for his Latin translation of the Bible, not the original Hebrew of the Old Testament but the Greek Septuagint, adding that any translator who insisted on working from the Hebrew would still be right only if he came up with a version that was in agreement with the Seventy (1972: 821; Schwarz 1955: 41).

Equivalence, which I will continue to interpret as meaning equality in value and status, is not a feature that can be extrapolated on the basis of textual comparison. Rather than being extracted from texts, equivalence is imposed on them through an external intervention in a particular institutional context. In other words, equivalence is proclaimed, not found. As we will see below, the proclamation is effective only if the conditions are right. Moreover, a translation raised to equivalent status with its original will necessarily be recognised as a correct representation of it, indeed it is of necessity the only correct representation. This explains why Moroni forbade Joseph Smith to retranslate the 116 pages which Martin Harris's family had allegedly mislaid or destroyed. A new translation would run the risk of throwing up divergent renderings and these would undermine the claim of divine inspiration if the Harris family were acting in bad faith and intended to entrap Smith by producing the initial translation at a later date. With reference to the Septuagint the 'Letter of Aristeas' mentions that after the translation of the Seventy had been presented and approved, an imprecation was pronounced on any who dared add, omit or alter anything at all in the Greek text (in Robinson 1997: 6).

Equivalence does not preclude differences in meaning. Augustine knew perfectly well that a close comparison between the Greek Septuagint and the Hebrew text of the Bible disclosed numerous divergences. He accounted for them most ingeniously by claiming, in *The City of God*, that if there were things in the Greek that were not in the Hebrew, God had wanted to say those things only in Greek; if there was anything in the Hebrew that was not in the Greek, God had wanted to say those things in Hebrew only; and if the Greek and the Hebrew said different things, God had wanted to say all those things, but some only in Greek and others only in Hebrew (Augustine 1972: 821-2; Schwarz 1955: 41-2). For Augustine, the Septuagint and the Hebrew Bible were fully equivalent authentic versions of the same message. God spoke with equal force, with equal directness and with equal authority in each version.

Relevance theory distinguishes between descriptive and interpretive use of utterances. Descriptive utterances are statements about the world, and they may be true or false (for example, "it is raining"). Interpretive utterances are statements that represent other statements, and they are judged by their degree of resemblance to those other statements (Sperber and Wilson 1986: 224-31; Wilson and Sperber 2004: 621). Ernst-August Gutt has used this distinction as a basis for his view of translation as interpretive use (Gutt 1991). With respect to the *Book of Mormon* and the Septuagint, we see the distinction collapsing, or, better perhaps, becoming irrelevant. For all we know, Joseph Smith's English resembles Mormon's script, but we cannot ascertain or measure the resemblance and so we read the *Book of Mormon* descriptively, not interpretively. And if God speaks with equal force in the Septuagint and in the Hebrew Bible, then the Greek may well resemble the Hebrew, but we may as well read either, for we can hear the divinely inspired word directly in both.

This takes us to the second aspect that needs highlighting. In these cases of wholesale equivalence, the translations have to all intents and purposes ceased to be translations. A translation which is declared to be, and is recognised as being, in all respects equal to its prototext, may well continue to be a translation in a genetic sense but it no longer functions as such. The user is now confronted with two wholly and exactly corresponding authentic texts embodying a single underlying intention. Talking of the Septuagint and Hebrew versions of the Bible, Philo of Alexandria suggested we should "speak of their authors not as translators but as prophets and priests of these mysteries" (Schwarz 1955: 23). It may have been accidental but it certainly was no less symbolic that Joseph Smith was first entered as 'author and proprietor' of the *Book of Mormon*.

Vienna's treaties

Nowhere do we see this practical and radical consequence of the positing of equivalence more clearly at work than in the very different, modern, juridical context of the Convention of Vienna. Delving into this topic means a change of scene as we switch from the history of religion to international law.

The Vienna Convention on the Law of Treaties is a United Nations convention first enacted in 1969 and revised in 1986. It deals with international treaties, including bilateral and multilateral treaties involving more than one language (Blix and Emerson 1973; Reuter 1995: 210-43; Sinclair 1984). A bilingual or multilingual treaty constitutes a single legal instrument, but it consists of versions written in different languages. The texts of such a treaty may have come into being as a result of parallel drafting in two or more languages, or it may be that a version in one language was agreed by all parties to the treaty and then translated into the other language or languages. Article 33 of the Vienna Convention concerns the interpretation of treaties that have been 'authenticated' in two or more languages. It runs as follows:

> *Article 33 Interpretation of treaties authenticated in two or more languages*
> 1. When a treaty has been authenticated in two or more languages, the text is equally authoritative in each language, unless the treaty provides

or the parties agree that, in case of divergence, a particular text shall
prevail.

2. A version of the treaty in a language other than one of those in
which the text was authenticated shall be considered an authentic text
only if the treaty so provides or the parties so agree.

3. The terms of a treaty are presumed to have the same meaning in
each authentic text.

4. Except where a particular text prevails in accordance with paragraph
1, when a comparison of the authentic texts discloses a difference of
meaning which the application of articles 31 and 32 does not remove,
the meaning which best reconciles the texts, having regard to the object
and purpose of the treaty, shall be adopted. (Reuter 1995: 261-2).[2]

Authentication is the key concept. It is defined earlier in the Convention, in
Article 10, as a procedure confirming that the text of a treaty is the correct and
authentic one. Authenticating the different language versions of a bilateral or
multilateral treaty means recognising each version as equally authentic, so that
each version is on a par with the other version or versions. An authenticated
version of a treaty is consequently "a version which the parties to the treaty
have officially approved and recognised as an interpretive source equivalent
to such other language versions as there may be" (van den Hoven 1998:
40; my translation of: *een tekstversie van een verdrag die officieel door de
verdragspartijen is vastgesteld en erkend als kenbron, gelijkwaardig aan de
eventuele andere taalversies*").

In other words, when a treaty has been produced in different language
versions, whether by means of translating one initial version or by simultaneously drafting parallel versions, the treaty-concluding parties authenticate
these various texts by recognising each individual version as equivalent to
the other versions. The recognition takes the form of an institutional act, a
performative speech act which posits and thereby creates "the fiction of total
equivalence and correspondence" (*ibid.*) between the various parallel texts.
The individual versions are declared to be equivalent, and therefore identical in meaning. This is exactly what paragraph 3 of Article 33 (above) of
the Convention states: "The terms of a treaty are presumed to have the same
meaning in each authentic text."

There are several things to be noted here. Firstly, authentication, the establishment of the principle of equal authenticity, is a precondition for the
different versions of a treaty to be recognised as constituting a single legal
instrument. Authentication grants each authentic text equal force of law. It

---

[2] Articles 31 and 32 deal with the 'General rule of interpretation [of treaties]' and 'Sup-
plementary means of interpretation', respectively.

bestows authority on texts. The Septuagint and the *Book of Mormon* invoked divine intervention to bring this about. In the world of international law, authentication is a pronouncement that carries legal force.

Secondly, since authentication makes something happen by means of words, it constitutes a performative speech act, more particularly what J.L. Austin called a perlocutionary speech act, one that achieves an effect (Austin 1962). Following Austin's original classification of performatives, the authenticating speech act would be an 'exercitive', "a decision that something is to be so, as distinct from a judgement that it is so" (Austin 1962: 154). As a speech act, it will succeed only if the felicity conditions for its success are fulfilled. Treaties are binding only if the correct procedures have been followed, and they oblige only the treaty-concluding parties. Not everyone outside the Mormon Church will feel the story of the gold plates and seer stones directly affects them, and few nowadays accept the miraculous account of the Septuagint. Authentication works best in strongly institutionalised environments, such as judiciaries and churches. In the context of international agreements it will normally be part of the felicity conditions that texts presented for authentication cannot be the work of translators alone but that the negotiators themselves must take responsibility for their phrasing.

Thirdly, authentication creates the "fiction of total equivalence and correspondence". The imposition of equivalence has as a consequence the presumption that the various authentic versions convey the same meaning. Umberto Eco has described translation as "saying almost the same thing" in another language (*Dire quasi la stessa cosa*, Eco 2003); authenticated versions, not being translations, all say *exactly* the same thing. It would appear, then, that authentication has a double effect. It makes two or more parallel texts equally authentic; and in so doing it creates the presumption of sameness of meaning between these texts. Although the two effects come about simultaneously, the former takes precedence over the latter. Equality of status instigates coincidence of meaning. The causal connection runs one way and not the other. It is not the observation that texts can be said to have the same meaning that leads to the conclusion of equivalence. Rather, equivalence is primarily a matter of status and only secondarily a matter of semantics or use value. Also, by creating the fiction of total equivalence and correspondence, authentication asserts the notion that collectively the different language versions constitute a single document or, in the case of international agreements and treaties, a single legal instrument.

Fourthly, if one or more versions of a treaty have come into being as a result of a process of translation from one initial version, authentication erases the memory of this process. Upon authentication, translated texts become authentic texts and must forget that they used to exist as translations. In fact, authentication strikes not only translations with amnesia, but also originals. If versions that were once translations are now parallel authentic texts on a par with all other versions, then the version that once served as the original is now also one authentic version among the other authentic versions that are its equals. Where there are no translations there are no originals – unless all are agreed to be originals. Nor, as we will see shortly, are there translators. It also follows from this that, unlike translations, parallel authentic versions are not metatexts that refer to one another. They speak in unison, and they are presumed to say the same thing, but they do not speak about each other. Each speaks for itself, without claiming to represent one or more of the others in the way translations represent their originals. Despite the similarity between them, parallel authentic versions offer instances of what Relevance theory calls descriptive rather than interpretive use.

Fifthly, because an international treaty represents an agreement concerning specific issues referred to by means of particular words, there will be only one authenticated version of that treaty in each language. In the same way there could be only one version of the Septuagint and only one English version of the *Book of Mormon*.

Sixthly, when differences in meaning between authenticated versions of a treaty are detected, the discrepancies must be resolved by appealing to the common intent of the treaty-makers. They emphatically must not be resolved by retracing the history of the different language versions. If some versions have originally come into existence as translations of a prototext in a given language, drawing on this knowledge in interpreting the treaty would privilege a particular language version over the others. Such privileging would jeopardise the principle of equality and hence the equal authority of all the other parallel authentic versions. That move is therefore not allowed. Articles 31 to 33 of the Vienna Convention provide the judiciary with rules of interpretation designed to safeguard the parity between the various authenticated versions. Indeed paragraph 4 of Article 33, which I quoted above, stipulates that in the case of divergences "the meaning which best reconciles the texts, having regard to the object and purpose of the treaty, shall be adopted' (Reuter 1995: 261-2). This is in line with the view of the International Law Commission (set up in 1948 under United Nations auspices), which holds that the unity of multilingual treaties and of each of their terms "is safeguarded by combining with the principle of the equal authority of authentic texts the presumption that the terms are intended to have same meaning in each text" (in Sinclair 1984: 148-9). It is a position that comes uncannily close to the way in which Augustine accounted for the discrepancies between the Septuagint and the Hebrew

Bible when he argued that both were imbued with the same spirit and voiced the same intent. The rules of interpretation stipulated by the Vienna Convention also show, however, that while the total equivalence and correspondence in meaning instituted by authentication may be a fiction, this fiction is a legal reality that has force of law. It permits some readings and prohibits others.

Finally, if some versions of a treaty have come about through a process of translation and they are not authenticated, they remain translations, and merely translations. Uncertainties or disputes concerning the interpretation of such a treaty will be resolved with reference to the officially recognised authentic version or versions, not with reference to a translation. A translation, that is, simply cannot have the same force of law as an authentic version. In this sense authentication makes a sharp distinction between authentic versions and mere translations.

The relevance of the concept of authentication lies in the conferral of authority. If different language versions of a treaty are authenticated, granting them equal force means recognising the equality in status of the treaty-concluding parties. Authenticating only one among several language versions privileges that version and the speakers of its language. The procedure of authentication thus addresses a much more general issue, the inequality between languages and communities. This issue obviously predates the Vienna Convention. As early as the first century CE the Roman writer Valerius Maximus observed in his *Memorable Doings and Sayings* that Roman magistrates would invariably insist on using Latin in their contacts with their Greek counterparts, obliging the Greeks to speak through interpreters, not only in Rome but in Greece and Asia also, as far as Roman imperial control extended. The Roman practice served as a reminder to the Greeks that "in all matters whatsoever the Greek cloak should be subordinate to the Roman gown" (Valerius Maximus 2000: 38-39).

Versions of authority

Authentication, as the proclamation of equivalence, can take different forms. In the case of the Septuagint, the entire account of its creation as told by Philo of Alexandria serves to authenticate the Greek version. The story of the *Book of Mormon* is very similar, but features the additional twin moments of the voice from heaven and the physical removal of the gold plates. In bilingual or multilingual legal instruments the authenticating statement tends to occur in the texts themselves, so that the specific agreement confirming that the various language versions of the single instrument enjoy equal status forms part of the broader agreement that is recorded in the document as a whole. Authentication then takes place, and equivalence takes effect, the moment the various parties sign the relevant documents.

The constitutions of bilingual or multilingual countries offer perhaps the clearest illustrations of this kind of authenticating statement embedded in the actual texts. For example, the Canadian Constitution Act of 1982, Article 52 of which proclaims it "the supreme law of Canada", states in Article 57 that "The English and French versions of this Act are equally authoritative". The French version states likewise that "Les versions française et anglaise de la présente loi ont également force de loi", the only inconsequential difference between the two versions being that the English mentions English first and the French puts French first (Canada 1982). The idea was not new in 1982; the Canadian High Court upheld the principle of linguistic equality for legal purposes as early as 1935 (Lavoie 2003: 122).

The Belgian Constitution, in its current incarnation as fixed in 1994, exists in three language versions, as its Article 189 confirms in each language:

> Le texte de la Constitution est établi en français, en néerlandais et en allemand.
> De tekst van de Grondwet is in het Nederlands, in het Frans en in het Duits gesteld.
> Der Text der Verfassung ist in Deutsch, in Französisch und in Nieder-ländisch festgelegt. (Belgium 1994)

When Belgium gained independence in 1830 the only language used for legal purposes was French. Although from 1898 onwards Belgian laws were drafted and promulgated in both Dutch and French, the Dutch version of the Belgian Constitution was not granted full legal status until 1967 (Brouckaert 1998: 33). The German text of the Constitution is of even more recent date, 17 February 1994. We can be certain that the Dutch was translated from the French and the German from both the Dutch and the French, nevertheless neither the Dutch nor the Geman versions are translations. While genetically they may have been translations at a certain stage, legally, as texts of the Belgian Constitution, they are not and cannot be, because of the principle of linguistic parity. All three are authentic texts, each version on a par with the other two.

International treaties and conventions involving several languages follow the same pattern. The practice has a history and, in Europe at least, appears together with the emergence of nation states and their national languages. During negotiations in 1682 between France and the Holy Roman Empire in connection with the French annexation of Strasbourg, French delegates are said to have asserted for the first time the principle that no sovereign state can impose a particular language on another and that each therefore has the right to use its own language of government, unless agreement can be reached on the use of a common tongue. Indeed a French *Mémoire* of 20 June 1682 insisted that "it appears reasonable among equals to agree for that purpose on one common language, or to make several originals" (Ostrower 1965, 1: 290-1; "il est raisonnable entr' égaux de convenir pour cela d'une langue commune, ou de faire plusieurs originaux", Brunot 1966, 5: 444-5).

The Treaty of Rome of 25 May 1957, which created the nucleus of what is now the European Union, states that it was "drawn up in a single original in the Dutch, French, German and Italian languages, all four texts being equally authentic" (Article 314 in the consolidated version of 24 December 2002; Rome 1957). The Accession Treaty of 25 April 2005, by which the then twenty-five European Union member states agreed for Bulgaria and Romania to join the Union, undoubtedly came into being in the two new languages as a result of translation, but it now exists in a single original in twenty-three languages, as Article 6 confirms:

> This Treaty, drawn up in a single original in the Bulgarian, Czech, Danish, Dutch, English, Estonian, Finnish, French, German, Greek, Hungarian, Irish, Italian, Latvian, Lithuanian, Maltese, Polish, Portuguese, Romanian, Slovak, Slovenian, Spanish and Swedish languages, the texts in each of these languages being equally authentic, shall be deposited in the archives of the Government of the Italian Republic, which will remit a certified copy to each of the Governments of the other Signatory States. (European Union 2005)

In the same way the Convention on the Prevention and Punishment of the Crime of Genocide stipulates in Article 10: "The present Convention, of which the Chinese, English, French, Russian and Spanish texts are equally authentic; shall bear the date of 9 December 1948' (Blix and Emerson 1973: 256).

However, in many cases not all the relevant language versions of a multilingual treaty are assigned equal status. When this is the case, the treaty will normally specify which versions are authentic and which are to be regarded as translations. The various Geneva Conventions of 1949, for example, which regulate the treatment of prisoners, of the wounded and of civilians in times of war, declare the English and French versions to be equally authentic, and make provision for official translations into Russian and Spanish.[3] Clearly, as far as

---

[3] Geneva Convention for the Amelioration of the Conditions of the Wounded and Sick in Armed Forces in the Field, Article 55; Second Convention for the Amelioration of the Conditions of the Wounded, Sick and Shipwrecked Members of the Armed Forces at Sea, Article 54; Third Convention Relative to the Treatment of Prisoners of War, Article 133; Geneva Convention Relative to the Protection of Civilian Persons in Time of War, Article 150 (Draper 1958: 136, 148, 181, 215).

interpretation and authority are concerned, authentic versions take precedence over translations, official or not. Only the authentic versions determine what the agreement actually says. Thus, political power and prestige are reflected in the choice of authentic language or languages of bilateral or multilateral agreements. The 1957 Cultural Agreement between Japan and Pakistan was "done in duplicate in the English language at Karachi", and the 1958 Air Services Agreement between Sweden and Sudan was likewise "in the English language, which shall be the authoritative language", with provision for an official translation into Swedish and Arabic. The Peace Treaty of 1958 between Indonesia and Japan was "[d]one in duplicate, in the Japanese, Indonesian and English languages" but added that "[i]n case of any divergences of interpretation, the English text shall prevail" (Blix and Emerson 1973: 254, 256).

The differences in status can be subtle. The Berne Convention for the Protection of Literary and Artistic Works (in the Paris text of 1971) was drawn up "in a single copy in the French and English languages" with "official texts" in Arabic, German, Italian, Portuguese and Spanish (Article 37); however the document goes on to say that "[i]n case of differences of opinion on the interpretation of the various texts, the French text shall prevail" (Berne 1971). Only exceptionally is the original language of drafting made relevant. The 1955 Protocol Amending the Warsaw Convention of 1929 was signed at The Hague "in three authentic texts in the English, French and Spanish languages" but added that in the case of any inconsistency "the text in the French language, in which language the Conventions was drawn up, shall prevail" (Blix and Emerson 1973: 256). In this case authentication appears not to have been absolute; I will return to this below.

The so-called 'Unequal Treaties' are a series of treaties forced upon China in the nineteenth and early twentieth centuries in the wake of military defeats inflicted by Western powers. They obliged China to cede territory, open up ports, pay indemnities, allow foreigners to remain outside its jurisdiction, admit Western missionaries, and a host of other things. The Treaties of Tientsin which China signed with a number of countries between 1858 and the mid-1860s, emphasise time and again the difference between authoritative authentic versions and mere translations, almost invariably privileging the language of the victors.

The preamble to the treaty which Britain signed with China on 26 June 1858 sounds lofty enough:

> Victoria, by the Grace of God, Queen of the United Kingdom of Great Britain and Ireland, Defender of the Faith, etc., etc., etc., [...] Whereas a Treaty between Us and Our Good Brother the Emperor of China

> was concluded and signed, in the English and Chinese languages, at
> Tientsin, on the Twenty-sixth day of June, in the Year of Our Lord One
> Thousand Eight Hundred and Fifty-Eight […]. (China 1908: 212)

Even the cordial reference to "Our Good Brother" may have beeen a back-
hander: traditionally, foreign ambassadors were required to kowtow before the
Emperor. Although both English and Chinese are explicitly recognised as the
languages in which the treaty was concluded and signed, Article 50 leaves no
doubt at all as to which language will take precedence should a dispute arise
over the meaning of the treaty:

> All official communications addressed by the Diplomatic and Consular
> Agents of Her Majesty the Queen to the Chinese Authorities shall,
> henceforth, be written in English. They will for the present be accom-
> panied by a Chinese version, but, it is understood that, in the event of
> there being any difference of meaning between the English and Chinese
> text, the English Government will hold the sense as expressed in the
> English text to be the correct sense.
>
> This provision is to apply to the Treaty now negotiated, the Chinese
> text of which has been carefully corrected by the English original.
> (China 1908: 226)

The treaty with France, signed on 4 July 1858, stipulates that only the French
text is authoritative (China 1908: 604). Treaties with other countries vary in
their language provision. For example, the treaty with the United States, dated
18 June 1858, is in English and Chinese and says nothing about language,
so we may assume both versions to be equally authoritative (China 1908:
509-31). The treaty with Denmark has a preamble and conclusion in Danish
but is otherwise in English and Chinese; it stipulates that "in the event of there
being any difference of meaning between the English and the Chinese text,
the Danish government will hold the sense as expressed in the English text to
be the correct sense", and adds that this provision "applies also to the present
Treaty, copies of which, both in the English and the Chinese languages, will
be signed and sealed by the Plenipotentiaries of the two High Contracting
Parties" (China 1908: 1043, 1058). The treaties with the Netherlands, Spain
and Belgium (signed in 1863, 1864 and 1865, respectively) are in Chinese and
Dutch, Spanish and French respectively, and declare that each side regards
the version in its own language as authoritative; that with Belgium adds that
"the Chinese translation has carefully been made to accord with the French
original" ("la traduction chinoise a été rendue soigneusement conforme au
texte original français", China 1908: 761).

The treaty with Russia, signed as early as 12 June 1858, is unusual in being in Russian, Chinese and Manchu, with the Russian being accompanied by a French translation ("as published by the Russian Ministry of Foreign Affairs") and the stipulation that "the Manchu text will be used as a basis for interpreting the meaning of the articles" of the treaty ("le texte Mantchou sera adopté comme base pour l'interprétation du sens des articles"; China 1908: lvx). The treaty with Germany, of 1861, is in German, Chinese and French and declares that all three versions have "the same sense and meaning"; interestingly, it goes on to say that, since every diplomat in Europe knows French ("mit Rücksicht darauf, dass die Französische Sprache unter allen Diplomaten Europa's bekannt ist"; "par la raison que la langue Française est connue de tous les diplomates de l'Europe"), the French version will be regarded as the original; it adds that, if there is any difference of interpretation between the German and the Chinese versions, the French version will be authoritative ("s'il y a quelque part une interprétation différente du texte Allemand et du texte Chinois, l'expédition Française fera foi"; "wenn eine verschiedene Auslegung des Deutschen und Chinesischen Vertrages irgendwo stattfinden sollte, die Französische Ausfertigung entscheidend sein soll", China 1908: 845-5).

While various multilingual treaties may play out the political inequality between languages, the versions that enjoy equal status are equivalent and are therefore presumed to have the same meaning. Is this the end of the matter? Not quite. Authentication and its effects are clear enough in principle. They enable multilingual treaties and contracts to appeal, in Jacques Derrida's words, to "a transferability already given and without remainder" ("une traductibilité déjà donnée et sans reste", Derrida 1985: 185, 229). Practice may be somewhat murkier. Occasionally, opinions are voiced in favour of 'historical interpretation', which would take the drafting process of a multilingual agreement into account in determining its meaning (Ostrower 1965, 1: 483ff). And there was also Waitangi, with plenty of remainder.

The historical interpretation was invoked, for example, in a case discussed in Ian Sinclair's *The Vienna Convention on the Law of Treaties* (1984). The case concerns a dispute which arose in 1980 about the meaning of the terms "depreciation" (English), "dépréciation" (French) and "Abwertung" (German) in the trilingual London Debt Agreement. When the matter went to legal arbitration the Tribunal upheld the principle incorporated in Article 33 of the Vienna Convention against the earlier practice of referring to the basic or original text as an aid for interpretation. However, there was also a dissenting minority view, held by three of the seven judges serving on the Tribunal, that reference to the original drafting language may sometimes be valid, especially when different language versions prove incompatible. The minority view pointed out that, in the particular case of the London Debt Agreement, it was the negotiators who had agreed the English-language text, while the other language versions were produced afterwards by mere translators (Sinclair 1984: 150-2).

The Treaty of Waitangi presents an altogether different case (Waitangi s.d.; Fenton and Moon 2002, 2004). One of New Zealand's foundational documents, it was signed in 1840 by William Hobson as the representative of the British Crown and by over five hundred Maori chiefs. It has been disputed up to the present day. William Hobson drafted the original English text and had it translated into Maori by the Anglican missionary Henry Williams. On 5 February 1840 Hobson and the Maori chiefs all signed the version in their language, so that, although no formal authentication appears to have taken place, this was effectively what happened. The differences in interpretation which subsequently arose concerned concepts like sovereignty and possession of land. The British understood – and intended – the treaty to secure British sovereignty over the territory, whereas the Maori read the corresponding term in their version of the treaty as meaning powers of governance only. References to 'possession' of land did not fit Maori conceptions at all, since land could not be owned; their corresponding term indicated control and authority, without implying a commodity to be owned or traded. In this case, then, even if both the English and Maori versions of the treaty are regarded as equally authoritative, it seems hard to establish a common intention that could serve as a basis for interpreting the treaty as a single instrument. Because the British and the Maori inhabited different conceptual worlds, their negotiators were talking at cross-purposes and neither side grasped the import of the other's terms. Insofar as discrepancies in interpretation resulted in dispute, the solution would be a matter of superior force. Whites began to outnumber Maoris in New Zealand in the 1860s, and only the English version of the treaty was implemented by successive governments. This continued to be the case until the establishment of the Waitangi Tribunal in 1975 (Fenton and Moon 2002: 42). The two different language versions of the Treaty of Waitangi may well have been nominally equal but power imbalances, cultural disparities and possibly cunning contrived to make one version take precedence over the other.

Still, the principle of authentication remains unaffected by these counterexamples. The tribunal that heard the London Debt Agreement case found ultimately in favour of the idea that translations, once authenticated, cease to be translations. In the case of the Treaty of Waitangi it could be argued that the two versions were nominally equal, even if in fact the power differential was such that one version effectively prevailed. In recent decades a more equitable view of the relation between the two versions emerged after all.

Authentication in a minor key

Authentication is a strong concept, and especially in its legal definition and context it refers to a clear-cut procedure resulting in concrete effects. Authentication confers authority and instigates equivalence. Translations that are authenticated cease to be translations and become authentic texts. In what follows I want to explore several weaker forms of authentication. Translations may be partially authenticated, or they may have a degree of authority bestowed on them without being fully authenticated. There are also situations in which the distinction between translation and original is simply no longer relevant and a form of authentication has occurred *de facto*.

The Council of Trent offers an instance of partial authentication of a particular Latin version of the Bible. The Council, convoked by Pope Paul III and held from 1545 to 1563 in the northern Italian city of Trento, initiated the Catholic response to the Reformation. Its canons and decrees reaffirmed Catholic doctrine; it also fixed the Tridentine mass and created the Jesuits as a militant order to combat Protestantism and other heresies. The fourth of the Council's twenty-five sessions took place in April 1546 and concerned the canonical scriptures. It had to decide which Biblical texts, and which version or versions, to accept as authoritative. It came down in favour of Jerome's Latin Vulgate:

> Moreover, the same holy council considering that not a little advantage will accrue to the Church of God if it be made known which of all the Latin editions of the sacred books now in circulation is to be regarded as authentic, ordains and declares that the old Latin Vulgate Edition, which, in use for so many hundred years, has been approved by the Church, be in public lectures, disputations, sermons and expositions held as authentic, and that no one dare or presume under any pretext whatsoever to reject it. (Schroeder 1978: 18)

As well as proclaiming the Vulgate "authentic" (*authentica*, Rice 1985: 185) the Council went on in the next paragraph to warn that no one should presume to interpret the scriptures "contrary to that sense which holy mother Church, to whom it belongs to judge of their true sense and interpretation, has held and holds" (Schroeder 1978: 19), thus reserving to itself the exclusive right to interpret the scriptures. In this way the Council secured both the text and its reading: only one version could be authentic, and only the Church was entitled to determine what it meant.

The Council members did not deny that the Vulgate was a translation and did not seek to undo its status as a translation, although they came close. They observed that the Vulgate was to be preferred above other versions as being the most ancient, the most used, the least biased, and also "as representing more correctly the state of the ancient copies of the Greek and Hebrew Scriptures than any other Latin version, or even, probably, than any other then, or now, existing Greek or Hebrew edition" (Waterworth 1848: lxxxix). This was a strong claim, but it operated purely at the level of philology. However, the Franciscan Andrés de Vega, of the University of Salamanca, immediately grasped the implication. He interpreted the decree which recognised the Vulgate as 'authentic' and as thereby asserting "that it was free from all errors against faith and morals, but not from such imperfections as are incidental to all translations" (Waterworth 1848: xci). After the Council the influential cardinal and sometime inquisitor Robert Bellarmine repeated, in a book on the subject (*De editione Latina vulgata...*, not published till 1749), that "there is no error in this translation in matters pertaining to faith and morals" (Rice 1985: 187). This view managed to have it both ways. The Vulgate remained a translation, vulnerable to error and not on a par with the divinely inspired original, but it was in the full sense of the word 'authentic' in respect of substance and doctrine, that is, in every respect that mattered as far as the Church was concerned. In these respects the Vulgate was more than a mere translation. Not surprisingly, occasional claims were also made at the time to the effect that the Holy Spirit had assisted Jerome in translating doctrinal matter but had left him to his own fallible devices "in places of less moment"; these views however did not become official Church doctrine (*ibid.*).

Self-translation bestows authority in ways similar to authentication. The phenomenon is well documented, especially in the literary domain, where bilingual authors like Vladimir Nabokov, writing in Russian and English, and Samuel Beckett, in English and French, have often been studied. The issue here is not primarily whether bilingual writers are really equally at home in two languages or not, or how closely self-translations match their originals. Brian Fitch argued in his study of Beckett (Fitch 1988) that the issue is ontological. Works translated by their own authors do not refer back to their originals in the way translations do. Rather, they share a common authorial intent with these originals. As a result, according to Fitch, translations and originals end up as parallel productions which generate independent critical discourses in each language. Elizabeth Klosty Beaujour concluded her study of bilingual Russian émigré writers by stressing the equality of original and translation when the latter was a self-translation. She celebrated self-translation as affording "the Mephistophelian pleasure of creating two mutually orbiting works in dynamic equilibrium"; she added that the voice addressing the reader in these self-translations "is unmistakably the same in both languages, and this very fact indicates that it emanates from a self which must exist *below* both languages" (Beaujour 1989: 175, 176).

The ontological perspective is not enough, though. It needs to be supplemented with institutional considerations, for only they effectuate the social valorisation of self-translations. When works are translated from one language into another by their own authors, both texts are recognised as emanating from a single source and, as a consequence, invested with equal authority. Some self-translating authors seek to give symbolic expression to this equality in status. Karen Blixen, for example, the author of *Out of Africa* who wrote in both English and Danish and translated much of her own work from her adopted language, English, into her native Danish, made strenuous efforts to have British, American and Danish editions of her books appear on the same day and with similar-looking covers. She also sought to revise the original English texts of some of her works on the basis of her own Danish renderings of them (Anderson 1997: 173-4). Both moves promote a view of parallel versions on a par with one another or even coalescing into a single work existing in two language versions simultaneously, in the way the different versions of a multilingual treaty or constitution make up a single legal instrument. Brian Fitch's examination of Beckett's self-translations closes in similar vein with the "tantalizing mirage" of parallel texts which together form a virtual work that does not exist in either language (1988: 138).

However, whereas in the context of international law authentication prompts the corollary that parallel versions have the same meaning, this point is not pushed in the case of self-translation. Instead, the assumption of a common intent underpinning different language versions is particularly prominent. In addition, the author-translator's sole ownership of both texts ensures that the restrictions which convention or copyright law may have placed on translation, fall away. This makes it hard for readers and critics to decide how to label these products, as the standard distinctions between creative and reproductive writing appear inappropriate. The Galician writer Suso de Toro translated some of his own novels into Spanish and added some twenty pages on one occasion, subsequently incorporating them into the original Galician version (Santoyo 2004: 230). Nabokov incorporated a story first written in French ('Mademoiselle O', 1936) into his autobiography (*Conclusive Evidence*, 1951), which was written in English and which he subsequently adapted into Russian (*Drugie berega*, 1954), only to rework this Russian text again in a second English version (*Speak, Memory*, 1966) (Grayson 1977: 10-11; Beaujour 1989: 112-14).

For some authors self-translation proves an impossible task all the same, despite prodigious linguistic skill. The Greek-born Swedish-language writer

Theodor Kallifatides, for example, finds himself incapable of translating his own work and reckons he thinks and feels like a different person when he uses a different language (Qvale 2003: 73). The Irish poet Nuala Ní Dhomhnaill is perfectly at home in English but does not self-translate because he does not see himself as a poet in that language (in de Courtivron 2003: 88-89). As a result, the question of parallel versions enjoying equal authority does not come up in these cases, even though Ní Dhomhnaill insists on bilingual editions of translations of his poems (*ibid.*).

The originally Czech writer Milan Kundera represents the opposite case. He moved to France in 1975 and became a French citizen in 1981, began to write in French, personally amended the French translations of all his Czech books between 1985 and 1987, and has since gone on to insist that the French versions of his work are the only authentic ones. In so doing he effectively transformed the French versions into originals, marginalised the original originals and ensured that translations – or, in some cases, retranslations – into other languages would be based on the French texts (Casanova 2004: 281-2; Woods 2006: 2-3, 41). Nabokov too used the later English versions of his early Russian novels as the basis for subsequent renderings into other languages, notably French (Beaujour 1995: 719-20; Grayson 1977: 8). As the author he also felt free to rewrite both his own translations of his work and those made by other translators. In this way he overrode Winifred Roy's 1936 translation of his originally Russian novel *Camera Obscura* with his own much freer version (published as *Laughter in the Dark*, 1938); he also made two very different English versions of another of his early Russian novels, *Otchayanie* ('Despair', 1936), first in 1937 and then again, decisively, in 1966 (Grayson 1977: 59-82), "thus rendering both the Russian novel and the first English translation retroactively incomplete", as Beaujour puts it (1995: 720).

Literature however is a weakly institutionalised field, in which pronouncements about the status of a text may be contested. The Canadian writer Nancy Huston has lived mainly in Paris since 1973, writes in both English and French and translates her own work from one language into the other. Her novel *Cantique des plaines* (1993), which she had reworked from her English novel *Plainsong* (also 1993), caused controversy when it won an award reserved for original writings. Some critics argued that the French version showed every sign of being a translation, while the author protested it was not a translation but a rewriting and therefore an original work (Klein-Lataud 1996: 220-22). The case is similar to that surrounding the London Debt Agreement above. Although the author's word put both versions on a par, the fact itself that dissenting voices were raised concerning the status of the chronologically later version suggests that the author's declaration is not necessarily the last word.

Authentication here remains open to challenge.

When authors collaborate with translators, some authorial authority is transferred to the translation. The Algerian writer Rachid Boudjedra has written in both Arabic and French and translated himself in both directions but now writes mostly in Arabic. When a translator translates his Arabic into French, he says, "I insist on working with him on the translation, because it has to be by Boudjedra, like the days when I wrote in French" (Casanova 2004: 268). The translation will not have the same status as the original, but the author's involvement in its creation lifts it above the level of ordinary translation and grants it at least quasi-equivalence. There are plenty of cases in which authors assist their translators, and in so doing control and authorise the result. The Polish writer Witold Gombrowicz, for instance, lived in Argentina for more than two decades and first translated his own work into Spanish, then collabo- rated with two French translators to produce French versions of other works originally written in Polish. The definitive French translation of James Joyce's *Ulysses* appeared in 1929 with a title page identifying the book as a translation by Auguste Morel assisted by Stuart Gilbert and revised by Valéry Larbaud jointly with the author (Casanova 2004: 143, 145). Nabokov also collaborated with other translators on his own work but always retaining complete control of the process, treating his translators very much as hired hands and reserving for himself as the author the right to make any changes he saw fit (Grayson 1977: 7; Beaujour 1989: 112).

Translations authorised by the original author's active participation in the constitution of the text are comparable to authorised biographies to which the subject of the biography has lent his or her cooperation. They flaunt the signs of privileged access to the source and can thus claim a degree of authenticity. In a sense, this is authentication in a minor key. In principle, of course, all translations made of contemporary or recent work and brought into the public domain are authorised. They have to be if they are to comply with international copyright law, which in its current form stipulates that works are protected up to seventy years after the author's death. In all countries that subscribe to the Berne Convention translations can be published only with the permission of the original author or copyright holder. The authorisation bestows status and signifies a stamp of approval. This is perhaps the weakest form of explicit authentication. Like author-assisted translations, authorised translations are undoubtedly translations, but they have one up on any other translations that may be circulating. Typically, there tends to be just one authorised transla- tion of a particular work in any one language; if there is more than one, the most recent is likely to serve as a corrective to its predecessor. When Michael Heim retranslated Milan Kundera's novel *The Joke* in 1984 (the first English translation of 1969, by David Hamblyn and Oliver Stallybrass, had drawn a furious public response from Kundera and had been revised in 1970), the author not only worked closely with his translator but eventually appended an approving note when the book was published, declaring this rendering to be "the first valid and authentic version of a book that tells of rape and has itself so often been violated" (in Woods 2006: 28-29, 38).

There is one further form of authentication that needs to be considered. It does not involve a pronouncement and comes about purely *de facto*. Although a decidedly weak form of authentication, it is quantitatively of huge importance. This is the case of all those translations that are used and handled as texts in their own right, without reference to the fact that they are translations. They have to all intents and purposes replaced their originals. They have become the pragmatic substitutes for their sources, and stand in for them so well that their being in fact translations is now irrelevant. To put it in terms of Relevance theory: their interpretive value has been whittled away by descriptive use and has fallen into oblivion. Of course, some translations fit more easily into this category than others. So-called 'covert' translations (House 1981), for example, which are keen to conceal their being translations, will have a better chance of passing for originals than texts that advertise their status as translations. Pragmatic equivalence means that a translation has managed to make everyone forget its origin. Whereas the Convention of Vienna imposed amnesia by judicial means, here authentication has taken place by default, as it were.

This is perhaps the closest that the approach to the question of equivalence which I am taking here comes to standard views of the matter. The traditional linguistic opinion assumed that equivalence was the result of sameness or similarity of meaning, however defined. It sought to infer equivalence from semantic relations between texts, and has now been largely abandoned in favour of more differentiated, communicatively-oriented approaches (Koller 1995, 2004; Neubert 2004). The latter prefer to posit equivalence in pragmatic terms as sameness or similarity of use value. Jelle Stegeman (1991), for example, argued that two texts were equivalent if no difference could be observed as regards their impact – inviting the thorny methodological problem of how to measure the impact of different texts in different populations. Anthony Pym (1995) and others emphasised that equivalence was a matter of a socially operative and enabling belief. Users commonly assume, Pym pointed out, that translations are equivalent to the texts they claim to represent, and indeed users of translation must be able to believe in some type of equivalence pertinent to the situation if translation is to function in a social context at all (Pym 1995: 166-7).

This belief is properly a suspension of disbelief. Many translations, and covert translations more than most, work hard to look like originals and to be able to function like the originals they re-enact. The more successful they are, the more effective the belief system, that is, the suspension of disbelief. The really successful ones, be they intricately rhymed poems or microwave oven manuals, look every bit the part of an original, and of *the* original. But it does not take much to puncture the illusion. The trigger does not even have to be textual, it may be paratextual or extratextual. Any reminder that the text in question is in fact a translation threatens the assumption of equivalence and tells the reader: oh yes, this is only a translation, not quite the same thing as the original, certainly not fully as authoritative as the original. The illusion of equivalence may have roughly the same pragmatic effect as authentication, but it remains much more vulnerable because it is based on convention and expectation only, that is, on a tacit agreement to maintain a fiction, not on an institutional or judicial injunction. In this sense it amounts at best to a weak form of authentication, one that cannot prevent a translation being put back in its place whenever someone takes the trouble to recall its origin. Needless to say, there are borderline cases similar to that of Nancy Huston's rewriting discussed above, in which it is more productive and enlightening to speak in terms of what Relevance theory calls descriptive rather than interpretive use (indeed Gutt 1991: 54-65 discusses some). The fact that there is such a grey area suggests that authentication has reached here its most diluted form.

Let me sum up the main argument I have pursued in this chapter. Equivalence between a translation and its original is established through an external, institutional, perlocutionary speech act. Rather than being an inherent feature of relations between texts, equivalence is *declared*. Establishing equivalence amounts to an act of authentication. A translation thus proclaimed to be equivalent to its parent text ceases to be a translation. Authenticating a translation means transforming it into an equivalent authentic text which, in its own particular sphere, can lay claim to the same authority as the original. To that extent equivalence authorises a translation to overwrite the original. Moreover, all equivalent texts are presumed to be consonant. They are taken to express the same intent, breathe the same spirit and speak with the same voice as the source. That is why an authenticated translation is also a definitive translation. It exists in one form only. There is only one Septuagint and each language has only one Book of Mormon and one legally valid version of each international treaty. A fully equivalent translation amounts to an authenticated translation, and, once authenticated, a translation has ceased to be a translation. Authentication and the positing of equivalence bring about translation's amnesia: they make it forget its origin and annul its own past. A translation may reach for equivalence but on attaining it the translation self-destructs as translation. Equivalence spells the end of translation.

It follows that a translation, for as long as it remains a translation, cannot be equivalent to its source.

2. Before the End

A translation that has not yet ceased to be a translation cannot be equivalent to its source. Nor can it be the definitive version standing in for this source. If a translation were to be the definitive version of a given original, it would have attained equivalence and no longer be a translation. Indeed there is only one *Book of Mormon*, one Septuagint, and one authentic version per language of multilingual treaties, contracts and constitutions.

Translations for their part remain forever repeatable, and therefore provisional. A new, improved rendering can always be attempted, either by the translator or by someone else. "If anyone makes of these books of chronicles a better and more profitable English translation, may God reward him" ("Yif eny man makith of these bokes of cronicles a bett Englissh translacioun and more profitable, God do his mede"), John Trevisa wrote in 1387 (Wogan-Browne *et al.* 1999: 135). According to a possibly apocryphal story told in Edward Hall's *Chronicle* of 1548, the English Bible translator William Tyndale was visited in Antwerp in the 1520s by the merchant Augustine Packington, who wanted to purchase the entire print run of Tyndale's recently published New Testament. Although Tyndale knew Packington was only buying the books so the Bishop of London could burn them as heretical, he expressed delight at the prospect of the transaction because "the overplus of the money," as he put it, would make him "more studious to correct the said New Testament, and newly to imprint the same once again" (Burke 1993: 47; Daniell 2003: 145).

One can always offer another translation of a text, the only practical and temporary impediment in the modern world being the restrictions imposed by copyright law. This also means that the convergence of meaning, the consonance of voice and the singularity of intent that are attributed to fully authenticated equivalent texts, lie beyond the grasp of translation. That is precisely why an external performative speech act is required to create the fiction of equivalence and in so doing lever translation up beyond itself to the status of an authentic version on a par with the original – which is then, in the same move, as we saw in the previous chapter, transformed into one among several authentic versions.

Discourses about translation tend to project equivalence as something translators ought to strive for and perhaps to achieve. The norm of the 'faithful translator' as laid down in numerous codes of conduct of professional translators' and interpreters' organisations insists on translators reproducing originals completely and accurately, without addition, deletion, distortion or intervention. It calls on translators to be so discreet as to spirit themselves away for the sake of the original's integrity, to bite their own tongues in the interests of consonance. Historical discourses about translation, too, abound in images and metaphors urging translators to make themselves unseen and unheard, to act as pure conduits. Only a translation purged of the translator's presence allows consumers to indulge the fiction of equivalence. The illusion of equivalence demands the elision of the translator as a subject in the text. Equivalence spells not only the end of translation but also the death of the translator. When a translation sublimates into an authentic equivalent version, it self-destructs as translation and takes the translator with it. There is a certain irony here: a translator may have to work very hard to create an illusion of equivalence, and a convincing illusion requires a translator so disembodied as to be invisible, or at least so impersonal as to be anonymous (as Pym 1992: 51-52 has it). When authentication makes equivalence a reality rather than an illusion, even bearing in mind that the reality in question is no more than a socially binding legal or institutional fiction, the translator is evacuated entirely. Equivalent versions are not translations.

For as long as a translation remains a translation, then, it will always have a translator's presence and therefore a translator's subject position inscribed in it, however well hidden they may be. There are several ways of showing this. One is by drawing on narratology. As a communicative act, a transla-tion must have an addresser as well as an addressee. This consideration led Giuliana Schiavi (1996) to posit the notion of an 'implied translator' as a counterpart to the 'implied author', a concept familiar to narrative theory. In Schiavi's model, the implied translator was the agent who directed the origi-nal message to the new receptor-language audience. In an article written in parallel with Schiavi's in 1996, I highlighted cases in which the translator's discursive presence could not help but become directly visible in the translated text (Hermans 1996). They included cases in which translators could be seen struggling with cultural references (not just by adding explanatory footnotes but also by providing manifestly redundant or inadequate information in the text itself), cases in which the self-reflexiveness of texts invoked the language in which the original was written, thus threatening the translation with self-contradiction, and cases of 'contextual overdetermination', where a particular phrase might become untranslatable because too many other textual elements depend on this or that exact phrase. In her booklength study *Le conflit des énoncés* (1991) Barbara Folkart had taken a similar line, casting translation as reported speech and hence as the translator's re-enunciation of another utterance.

The kind of forensic stylistics made possible by corpus studies offers a very different way of detecting the translator's hand in translated texts. In an exploratory essay Mona Baker (2000) compared the work of two translators,

Peter Clark and Peter Bush. Feeding a total of eight translated books, almost half a million words, into a computerised corpus of translations comprising around 6.5 million words at the time, Baker was able to show that, irrespective of the nature of the originals they tackled, each translator exhibited certain recurrent linguistic features to a degree that was statistically significant. Each translator, that is, left a personal thumb-print or stylistic signature on their translations. The signature was there in all their work, and was therefore independent of the original texts. Many of these choices must have been unconscious. They are linguistic tics, little idiosyncrasies or preferences that mark the way individuals use language. The same type of forensic stylistics had been used before, without reference to translation. For example, in 1995 it helped to identify and arrest the so-called Unabomber in the United States (the Unabomber, Ted Kaczynski, had been sending parcel bombs to airlines and universities for around fifteen years; when US newspapers published his political manifesto in 1995, his brother thought he recognised the style of writing and informed the FBI; linguistic analysis of personal and other documents written by Kaczynski confirmed him as the author and led to his arrest).[1] In 1996 the technique also correctly picked out *Newsweek* columnist Joe Klein as the author of the anonymously published novel *Primary Colors*, a fictionalised account of Bill Clinton's early career in Arkansas, showing detailed knowledge of the Clintons and their world; the author was identified by using a computer to locate similarities in linguistic usage between the novel and the assorted writings of a large number of people belonging to the Clinton circle.[2]

In what follows I want to try another approach, starting from the particular choices translators make as they translate. The underlying idea is simple. The translating subject cannot be elided or eliminated from translations because, as a form of text-production, translating requires the deployment of linguistic means in the host language, and this will involve dimensions other than those of the original. As a result, the translator's utterances are necessarily marked, revealing a discursively positioned subject. I will go on to argue that the intertextual and self-referential dimension of these choices renders translation self-reflexive. Translations speak about themselves

Hostile dynasties

Let me begin with a transparent example. In a collection called *Women Writing in Dutch* published in 1994, Laureen Nussbaum presented fragments from the diary of Anne Frank in English translation (Nussbaum 1994). The

---

[1] http://en.wikipedia.org/wiki/Theodore_Kaczynski.

[2] http://en.wikipedia.org/wiki/Primary_Colors

section was extensively introduced and annotated. Nussbaum explained that in her opinion the standard English translation of Anne Frank's diary by B.M. Mooyaart-Doubleday was unsatisfactory: "the Doubleday translation tends to be too literal, which makes for awkward reading, and quite often it is downright wrong" (Nussbaum 1994: 572). She had corrected the alleged errors in her own translation, which she wanted to publish. Unfortunately, the copyright holders, the Doubleday publishing company in New York, refused permission for Nussbaum's alternative version to appear in print. She therefore faced a choice: either reprint the standard translation she disapproved of, or leave the Anne Frank chapter out of the collection altogether.

No doubt thoroughly annoyed, Nussbaum decided to print the Mooyaart-Doubleday version. However, she also inserted her own corrections into it, as a kind of running commentary. The results can be seen in a brief passage like the following. The main text represents Mooyaart-Doubleday's translation, the italicised words and phrases are Nussbaum's suggestions for alternative renderings (between square brackets) and additions (between accolade marks):

> I must keep my head high and be brave, those thoughts will come *{all the same}*, not once, but oh, countless times. Believe me, if you have been shut up *[confined]* for a year and a half, it can get too much for you some days. In spite of all justice *[fairness]* and thankfulness, you can't crush *[repress]* your feelings. (Nussbaum 1994: 552)

Nussbaum realised that the parentheses were intrusive and would make the reading of the translation "somewhat cumbersome", but she felt they were necessary "to do justice to the text that Anne really wrote" (1994: 573). In the passage above there are several parentheses in quick succession. Each intervention points to Nussbaum's disapproval of the Mooyaart-Doubleday rendering, so that we become aware of an ongoing discussion between the main text and the italicised parentheses. The words and phrases between square brackets and accolades contain obvious criticisms of the previous translator's choices and alleged omissions. In other words, the dialogue is polemical and its subject concerns the question how best to do justice in translation to what Anne Frank originally wrote. Nussbaum kept up her criticism in a series of searing footnotes. The critical exchange, or the slanging match, is one between translators, and also, arguably, between Nussbaum and the publishers Doubleday as the copyright holders whom Nussbaum wants to expose for protecting a translation she deems to be inferior. These remonstrations fly back and forth over the original author's head, as translators and publishers fight about how to translate Anne Frank. Nussbaum's interventions refer back to the original Dutch but they are aimed just as much at the perceived inadequacies in the existing translation. Her alternative choices and additions are manifestly oppositional, even if for legal copyright reasons they have been condemned to lead a grouching interstitial existence confined to brackets and footnotes.

I am not interested in establishing the rights and wrongs of Nussbaum's case against her fellow translator. Instead I want to follow up on the way the polemic lends Nussbaum's rendering a double edge. There is more than one palimpsest discernible beneath Nussbaum's words. Her version has one eye on the Dutch and the other on the preceding translation. She speaks simultaneously for Anne Frank and against Mooyaart-Doubleday. The former dimension bears on the translation as an interpretation and re-enactment of the underlying original, the latter on the translation as a critique of another translation. Both dimensions instigate difference and dispersal, and they imply self-reference and self-reflexivity.

There is no need to linger on the issue of interpretation, which has been discussed many times before. All interpretation implies an interpretive angle, a vantage point or subject-position from which things are observed and made sense of. Indeed modern hermeneutics since Heidegger has emphatically confirmed that prejudice, in the literal sense of pre-judgement, the observer's pre-existing horizon of assumptions and expectations, is a prerequisite for interpretation (Gadamer 1989: 268ff., 278ff.). For this reason individual acts of interpretation remain partial and open-ended; they cannot hope to exhaust the meaning of a text, not so much because texts are so rich as to be inexhaustible but because they are read from changing vantage-point in changing contexts.

Translation reflects interpretation. And because translation, for as long as it does not cease to be translation, remains repeatable, successive translations embody different interpretations. Dispersing in time and space, different translations, each in its own way, flesh out the interpretive potential of a given text. It is not just that each translation exemplifies a particular reading. Together they thematise the interpretive differences between them as they shift from one reading to another. Insofar as a text can always be translated again and no translation can lay claim to a definitive reading that would bring interpretive closure, translation figures interpretive difference. Each rendering exhibits its own reading and, in so doing, marks its difference from other readings, other interpretations. This marking constitutes a self-referential moment.

As we saw in the previous chapter, the modern world possesses an instrument to stop translation living out the centrifugal open-endedness of interpretation. The instrument has a name. It is called copyright law. It was at work, not very effectively, in the Anne Frank example just now. Insofar as translation embodies interpretive difference, the law grants the copyright holder a monopoly on the number and kind of interpretations that can enter the public domain in the form of translation.[3] At the very least it can push alternative readings into the margin of an approved reading, as the Anne Frank case shows. It is thus able to bring about a degree of interpretive closure, but only temporarily, up to seventy years after the author's death. Whereas translation celebrates the heterogeneity and proliferation of meaning, copyright law enables authors to impose what Jacques Derrida in a different context called "the hegemony of the homogeneous" (1998: 40). Insofar as the law permits translation to bring multiple interpretations into the open, each translation flaunts it identity through the difference with other translative interpretations.

The other dimension of Laureen Nussbaum's translation concerns not so much the way in which it refers back to its parent text and embodies a particular reading of it, as the way in which it highlights a particular mode of translating. Nussbaum's critique of the Mooyaart-Doubleday version was voiced in a paratextual note but it also crept into the translation itself. The visual presentation of the text with its numerous italicised parentheses left little doubt that Nussbaum's alternative choices were intended polemically to demonstrate a mode of translating assumed to be better suited than her predecessor's to this particular prototext. However, if the presentation had not visually dramatised Nussbaum's disagreement with her fellow translator, the polemic would still have been there. In any case, Nussbaum would obviously have preferred to see her own version printed in full rather than confined to the margins of Mooyaart-Doubleday's. Had she been granted permission to do this, the passage quoted above would have looked like this:

> I must keep my head high and be brave, those thoughts will come all the same, not once, but oh, countless times. Believe me, if you have been confined for a year and a half, it can get too much for you some days. In spite of all justice fairness and thankfulness, you can't repress your feelings.

This version incorporates Nussbaum's addition of "all the same" and everywhere else replaces Mooyaart-Doubleday's choices with Nussbaum's suggested alternatives. The challenge to the preceding translation is just as forceful and as pertinent, but since the text being targeted is no longer provided, the exact nature of the criticism and hence the confrontational aspect

---

[3] To quote just one rather striking example, in a letter to the *Times Literary Supplement* of 9 November 2000, George Steiner, author of the translation studies classic *After Babel* (Steiner 1975), reaffirmed his refusal to grant German or Hebrew translation rights to his novel *The Portage to San Cristóbal of A.H.*

of Nussbaum's choices must remain a matter of speculation, unless one were to fetch the Mooyaart-Doubleday version and compare it line by line with Nussbaum's. Even if Nussbaum had not supplied a footnote identifying Mooyaart-Doubleday's translation as the one against which her own version asserted itself, her choices would still be polemical, but the antagonism would have remained under the surface, discernible only to readers aware of the intertextual connection.

As mentioned above, the debate between the translators, regardless of its degree of visibility in Nussbaum's text, rages over the head of the original author. It concerns in the first instance a number of specific choices at the level of words and phrases. But it is about more than this. Nussbaum's angry reference to the Mooyaart-Doubleday translation, whether advertised in the text or in the shape of silent allusion, qualifies as an instance of specific intertextuality in the French critic Gérard Genette's classification (Genette 1979: 81-83; 1982: 1-7). It has a metatextual aspect in that it constitutes a critical commentary on the previous translation. However the relation between Nussbaum's text and Mooyaart-Doubleday's goes beyond the issue of specific word choices and their intertextual echoes. It extends to that of the appropriate kind of translation that would be required to adequately represent this particular original and presumably other originals like it. If we accept this extension we can expand the idea of intertextuality from the level of relations between particular texts to generic connections. This, then, is the level of generic intertextuality. And once this extension is granted, it is not hard to see the polemical edge of Nussbaum's text involving the even broader question of what makes a good or a valid translation as such. This is what Genette calls an architextual relation, one which ties a text to an entire category or text type, "the entire set of general or transcendent categories – types of discourse, modes of enunciation, literary genres – from which emerges each singular text" (1982: 1).

Every text exhibits, or has attributed to it, a relation to a genre and a type of discourse. Nussbaum's translation highlights this relation by casting aspersions on its predecessor. Criticising Mooyaart-Doubleday is for Nussbaum's text a way of staking a claim to be a superior instance of a certain type of translation (however defined: overt translations aiming at textual accuracy, stylistically adequate translations, translations of world classics, of war testimonials, of autobiographical writing, of diaries written by teenage girls,…) or, at the very least, to be an equally valid translation. There is, then, also a double dynamic at work in Nussbaum's translation on this intertextual level. On the one hand it inflects the translator's 'differential voice' (the term is Barbara Folkart's, 1991: 394) in opposition to another translation or possibly another mode of translating. On the other, it appeals, architextually, to a historically sedimented, socially accepted notion of translation as a type of text of which it presents itself as a token. The former dynamic is necessarily more specific than the latter, because it eyes a particular target.

The dynamic itself bypasses the original. Instead, it is played out in a metadiscursive domain in which translators observe their own translations and those of others, and comment on them through the differential choices they make. The distinction that Cecilia Wadensjö has drawn between representation by displaying and representation by replaying may help to clarify the point (Wadensjö 1998: 247). When translators replay an original, they re-enact it in such a way as to minimise any distance between the figure they are voicing and their own speaking selves. Displaying, by contrast, seeks to alert the audience to the enacting self and the particular way the original is being represented. Whereas replaying invites the translator's voice to be subsumed under that of the original speaker, displaying holds the translated discourse up for inspection as having been rendered in a certain manner. For the argument I am developing here (I will return to Wadensjö's distinction in the next chapter) it is important that either way the translator is keying the utterance in a certain manner, and this keying cannot be entirely reduced to the act of representation. Translators may flaunt their individual style of translating or they may quietly follow convention. Even if they never signal their agenda in a paratext, they show their hand in the choices they make. The element of display in every replaying reveals the translator's interaction with other translators. It is part of the claim that every translation makes: the claim to legitimacy as a translation.

There are countless other translations, apart from the Nussbaum case, in which a similar dynamic is in evidence, so much so that picking further examples is a matter of making a random selection. Vladimir Nabokov's rendering of Pushkin's *Eugen Onegin* (Pushkin 1975) is a particularly flamboyant exercise. Its paratexts pour scorn on every existing English version and champion literal translation as the exclusive form of genuine translation. Nabokov occasionally quotes his predecessors' versions in his footnotes, with the sole aim of demolishing them. The defiant literalism of his own wording, so emphatically at odds with earlier renderings, sends a double and perhaps contradictory message. It suggests that translation can be done in more ways than one and that some ways may be better than others, while claiming in the same breath that there is in fact only one correct way of doing it, which is Nabokov's way. Nabokov's *Onegin* seeks to redefine not just what a good translation is, but quite simply what translation is. Even without the huge critical apparatus with which he festooned his version, that message would be clear. Either way the polemical, oppositional, differential nature of his choices as a translator amounts to a running commentary on how Pushkin's original is to be read and how it is to be represented in English translation. And it is important to realise that this running critical commentary about fellow translators and about translation that is inscribed in Nabokov's aggressive choices constitutes its own discursive dimension, one which is not part of the representation of Pushkin but parasitical on it. It is in this discursive dimension that Nabokov the translator attacks other translators in and through the particular wording of his version.

Here are some more cases, in descending order of eccentricity. The celebrated homophonic renderings of Catullus by Louis and Celia Zukofsky virtually demand to be read as parodic and carnivalesque inversions of the standard modes of poetic translation. Their bilingual Latin-English layout not only invites the reader to assess the English poems as representations of the Latin parent texts but is also designed to show the extent to which the Zukofskys' strategy of privileging sound over sense destabilises the prevailing conventions of poetry translation, as indeed the translators announce in their preface (Zukofsky 1969). As mentioned in the previous chapter, Nabokov wrote his early novel *Camera obscura* in Russian, was dissatisfied with the English translation that Winifred Roy made of it in 1936 and produced his own, *Laughter in the Dark,* in 1938 (Grayson 1979: 5). The reworking amounted to a demonstration of how he wanted translations of his work to be done. The 'abusive fidelity' which Philip Lewis preaches and the 'minoritising' mode of translation that Lawrence Venuti practises are more ideologically motivated but equally emphatic in flaunting particular styles of translating intended as a criticism of mainstream ways of doing things (Lewis 1985; Venuti 1998).

The mainstream itself behaves in much the same way. When David Luke retranslated Thomas Mann's *Death in Venice* in 1996, he concluded his preface with a six-page catalogue of alleged errors in Helen Lowe-Porter's standard version of the novella (Mann 1996). As a result, the choices Luke makes in his own translation gesture not only to Thomas Mann but also, polemically, to Lowe-Porter, whose standard of accuracy Luke so virulently questioned. The history of translations of Freud is littered with such revisions and polemics, not just in English, where James Strachey's standard version has been praised as well as reviled and revised, but in other languages as well. The Spanish translation by José Etcheverry published in 1978-82 was consciously designed as more literal and internally consistent than the 1948 *Obras completas* of Luis López-Ballesteros and than those of Ludovico Rosenthal which date from 1952-56. The new French version by Jean Laplanche and his team mounted an elaborate defence of literalism that repudiated Strachey, quoted Chateaubriand and André Chouraqui with approval, and would have delighted Nabokov

(Ornston 1992: 114-90; Laplanche 1992: 14, 16, 207-08). In all these cases the paratexts measure and explain the critical distance from the predecessors, and this distance is then rehearsed in the differential choices that make up the actual translations. Again, the critical distance, and the intertextual links, would be there even if there were no paratext to announce them. We are dealing with a metatranslative dimension inherent in every translation.

The perception of intertextuality may be in the eye of the beholder. Indeed any accusation of plagiarism between translations is likely to involve someone having to prove that the similarities between two translations are due not to two translators having independently rendered the same original in the same way but to one translator having surreptitiously copied another. If in this case demonstrating a specific intertextual relation is part of the burden of proof, more generic linkages are also possible. When Friedrich Hölderlin's renderings of Sophocles appeared in print in 1804, several reviewers thought they were the work of someone who was mentally disturbed. One critic, Johann Heinrich Voss jr. (the son of the translator Johann Heinrich Voss), wondered in a private letter: "What do you make of Hölderlin's Sophocles? Is the man mad or does he just pretend, and is his Sophocles a veiled satire on bad translations?" (in Fioretos 1999: 277). Either way, it appears, Voss jr could not quite fit a text that was so wholly beyond the pale into the category 'translation' as he knew it; the closest he could come was by suggesting satirical intent. Whether this was the translator's aim remains a moot point. Still, judged by the prevailing standards of German literary translation from the classical languages, Hölderlin's extraordinary version could be seen as a deliberate inversion of these standards, and this was evidently a possibility Voss considered.

The intertextual relation that ties one translation to another does not have to establish what Jorge Luis Borges, speaking of the translators of *The Thousand and One Nights*, called a "hostile dynasty" in which a subsequent translator translates with the express aim of discrediting a predecessor (Borges 2004: 94). In fact, the overwhelming majority of translations fall in with existing translations and prevalent modes of translating. This is so obvious that it is only rarely made explicit. Hugh Tomlinson and Barbara Habberjam, who translated the *Dialogues* of Gilles Deleuze and Claire Parnet, for example, mention in their 'Translators' Introduction' that they have rendered key terms pertaining to Deleuze's thinking in a way consistent with recent translations of Deleuze's other works (Deleuze and Parnet 1987: xii-xiii). Perhaps the most striking practical application of this kind of translative intertextuality however lies elsewhere, in the use professional translators today make of computerised translation memories. Since these memories have the capacity to store vast numbers of existing translations, new translation jobs can be fired at the collection to see what kind of matching will result. Regardless of the size of the memory, the principle is generic intertextuality in action: previous translations furnish a larger or smaller part of the fabric of the new translation to be made.

Friendly filiations may combine in complex ways with hostile stand-offs. In 1768 Edward Harwood published an English rendering of the New Testament which, as the title had it, sought to translate the sacred writings "with the Freedom, Spirit, and Elegance, with which other English Translations from the Greek Classics have lately been executed". In his preface Harwood explained that this was "*not a* verbal *translation, but a* liberal *and* diffusive *version of the sacred classics*" (Harwood 1768: iii). His aim, he said, was to give "a fair and honest version of the divine Volume, just as if I had sat down to translate *Plato, Xenophon, Thucydides, Plutarch,* or any other Greek writer" (1768: vi). By aligning himself with secular translation he could claim, on the one hand, philological impartiality and dispassionate judgement in establishing the "*true* signification of the Original," and, on the other, freedom from the sectarian tendentiousness of "false translations" (1768: iv, viii).

As his model Harwood invoked Sebastien Castellio's Latin Bible translation of 1551, an eminently accessible version which had pursued a Ciceronian standard of eloquence and used classical substitutes for traditional Biblical terms (for instance, *collegium* instead of *synagoga* and, strikingly, *respublica* instead of *ecclesia*; 1768: v; Daniell 2003: 611-12). Harwood wanted to represent the words of the Apostles "with that propriety and perspicuity in which they themselves, I apprehend, would have exhibited them had they *now* lived and written in our language" (1768: iii). To this end, and to counter the "bald and barbarous language" of earlier translations, he employed a distinctly modern idiom ("the vest of modern elegance") and the kind of explanatory paraphrase typical of much eighteenth-century translating ("perspicuous and explicit … upon rational principles", 1768: iv-vi). The famous opening sentence of the gospel according to John, which in the King James Bible reads: "In the beginning was the Word, and the Word was with God, and the Word was God", appears in Harwood's version as: "Before the origin of this world existed the LOGOS – who was then with the Supreme God – and was himself a divine person" (1768: 281). As the use of dashes indicates, and as David Daniell has shown (2003: 607-8), Harwood's style also echoes that of contemporary English novelists. Overall, Harwood's intertextuality is a web of allegiances and antagonisms which tie his version not only to its prototext and to original writings in the receptor language, but also to a network of pre-existing translations and modes of translating. The appeal to that network is part of Harwood's metadiscourse as a translator; and it is so with or without his paratexts.

Self-reference

The constant dialogue among translators about what can pass as (valid, appropriate, legitimate) translation, and the differential edge that each individual rendering possesses, constitute a translation-specific intertextuality which emerges as translators praise or berate one another in and through the very way in which each translator translates. It is this intertextuality which provides translation with its self-referential and self-reflexive dimension.

Self-reference lies dormant in every utterance. The present sentence implies the self-referential statements that it is a sentence and that it is a sentence in English. Self-reference involves a degree of self-observation. The sentences you are now reading know they are in English. Self-reference can be raised to a higher level of explicitness in the form of self-reflexivity and self-description. In most of the examples above (Nussbaum, Nabokov, Zukofsky, Luke, the Freud translators), the paratexts and the differential choices made in the translations themselves brought into view ongoing debates and expectations about how to translate, what can or should be accepted as translation, the regulative and constitutive norms of translation, its prescriptions, proscriptions, preferences and permissions, in short, the entire system of translation underpinning the decisions being made by individual translators as they go about their business.

Before exploring the self-referential dimension of translation further, let us inspect the idea of self-reference a little more closely. Consider the following passage, which occurs a few pages from the end of David Lodge's 1993 novel *Changing Places*. The scene shows two fictional characters, Philip and Morris, who are discussing how novels end. Both speakers are university professors specialising in literature and both are very familiar with the work of Jane Austen. Their conversation is presented, unusually, in the form of drama:

> PHILIP: [...] I mean, take the question of endings. [...] You remember that passage is *Northanger Abbey* where Jane Austen says she's afraid that her readers will have guessed that a happy ending is coming up at any moment.
> MORRIS: (*nods*) Quote, 'Seeing in the tell-tale compression of the pages before them that we are all hastening together to perfect felicity.' Unquote.
> PHILIP: That's it. Well. That's something the novelist can't help giving away, isn't it; that his book is shortly coming to an end? (Lodge 1993: 218)

The passage can hardly avoid being read self-referentially, as an ironic comment within the novel on the ending of novels, and therefore on the ending of this novel too. The reader realises that Philip and Morris may be knowledgeable about how readers can tell that novels are coming to an end even though the fictional characters in these novels cannot see this, but being characters in a novel themselves they do not know that the reader of *Changing Places* can tell from the tell-tale compression of the pages that their own story is about to end as well (actually, in the edition I am quoting from, *Changing Places* is the first of three novels bound in one volume; it ends on page 218 of 897). The fact that the scene is presented according to the conventions of theatrical texts rather than in the more usual form of narrative, heightens the self-reference and draws attention to the conventions of the genre.

If, as a genre, the novel is thought of as a particular form distinct from other forms, then thematising this form within the form renders it self-reflexive. In the scene above, the novel can be seen to observe its own form by reminding itself both of the material object it is – a volume with numbered pages that readers work through as they read – and of the conventions governing the discursive presentation of its narrative. In addition, we as readers can appreciate our ability to look into a fictional world precisely because the fictional characters cannot see their own fictionality even though they evidently appreciate other fictional worlds like Jane Austen's.

Self-reference and its heightened version, self-reflexiveness, come in a variety of manifestations. The present sentence, for example, contains ten words (count us!). This one has four. These sentences are in English. René Descartes' emphatic declaration, in the penultimate paragraph of his *Discours de la méthode*, that he has written his book in French and not in Latin, reminds readers of what they already know, because the claim that the book's language is French is indeed expressed in the French language. As Derrida has noted, Descartes' statement "Et si j'écris en français [...] plutôt qu'en latin" (And if I write in French [...] rather than in Latin) is, in the French formulation in which Descartes wrote it, a performative as well as a constative: it enacts what it states, for indeed it is not in Latin but in French (Derrida 2004: 1).

René Magritte's well-known painting *Ceci n'est pas une pipe* ('This is not a pipe') shows a very real-looking meerschaum pipe, in almost naturalistic detail, with under it the caption "Ceci n'est pas une pipe". The painting is paradoxical because the caption appears to contradict the picture. It can be read in more ways than one, and all invoke self-reference. The words of the caption may be read as saying that they are unlike the iconic image of a pipe. They can be taken literally as meaning that "Ceci" ('This') is indeed not a pipe, it is a word. The standard interpretation of the painting sees the caption as commenting on the fact that the iconic image is not a pipe but a painted two-dimensional representation of a pipe. In this case the painting is also commenting on the nature of painting.

Consider *Figure 1*. It is a painting by the seventeenth-century Flemish artist Cornelius Gijsbrechts. Not much is known about Gijsbrechts, except that he worked in Germany and the Scandinavian lands in the 1660s and '70s (Koester 1999: 12-17). Look at it closely. The painting is a still-life showing two dead birds hanging upside down against a rather dark wall. It appears not to have been framed and looks unfinished; perhaps it was abandoned before it was finished. The canvas is nailed to a fairly rough piece of wood; the top left corner has come away and hangs down over the picture. Nevertheless the birds have been drawn with care and in exquisite detail.

Figure 1: Cornelius Gijsbrechts, Still Life of Two Dead Birds
Hanging on a Wall, c.1672
(By permission of Statens Museum for Kunst, Copenhagen)

Now look again. The painting is unframed, but is not an unfinished work at all. Nor does it consist of a layer of paint applied to a piece of canvas that is frayed at the edges and stuck to a piece of wood. In fact, the wood too is painted and it forms part of the painting. What we have is a typical *trompe-l'oeil* performance. The picture is meant to be left unframed, and it shows a painted canvas which appears to be nailed to a piece of wood.

Gijsbrechts was a master of this kind of trickery. *Figure 2* looks like a photograph of the reverse of a framed painting. However it is not the reverse of one of Gijsbrechts's paintings. The wooden frame that we see, and the canvas it holds, are both painted. The painting consists of a picture of the back of a painting, drawn with uncanny precision, including the painted number 36 on the little piece of paper apparently fixed to the canvas with red sealing wax.

*Figure 2: Cornelius Gijsbrechts, The Reverse of a Framed Painting, 1670
(By permission of Statens Museum for Kunst, Copenhagen)*

Both these paintings by Gijsbrechts are self-reflexive, and thus more than merely self-referential. They consciously exploit the illusionistic effect brought about by their realistic depiction. The painted frame can easily be mistaken for a real frame, and the painted wood and nails for real wood and nails. But the painted truth that we think we see is deceptive, for the canvas with the dead birds of *Figure 1* cannot be removed from the wood and framed, and the painted frame of *Figure 2* cannot be turned around to reveal the front of the painting since it actually is the front, only made to look like the back. In both cases the care lavished on the representation is turned ironically against the viewer, who is reminded that the pictures are visual puns, representations playing on the idea of representation, playful pictorial comments on the painter's craft. Crucially, what makes the paintings work is both the natural likeness and the implicit reference to convention. We normally expect paintings to be framed, and to be hung with the front, not the back, facing the viewer. We are momentarily wrongfooted when the paintings deliberately thwart these expectations by refusing a frame or by integrating it into the painted surface.

Metatranslation

Translation too is inherently self-referential form. The form is framed by the entry on the title page identifying the text as a translation. That entry invites the reader to enter into a contract, an agreement to read the text as simulating a discourse in another language. The contract allows the reader's awareness of the original as being distinct from the translation to remain latent for as long as the translation illusion, the illusion of equivalence, lasts. The illusion can never be complete. If it were, the translation would cease to be a translation, as we saw in the previous chapter. But together with the contract on which it is based it permits us to state, casually and elliptically, that 'I have read Dostoevsky', when in fact I know I have read a translation of Dostoevsky.

Self-reference can be thrown into relief. This happens as soon as a text is recognised as a translation. The label tells us that someone is reporting or relaying someone else's words. The announcement that the text to follow is a translation frames the re-enactment that follows, if only by activating a particular set of expectations which may or may not subsequently be satisfied. A translator's preface will make the difference between the frame and what is contained within it even more emphatic. It draws attention to what Wadensjö called the display, at the expense of the replay. The translation itself then merely exemplifies one way of translating among others, one translative mode selected from a range of available modes.

To put this more strongly: approached through the preface that frames it, a translation dramatises one particular type of representation among others, and what matters is the particular kind of representation on display rather than the absent original. What is at stake when things are seen from this angle is not so much the reproduction of this or that original, but the choice of one mode of reproduction in preference to other existing or available modes. That choice is typically stated in the translator's preface, and it is enacted in the translation itself. In this way a translator's preface prevents an uninhibited reading of the translation because its echo can still be heard while the performance is under way. The actress who tells us how she is going to play Ophelia, will go on to play Ophelia like an actress playing Ophelia. What we then witness is an Ophelia played by a certain actress in a certain way. The curtain-raiser, the preface, makes us complicit in a self-conscious, double-edged performance.

The latent self-referentiality of translation is also raised as soon as we are reminded, in a translation, of the translation contract itself, or when a translation emphatically gestures to other translations or to particular modes of translating, that is, when its translation-specific intertextuality comes to the fore. At that moment we consider not so much the way in which the translation re-enacts its donor text, but the way it interacts with existing translations and with expectations about translation. The self-referentiality of translation is raised to self-reflection when the translative act itself is rehearsed within a translation, when the form – translation as a form distinct from other forms – re-enters the form and the translation contract is renegotiated within the text. This happens when the performance of translation is thematised in a translation itself and metatranslation invades the translated text.

Arthur Conan Doyle's story 'The Greek Interpreter' (Conan Doyle 1951) can be read as containing ironies of this kind. The story is perhaps not widely known, so here is the plot line. Melas, a Greek interpreter, accosts Sherlock Holmes in a London street with an account of how, two days ago, he was kidnapped in broad daylight and taken to a house somewhere on the outskirts of the city. There two Englishmen forced him, under threat of grievous bodily harm, to interpret for them. They produced someone they were holding prisoner, a pale and emaciated figure, his face covered in sticking plaster, with one pad covering his mouth. The prisoner, it turned out, was Greek; he had arrived in Britain only recently, and spoke no English. The two Englishmen, being English and villainous, did not speak any foreign languages. Melas had no choice but to interpret between the villains and their prisoner. At the end of the session he was taken away and dropped on Wandsworth Common; from there he made his way to Clapham Junction and caught the last train back to Victoria Station. Later on in the story it becomes clear that the prisoner, named Kratides, was the brother of a Greek girl whom one of the English villains had carried off and wanted to marry for her money. Kratides, the trustee of his sister's fortune, had inadvertently fallen into the villains' hands. He refused to sign his sister's money over to them, and to compel him they were starving him to death. Because the girl was being held in the same house, the villains had covered Kratides' face with sticking plaster, hoping she would not recognize him should she happen to see him. Despite Sherlock Holmes' best efforts the story ends tragically with Kratides dead and the villains fleeing abroad, taking the girl with them. Poetic justice is done when some months later a report arrives which tells of the two villains killing each other after a quarrel, although Holmes prefers to believe that the girl probably dispatched both her captors.

The interpretation scene, the central episode in the story and the one from which Holmes derives all his clues, is a peculiar specimen of dialogue interpreting. Melas, the unwilling intermediary, stands between the two English villains and the Greek prisoner. The latter is bound and gagged. The villains untie one of his arms and hand him a slate, on which he will write down, in Greek, his answers to Melas's spoken words. What follows is therefore an exercise in bimedial as well as bilingual interpreting. Melas hears English which he interprets into spoken Greek, then he reads the written Greek answers and interprets them into spoken English. We, the readers, read all this on the page, in English only.

As the conversation unfolds and Melas interprets, he realises that the villains do not understand Greek and are unable to check on the words he speaks in that language. So he starts playing a dangerous game, tagging brief questions of his own to the translated words he addresses to the prisoner. Kratides quickly catches on, and the two Greeks engage in a private monolingual conversation that takes shape entirely in the margin of the bilingual spoken and written exchange. As Melas recounts it to Sherlock Holmes afterwards, the conversation ran like this:

> 'You can do no good by this obstinacy. *Who are you?*'
> 'I care not. *I am a stranger in London.*'
> 'Your fate will be on your own head. *How long have you been here?*'
> 'Let it be so. *Three weeks.*'
> 'The property can never be yours. *What ails you?*'
> 'It shall not go to villains. *They are starving me.*'
> 'You shall go free if you sign. *What house is this?*'
> 'I will never sign. *I do not know.*'
> 'You are not doing her any service. *What is your name?*'
> 'Let me hear her say so. *Kratides.*'
> 'You shall see her if you sign. *Where are you from?*'
> 'Then I shall never see her. *Athens.*' (Conan Doyle 1951:316)

The italicised words are exchanged between the two Greek speakers only and they remain intelligible only to them. The rest takes on bilingual form. There was no risk, incidentally, of the villains catching names like 'London' or 'Athens' and becoming suspicious, because Kratides would have written them as *Λονδον* and *Αθιναι* (or possibly, in capital letters, *ΛΟΝΔΟΝ* and

ΑΘΙΝΑΙ). From an ethical point of view, of course, Melas's behaviour flouts all the deontic principles of the interpreting profession. He manifestly abuses his linguistic monopoly to gain information of benefit to himself. But then, he is justified in doing so, since his employers are criminals and Melas, having been dragged into the situation against his will, is bravely attempting to assist an innocent victim.

The unusual juxtaposition of translated and untranslated discourse within one half spoken, half written conversation, however, cannot fail to alert the reader to the difference between the two discourses. It is emphasised typographically by the use of italics. It calls for increased attention, as the reader needs to separate out the bilingual from the monolingual exchange and the respective recipients of each. In focusing on that difference, the translated nature of the non-italicised words catches the eye as much as the non-translated nature of the italicised ones. Each part of the exchange flaunts its own status, contrastively and, since both parts come to us in English only rather than in English and Greek, ironically.

The monolingual representation of a bilingual scene cannot help attracting attention to its medium. In the say way, a text that contains words or phrases already in the language into which it is being translated presents particular problems for the translator. In the letters of Vincent van Gogh, for example, we regularly encounter English phrases interspersed in the Dutch text. They stand out, as foreign bodies in an otherwise linguistically uniform whole. In the Penguin translation of van Gogh's letters (van Gogh 1996) these English phrases appear unaltered. It would not be right to say they have been left untranslated, since they are clearly part of the process of translation that the text as a whole has undergone. We might say they have been translated into themselves, into a form identical to their original form. However, being now commonplace English phrases in an English text, they no longer stand out. So, in order to convey to the Anglophone reader the surplus value of English words featuring as foreign bodies in a Dutch text, the translator, acting as an editor of sorts, inserted footnotes in the English version informing the reader that those particular phrases were already in English in the original. The footnotes rather conspicuously introduce a new speaking voice in the margins of the English text, and they tell the reader of a particular translation problem – not only that of translating into English phrases that were already in English, but, in addition, the extra relief English words acquire when they function in a Dutch text. Still, each footnote plays out a little paradox. Stressing the Englishness of a phrase which reaches readers in English anyway risks an absurd level of redundancy, which those readers can only dispel by reminding themselves that the surrounding text was originally not in English. It cannot therefore have been van Gogh who wrote all those other English words that are not footnoted in the translation.

Jacques Derrida's essay 'Signature Event Context' as translated into English by Samuel Weber and Jeffrey Mehlman (Derrida 1977) abounds with bracketed French words signalling the limits of translatability as perceived by the translators. Some interventions are explicitly identified as stemming from '*trans.*', that is, the translators. One famous crux appears with a bracketed amplification as "*différance* [difference and deferral, *trans.*]" (1977: 179). To render the Derridean "différance" as "*différance*" was not yet an obvious choice in 1977, and the translator's addition of the two meanings that are collapsed in the French neologism explains the nature of the problem to the reader. On other occasions the English text shows a degree of lexical variation which the translators appear to regard as perhaps unfortunate but inevitable. The repeated insertion of the same French term to match a variety of English renderings suggests as much. We read of "his intentions [*vouloir-dire*]", "the desire to mean what one says [*vouloir-dire*]", "its 'original' desire-to-say-what-one-means [*vouloir-dire*]", "the presence of meaning [*vouloir-dire*]" and "the exchange of intentions and meanings [*vouloir-dire*]" (1977: 177, 181, 185, 191, 194). The translators' presence makes itself felt through the marked contrast between the stability of the French term and the mutability of its various context-bound approximations in English.

These variations and supplements mark an impasse in the passage from one language to another, the passage also to translation. Put differently, they signal not so much the *difficulty* of translation, as the difficulty of *translation*. The problem, that is, lies in translation as a social construct, more particularly in the expectations audiences bring to texts labelled 'translation'. The translators are perfectly capable of glossing the original and devising corresponding expressions. Had they but world enough and time, they could catch the original's every nuance – but it would take forever, literally. The translators' problem lies in meeting the distinctive audience expectation commonly associated with the idea of translating, namely that the translation supply a single linear discourse matching the single linear discourse of its model – the 'quantitative' measure of translation, as Derrida would later put it (2004: 428). The contingency of the expectations associated with translation is highlighted precisely in those instances where the translation seems unable to live up to this quantitative measure. Through the way they deal with individual problems, the translators are throughout commenting on translation.

In 'Limited Inc abc . . . ' (translated by Sam Weber), Derrida's lengthy response to John Searle's attack on 'Signature Event Context', Derrida states in so many words that he is writing in French ("I am trying to respond in French",

1977a: 173) – but since we read these words in English, the incongruity of the statement already highlights the presence of more than one voice inhabiting the translated discourse. A couple of pages earlier Derrida had introduced the French acronym "Sarl" (*'Société à responsabilité limitée'*), which puns on the name of his opponent, Searle. Knowing that his essay would be translated into English, Derrida had directly addressed the translator with a request: "I ask that the translator leave this conventional expression in French and if necessary, that he explain things in a note" (1977a: 170); the request is translated, and indeed it is met, leaving the duly italicised and untranslated acronym as the visible evidence of the translator's cooperative handiwork. Speaking positions are thereby dramatised in the very performance of translation.

In 'Signature Event Context' the French words *éventualité* and *possibilité* had both been rendered as "possibility". The reader of the English, of course, would not have known that behind "possibility" lay two different French words. In Derrida's altercation with Searle however the difference between the French terms as they appear in the essay's original French version becomes relevant. In the second essay therefore the translator corrects the earlier conflation of the two words. Where the earlier essay said at one point that "Austin excludes this possibility" (1977: 189-90), the later essay first points out the translation error ("it is regrettable that the distinction [...] was not rendered in the English translation", 1977a: 229) and then quotes at some length from the first essay, recuperating its wording and simultaneously obliging the translator to amend the earlier rendering of the key term in a bracketed addition: "Austin excludes this *eventuality* [*éventualité*, initially translated as 'possibility']", 1977a: 229). Here again the issue of translation is being thematised within the text itself – in this case both the original and the translated text. Not only that, the repeatability of translation is being both talked about and acted out – but acted out in the translation only.

More paradoxical is the passage in 'Limited Inc abc...' where Derrida, having used the term "fake-out" ("What a fake-out, leaving me flat-footed..."), carries on for a couple of sentences and then suddenly retraces his steps, wondering, "I cannot imagine how Sam Weber is going to translate 'fake-out'" (1977a: 213). It is a peculiar statement to make, for in the translation we are reading the term has already been translated by Sam Weber, a few sentences earlier, and without a hitch ("What a fake-out, leaving me flat-footed..."). To explain what he assumes is going to pose a problem for the translator, Derrida first gives his personal understanding of it as a football term. He then returns to the French word which apparently sits behind "fake-out", namely "contre-pied" (which now appears in the English text in French, as it is emphatically to the French word that Derrida is referring) as French lexicographers understand it. He quotes the definition of it offered in Littré's dictionary. This definition however we read quoted in English, down to a citation from La Fontaine (except for the key-word *contre-pied* in the citation: "'People have taken precisely the *contre-pied* of the will.' La Fontaine"; *ibid.*) – when "fake-out", on its first occurrence in the English text we are reading, already covered Derrida's private understanding of *contre-pied* in a straight, unmarked, one-to-one matching. In anticipating what subsequently turned out to be a non-problem for the translator, Derrida has not only implicated the translator in the translation, but allowed us to register Weber's discursive presence in the curious situation where, having already and perfectly adequately dealt with *contre-pied* as 'fake-out', the translator is taken back to the corresponding French term which he is now obliged to put back into its French form as the problem it never was. As a result we end up reading, incongruously, because in English, the definition of a French word in a French dictionary. Translation is being thematised here in more ways than one.

Absence may be as telling as redundancy. In the summer of 2001 a US spy plane collided with a Chinese jet fighter in the skies above southern China; the Chinese pilot died in the accident. The US plane was forced to land on Hainan Island and a diplomatic tussle ensued between the American and Chinese authorities. The US demanded its plane and crew back, the Chinese insisted on an apology first. The situation was eventually defused by means of an exquisitely ambiguous form of words: the Americans said they were "very sorry" about the loss of life and "very sorry" about the whole incident. According to US diplomats, their side only intended to express regret, without implying an apology. The Chinese preferred to take the words as an apology. The Chinese interpreter however faced a dilemma, as (apparently) the double meaning of 'sorry' cannot be sustained in Chinese and different expressions would have to be used to convey either regret or apology. In the event, the interpreter left the words "very sorry" in English in his Chinese translation.[4] His decision not to translate, and hence not to choose between the two possible renderings, signals a cautious unwillingness to resolve a calculated ambiguity, and as such it entails a comment about the role of diplomatic interpreters. The comment may be read as signalling a principle of non-intervention, or one of respecting speakers' intentions, or a refusal to lay oneself open to possible blame afterwards, but it is a comment nevertheless. It appeals to a long history

---

[4] With thanks to Chuanyun Bao, Monterey Institute of International Studies (personal communication, October 2005). See also http://www.pacom.mil/pages/ep3photos.htm, http://archives.cnn.com/2001/US/05/01/china.us.plane.04/, http://www.globalsecurity.org/military/world/china/lingshui-ep3.htm, http://www.pbs.org/wgbh/pages/frontline/shows/china/etc/script.html.

of official interpreting, and would not be possible without it.

Finally, here is a little practical exercise. Unfortunately it will not work if you can read German, because you will see the point straight away. If you are lucky enough not to have any German, please read on. In one of his case histories Sigmund Freud writes about a neurotic patient, the so-called Rat Man, who was passionately in love with a woman. The lady had an English cousin named Richard, or Dick for short. One day the patient, who was intensely jealous of this Richard, suddenly became obsessed with the idea that he, the patient, was too fat and had to lose weight at all costs, and so he began to exercise madly. Here is Freud's account, exactly as he wrote it, except that I am giving it here in English. The few sentences I have left out (indicated by [...]) do not affect the passage or the exercise in any way. Please read the passage carefully and try to answer the questions that follow:

> One day while he was away on his summer holidays the idea suddenly occurred to him that he was too fat and that he must *make himself thinner*. So he began getting up from table before the pudding came round and tearing along the road without a hat in the blazing heat of an August sun. Then he would dash up a mountain at the double, till, dripping with perspiration, he was forced to come to a stop. [...]
> Our patient could think of no explanation of this senseless obsessional behaviour until it suddenly occurred to him that at that time his lady had also been stopping at the same resort; but she had been in the company of an English cousin, who was very attentive to her and of whom the patient had been very jealous. This cousin's name was Richard, and, according to the usual practice in England, he was known as *Dick*. Our patient, then, had wanted to kill this Dick.

Clearly, the patient envies Richard alias Dick because he sees the English cousin as a rival. He wants the rival out of the way, to be rid of him, hence the suppressed wish to kill Dick. So far so good. But why the frantic jogging? How will you connect the jogging with the desire to see Richard dead?

Various explanations suggest themselves. Perhaps the patient simply wanted to make himself more attractive? Perhaps Richard, too, was thin and the patient was eager to match his rival's thinness? Perhaps being thin would give the patient a better chance of killing Richard, or of gaining the lady's favour? All these explanations are plausible and sensible, and all are wrong. Nevertheless the passage above translates into English exactly what Freud wrote in plain, intelligible German. Why then does it remain impenetrable in English while Freud's German makes perfect sense? There is a solution, and it hinges on a single short word. Read the passage again and you will see:

> One day while he was away on his summer holidays the idea suddenly
> occurred to him that he was too fat (German: *dick*) and that he must
> *make himself thinner*. So he began getting up from table before the
> pudding came round and tearing along the road without a hat in the
> blazing heat of an August sun. Then he would dash up a mountain at
> the double, till, dripping with perspiration, he was forced to come to
> a stop. [...]
> Our patient could think of no explanation of this senseless obsessional
> behaviour until it suddenly occurred to him that at that time his lady had
> also been stopping at the same resort; but she had been in the company
> of an English cousin, who was very attentive to her and of whom the
> patient had been very jealous. This cousin's name was Richard, and,
> according to the usual practice in England, he was known as *Dick*. Our
> patient, then, had wanted to kill this Dick. (Freud 1963: 31-32)

The difference between this passage and the first one is that a German word
has been added between brackets; the word is also explicitly identified as being
a German word. It is in this form, with the bracketed aside, that the passage
appeared in print. As soon as the reader connects the bracketed German word
with the English cousin's popular name, the riddle is solved. If the case study
represents historical truth, the connection also gave Freud his breakthrough
when he was treating the patient. Freud, that is, explains the patient's behaviour
as a case of transference, an association of 'fat' with the name 'Dick'. In German the two words sound the same, hence the ready association of one with the
other. In English the link remains entirely opaque – indeed if the patient had not
spoken German he would not have gone jogging. The translator, Philip Rieff,
obviously saw the problem coming and intervened by informing the reader
in the bracketed aside that the word for 'fat' in German is 'dick'. We can now
understand the connection in the patient's mind between losing weight and
killing Dick. The urge to kill off the fat in his own body transfers to a culturally
acceptable plane the repressed murderous intent towards the rival.

The translator's aside stands out from the rest of the text. We know the
bracketed words represent an intervention by the translator because in uttering
them the translator is not translating. The word *dick* repeats Freud's German
word, untranslated, and the word 'German' does not occur in Freud's text, it
is the translator's label to denote the language he is translating from. In the
bracketed aside the translator briefly leaves his translating behind and addresses
the reader in his own name to offer much needed help: the reader needs to be
told to remember that 'fat' in German is 'dick', so the connection with the
name Dick later in the passage can be made.

Of course, the problem only arises because in English the adjective 'fat' does not sound like 'Dick' and there is no readily available alternative that fits the bill. This is the translator's bad luck. As a result, he is forced to interrupt his own performance and, breaking cover, explain the problem to the reader. In other words, the problem of translating into English the similar-sounding words 'dick' and 'Dick' as they occur in the German, here invades the translation itself. As a result, the passage as printed in English reveals two separate active voices, Freud's and the translator's, and the latter, not Freud, is reflecting on an insurmountable translation problem, an instance of homophony as fortuitous linguistically as it is crucial for Freud's entire project. The reflection evidently extends beyond the two bracketed words that the translator has added to the passage. It is not until the end of the second paragraph that the reader realises why it matters that 'dick' happens to be German for 'fat'. At the same time, the translator's recourse to brackets comprising a minimal and unattributed explanation is a relatively discreet solution, less intrusive than a footnote and less presumptuous than a wholesale rewriting of the entire scene. To that extent the particular way in which the translator thematises the translation problem within his translation suggests a particular view of how translators should behave.

If the passage is self-reflexive in confronting the reader directly with a translation problem and a proposed solution, it offers another, more oblique comment on translation as well, and again it is the translator who is making the comment over the original author's head. In English, 'dick' happens to be a slang word for penis. In Freud's German text this connotation plays no part. What matters there is that 'dick' means 'fat' and sounds like the name Dick, for this homophony is what makes the patient attack the flab in his own body. In English however the fact that 'dick' connotes 'penis' is impossible to ignore, especially in a case study which revolves around sexual obsession and repression. In making no reference at all to the slang meaning of 'dick', the English text demonstratively refrains from accommodating an obviously meaningful element. The translator's reticence amounts to a significant omission, and hence a statement. The translator evidently does not see it as part of his job to articulate a dimension of meaning absent from the original, however urgently the discourse in English may invite it. The statement, in other words, consists of an eloquent silence, and it concerns the limits of the translator's task as this translator sees them.

Perhaps the translator's unspoken comment is the more significant of the two. It shows that self-referential statements about translation occur in translations without having to be stated in prefaces, footnotes, bracketed parentheses or other paratexts. They are inscribed in the choices translators make as they

translate. These choices invoke, intertextually and architextually, other translations and a concept of translation as perceived by an individual translator.
By adopting a position vis-à-vis that body of translations the translator marks
not only a discursive presence but also a critical viewpoint. And since translations necessarily contain these positionings, they speak about themselves,
with more or less emphasis.

Let me conclude. Self-reference accompanies, in latent form, all translation. It is raised to metatranslative self-reflection when translation observes its
own operations and the factors conditioning those operations. This observing
reveals the observer's – that is, the translator's – subject-position in the text.
Self-reference may be raised to self-reflexiveness in paratexts, in discursive
interventions by translators breaking into the texts they are transmitting and in
translators' defiantly unconventional choices, but it is also there in everyday
conventional choices. Even when self-reference remains latent and submerged,
we can tease it out by focusing on translation-specific intertextual links and on
the provisionality of every rendering, and by reading translations differentially,
based on choices which fall in with or diverge from prevailing patterns and
expectations.

The self-reference of translation brings into view a metadimension where
translation speaks about itself. Self-reference and self-reflection allow us to
appreciate not only the individual signature of a given version, but also the
particular expectations to which it responds, irrespective of whether the response takes the form of compliance or defiance. To the extent that the interplay
between expectations, responses and adjustments determines what counts as
translation, when and where, self-reference yields insight into the internal
structure, the boundaries and the temporality of translation – in Chapter Five
I will come round to saying: the internal structure, the boundaries and the
temporality of translation as a social system.

Metatranslation stands for the way translations reflect about themselves
as translations. There is an ethical side to this, which we will explore in the
next chapter.

3. Irony's Echo

Let me suggest that if a typical book looks like the illustration on the left, the typical translation looks like the picture on the right:

Figure 3: *Adolf Hitler, Mein Kampf, 1925-26* Figure 4: *Adolf Hitler, Mijn kamp, translated by Steven Barends, 1939*

(By permission of Bayerisches Staatsministerium der Finanzen, Munich)

It may seem a little perverse to call *Mein Kampf* a typical book. However, I choose this example for its directness. Its cover shows the author looking straight at us, both in the original German and in its Dutch translation. When we start reading the book, the author, Adolf Hitler, speaks directly to us, in the first person singular, both in the original German and in the Dutch translation. Here are the opening sentences of the book's preface:

Am 1. April 1924 hatte ich, auf Grund des Urteilsspruches des Münchner Volksgerichts von diesem Tage, meine Festungshaft zu Landsberg am Lech anzutreten. Damit bot sich mir nach Jahren ununterbrochener Arbeit zum ersten Male die Möglichkeit, an ein Werk heranzugehen, das von vielen gefordert und von mir selbst als zweckmäßig für die Bewegung empfunden wurde. (Hitler 1925-6, vi)

Op den 1en April van het jaar 1924 werd ik, tengevolge van het vonnis dat het Münchener Volksgericht dienzelfden dag over mij velde, te Landsberg a/d Lech opgesloten, teneinde mijn vestingstraf te ondergaan. Hierdoor kreeg ik, na jaren van onafgebroken activiteit, voor het eerst den tijd, om mij te wijden aan een werk, dat velen van mij hadden geëischt, en dat mijzelf ook nuttig scheen voor de beweging. (Hitler 1939a: xxvii)

The German first-person singular pronoun 'ich' ('I') in the first line refers as unmistakably to Adolf Hitler as the Dutch 'ik' (in the second line of the Dutch text). Yet the Dutch words were not written by Hitler himself but by the Dutch translator of *Mein Kampf*, Steven Barends. Nevertheless there are good reasons for assuming that the voice addressing us not just in the German but in the Dutch as well is meant to be Hitler's. Not only is the Dutch version an authorised translation, as the title page announces ("Geautorise-erde uitgave"), but the packaging of the book indicates that the translator is evidently in sympathy with Hitler's views. The publishing house specialised in propaganda for the extreme right, and the back pages advertised some of Steven Barends's own publications: poetry collections with rousing New Order titles like *Ochtendappèl* ('morning parade') and *Viva la muerte!*, together with a semifictional "story of blood and borders" called *Brown Rebels in Austria*. During the Second World War Barends would join the SS. After the war he was banned from publishing his own work for ten years but had a lifelong ban on publishing translations imposed on him – his translating was obviously considered to be even more obnoxious that his original writing.[1]

If we feel entitled to read the 'I' that Barends writes as coinciding with Hitler's 'I', this is because there is very little to separate Barends's voice from Hitler's. The Dutch *Mijn kamp* is identified as a translation on the title page, but that is all. There is no translator's preface or epilogue, and in the text itself the translator also keeps in the background. The paratexts at the back of the book, and the name of the publishing house reveal Barents as a Nazi supporter. This ideological alignment of translator and author strengthens the consonance of voice. This is not to say that the translator does not have a presence or does not take up a position in the translated discourse itself. However this position is never profiled as diverging from the author's, and so it tends to be subsumed under it. More than that, everything suggests Barends was perfectly happy to act as Hitler's little local helper.

Things are very different with the American translation which a team led by Alvin Johnson brought out in New York in 1939. This version, a "fully annotated", "complete and unabridged edition," had been sponsored by a committee including Pearl Buck, Theodore Dreiser, Albert Einstein, Thomas Mann, Eugene O'Neill and others (Hitler 1939: n.p.). The translation was by Helmut Ripperger and others, as the Publishers' Note acknowledges (*ibid.*). The book featured a map, printed opposite the title page and showing Nazi Germany as a black oilslick ominously expanding beyond its borders. It is reproduced here as *Figure 5*.

---

[1] http://www.poeziemarathon.nl/dichters/barends.html

Figure 5: From Adolf Hitler, Mein Kampf, ed. Alvin Johnson et al., 1939
(By permission of The Random House Group Ltd)

The date on the map, "January 1, 1939", served as reminder of recent events:
the *Anschluss* with Austria of March 1938 and the annexation of the 'Sude-
ten' areas of Czechoslovakia in the autumn of 1938, among other things. The
introduction to the translation, signed by the editorial team, left the reader in
no doubt about the editors' opinion of the qualities of *Mein Kampf* and their
view of the book's message:

> The reader must bear in mind that Hitler is no artist in literary expres-
> sion, but a rough-and-ready political pamphleteer often indifferent
> to grammar and syntax alike. [...] *Mein Kampf* is a propagandistic
> essay by a violent partisan. As such it often warps historical truth and
> sometimes ignores it completely. We have, therefore, felt it our duty
> to accompany the text with factual information which constitutes an
> extensive critique of the original. [...] The separation between text
> and commentary is clearly indicated, so that the reader will have no
> difficulty on that score. (Hitler 1939: viii-x)

A further editorial note explained that the typography of the translation followed that of the first German edition and that passages which were left out

of the first English translation of *Mein Kampf,* the radically abridged version by E.T.S. Dugdale published in London in 1933 (Barnes and Barnes 1980: 2-18), had been marked with typographical symbols in the margin; there are many such passages in the book.

When we start reading this translation, it is impossible simply to superimpose Hitler's first person on the 'I' that speaks in the English text:

Am 1. April 1924 hatte ich, auf Grund des Urteilsspruches des Münchner Volksgerichts von diesem Tage, meine Festungshaft zu Landsberg am Lech anzutreten. Damit bot sich mir nach Jahren ununterbrochener Arbeit zum ersten Male die Möglichkeit, an ein Werk heranzugehen, das von vielen gefordert und von mir selbst als zweckmäßig für die Bewegung empfunden wurde.	On April 1, 1924, because of the sentence handed down by the People's Court of Munich, I had to begin that day, serving my term in the fortress at Landsberg on the Lech. Thus, after years of uninterrupted work, I was afforded for the first time an opportunity to embark on a task insisted upon my many and felt to be serviceable to the movement by myself. (Hitler 1939: n.p.)

The way the translation is framed by editorial introductions and annotations highly critical of *Mein Kampf* emphasises the ideological divide separating translator and editors from Hitler. Formally, the American translation of the actual text of *Mein Kampf* looks exactly like the Dutch one in that both present Hitler as speaking in the first person singular. In both cases the translators relay Hitler's words as if quoting them in direct speech. They both account for the fact that they have Hitler speak in a language other than his native German by affixing the label 'translation' to their texts. The key difference between the Dutch and the American translation is that the latter makes the quotation marks clearly visible. Steven Barends's version can be read as tending towards free direct speech, the kind of speech situation in which someone's words are reported in the form of direct quotation but the discourse which introduces and frames the reported discourse has been removed. True, Barends's version announces itself as a translation, but it uses its paratexts, including the label "authorised edition", as a quality badge to signal a philological and ideological allegiance that allows the translator to stand in the author's shadow, indeed behind him, out of sight. This discretion sustains the illusion that we are reading Hitler speaking in Dutch. It all but cancels out the distraction caused by the knowledge that there is someone voicing Hitler's words for us in a different tongue.

The American translation separates the philological from the ideological.

It too claims philological accuracy but makes it a part of the wider agenda that informs the venture as a whole. This agenda is anti-Nazi. It requires a full, unexpurgated, scrupulously accurate rendering of Hitler's words, so as to expose them for what they are – to the extent, of course, that translation is able to show them for what they are. It also requires a clear statement of ideological difference with Hitler's message. As a result, the editorial paratexts make the actual translation into an object of contemplation, not just as regards the book's message but also it style. The Book-of-the-Month Club prefaced its edition of the translation with an appraisal by Dorothy Thompson which warned: "The reader will find the English writing rhetorical, turbid, and digressive, and the text disorganized. Do not, however, criticize the translators" (Hitler 1939: n.p.). Stylistically, that is, the translators have chosen to write an idiom they would not otherwise have written, and the reader is meant to make allowance for this. Most importantly, of course, the anti-Nazi stance in the editorial team's introduction and extensive annotations (some 80,000 words in all) draws a sharp line between their values and Hitler's. In that sense Hitler's own words are held up for inspection and put as if between quotation marks. In Cecilia Wadensjö's terms: the replay recedes in favour of the display (1998: 247).

Despite this formal separation between the framing discourse and Hitler's words, the clash of values articulated in the translation's paratexts permeates the translation itself. Even as they move from the frame to the translated text, readers are meant to remain aware that the translator does not wish to be associated with either the style or the ideas of the original. This punctures the pretence that translators suspend their own identity as they usurp the first person singular in translation. The 'I' that addresses the reader in English refers exclusively to Hitler and not to the translator, even though it was the translator who wrote "I". The first-person pronoun therefore carries a double load: the translator's implied 'I' is the face behind the mask. The figure being voiced is to be distinguished from the self that is doing the voicing, indeed the latter insists in keeping its distance from the former, and the way the translated discourse as a whole is keyed makes this abundantly clear (Wadensjö 1998: 243-5).

The 1939 American translation of *Mein Kampf* illustrates the issue I am concerned with in this chapter. It is that of conflicts of value. What happens when translators translate texts they strongly disagree with or disapprove of, especially when ideological or moral values are at stake? It is normally ex-pected of translators either that they are in agreement with what they choose or consent to translate, or that they adopt a position of neutrality. In a short reflection of 1897, 'A Plea for the Translator', Mary Serrano, the translator of an abridged version of Marie Bashkirtseff's diary, put this demand in all its starkness. A translator, she declared, must be absolutely unselfish, content to live a reflected intellectual life, thinking always the thoughts of others, reflecting, like a mirror, the beauties of others, for which he receives no credit, and their defects, which are attributed to the distorting medium of his translation; held responsible for opinions which may be diametrically opposed to his own, for faults of taste which shock his aesthetic senses, and for views on morals and on life which he holds in detestation. He must be conscientious beyond all proof, capable of resisting the temptation to alter or to modify in the slightest degree his author's meaning, though to render it faithfully may be bitterer to him than wormwood. (in Kartman 1999: 67)

Approval or indifference are probably the default positions. In situations where a conflict of values may arise, professional ethics prescribe impartiality, the translator's conscious suspension of personal views and values. Codes of conduct and definitions of professional roles governing interpreting are particularly revealing in this respect. To take just one random example, the National Register for Public Service Interpreters in the United Kingdom issues a code of conduct for public service interpreters which stipulates that they should "not enter into the discussion, give advice or express opinions or reactions to any of the parties", and that they should "act in an impartial and professional manner" (Phelan 2001: 44-45). In nearly all cases this stipulation follows the requirement that interpreters shall interpret truthfully and faithfully what is said, without addition, omission or alteration.

The suspension of personal views and values is not always easy to achieve for translators or interpreters, even when they are in sympathy with what they translate. The use of the first person in particular may bring about a degree of identification with the anterior speaker's position that affects the translator emotionally. Writing about the hearings of South Africa's Truth and Reconciliation Commission in the 1990s, Antjie Krog reports on a young Tswana interpreter traumatised by his work; he found interpreting the victims' testimonies particularly harrowing "because you use the first person all the time. I have no distance when I say 'I'... it runs through me with 'I'" (Krog 1999: 195).

In the following pages I am interested in translators who object on moral, religious, ideological or other grounds to all or part of what they are translating. I will restrict myself to written translation, where it is often easier for translators to act as gatekeepers, especially for texts that are out of copyright. I will assume that the majority of translations are made for audiences that have no access to the original texts. I am therefore interested only in translations that show evidence, of one kind or another, of a translator intervening in a text to mark disapproval or reservation or an unwillingness to write what might have been written had there been no conflict of values. I will leave aside all those cases where only a comparison with the original could identify an intervention by the translator. I will begin by reviewing a few more examples and then attempt to construct a model that can deal with situations of this kind. The model will first explore the idea of translation as quotation before taking up the concept of irony.

In the paratexts of the 1939 American translation of *Mein Kampf* the editors and translators dissociated themselves from Hitler's book and thus ensured a critical reading of the translation itself. The translation is directly affected by the frame that surrounds it. This is also the case in the later English translation by Ralph Manheim, first published in 1943 and reprinted several times since. Unlike Ripperger, Manheim intervenes in the actual translation by inserting the occasional footnote to clarify stylistic issues. Hitler's style and sometimes grammar and logic are so poor that the English also looks substandard; Manheim covers himself against the charge of writing substandard English by quoting the original German of which the English is a close reproduction (Hitler 1995). Another wartime translation, *The Speeches of Hitler*, published under the auspices of the Royal Institute of International Affairs, is framed in a similar way. Looking outwardly like what Christiane Nord would call a 'documentary' translation (1997: 47-50), its framing makes it into a political weapon turned against its original author, as indeed the Foreword states:

> This book may give to the English student, in some measure, material on which to form a conception of Hitler's thought and methods. From this he will learn what it is that we are fighting, especially when he remembers the extent of the deception practised by Hitler. If it should succeed in doing this, its purpose will have been fulfilled. (Hitler 1942: iii)

In a very different context, a very similar form of framing the translation of a text regarded as belonging to a hostile camp is offered by the first English translation of the Qur'an. This was Alexander Ross's rendering of 1649, based on the 1647 French version of André du Ryer. In his preface ('The Translator to the Christian Reader') Ross warns his readers:

> Thou shalt finde it of so rude, and incongruous a composure, so farced with contradictions, blasphemies, obscene speeches, and ridiculous fables, that some modest, and more rationall *Mahometans* have thus excused it, that their Prophet wrote an hundred and twenty thousand sayings, whereof three thousand only are good; the residue [...] are false and ridiculous. (Ross 1649: A2v)

Positioning himself as a stout Christian addressing fellow Christians, Ross is aware of the potential danger of allowing the primary text of a rival religion to speak for itself. He remains confident however that "if thou hast been so a true Votary to orthodox Religion, as to keep thyself untainted by these follies; this shall not hurt thee" (Ross 1649: A3r). He concludes his preface by turning the tables on anyone who might doubt the wisdom of his enterprise and argues the book will serve as an antidote: seeing the absurdities and poison in these writings at first hand will actually strengthen Christians in their faith:

> Such as it is, I present to thee, having taken the pains only to translate it out of *French*, not doubting, though it hath been a poyson, that hath infected a very great, but most unsound part of the universe, it may prove an Antidote, to confirme in thee the health of Christianity. (*ibid.*)

Since Ross follows Du Ryer rather than the original Arabic, he has also translated Du Ryer's preface. The opening of 'The French Epistle to the Reader' chimes with Ross's own line: "The Book is a long conference of God, the Angels and Mahomet, which that false Prophet grossly invented" (Ross 1649: A3v); it ends in an equally hostile manner: "Thou wilt wonder that such absurdities have infected the best part of the world, and wilt avouch, that the knowledge of what is contained in this Book, will render that Law contemptible" (Ross 1649: A4r). Bound in at the end of the volume, after the translation, are fifteen densely printed, unnumbered pages entitled 'A needful Caveat or Admonition, for them who desire to know what use may be made of, or if there be danger in reading the *Alcoran*. By Alexander Ross'. Here too the translator makes quite sure his opinion of the original will not be mistaken: "I suppose this piece is exposed by the Translator to the publike view, no otherwise then some Monster brought out of *Africa*, for people to gaze, not to dote upon" (Ross 1649: n.p.). Even more striking perhaps than the image of the (human? animal?) monster is the evocation of the desired reception: the translation is to be gazed upon in wonderment and disgust, an alien body to be looked at from a safe distance, not something that could ever be part of one's own life.

With frames as crude as these, every word in the translation lives under the cloud of the translator's disdain for the original. However, the frame does not have to affect every aspect of an original. It can be selective and isolate only certain aspects of a foreign text rather than the text as a whole. Not wanting to be seen to harbour sympathies for the Christian ideas in Daniel Defoe's *Robinson Crusoe*, the early twentieth-century Chinese translator Lin Shu commented in his preface:

> In the book, there are many descriptions of religious matter. It looks as
> if the translator is devoted to that religion. This is not true. Translating
> a book is different from writing one. A writer can express his views
> freely, and he can write out of his imagination. But when you translate,
> you are recounting what has happened. How can you put in your own
> opinions? This book talks about religious matters. How can I, as the
> translator, avoid them and delete them? I have to follow what was said
> in the book. (in Wong 1999: 33)

By invoking the translator's ethos Lin Shu hopes to be absolved from responsibility for the ideas contained in the text he has nevertheless written. At the
same time, readers are informed that whenever religious ideas come up in
the story, they should remember the translator's misgivings about them and
read those passages not just for what they say but also for what the translator said of them. The appeal to the audience matters in another way too. The
translator's expression of his reservations positions him with respect to the
values he shares with his audience. It establishes a bond with them. The "we"
that was used in the Foreword to *The Speeches of Hitler* above had the same
effect, just as Alexander Ross and André du Ryer were obviously projecting
themselves as Christians speaking to Christians, thus reinforcing their shared
sense of self and community in contrast to the outsiders, the others, the world
of alien and objectionable ideas.

Framing is one device for signalling the dissociation from alien and the
affirmation of indigenous values. Here is another. As an illustration, let us look
at J.M. Rigg's 1903 translation of Boccaccio's *Decameron*. Having reached the
tenth story of the third day, in which the hermit Rustico persuades the innocent
Alibech to 'put the devil back into hell', the reader encounters this passage:

> So, probing her by certain questions, he discovered that she was as
> yet entirely without cognizance of man, and as simple as she seemed:
> wherefore he excogitated a plan for bringing her to pleasure him under
> colour of serving God. He began by giving her a long lecture on the
> great enmity that subsists between God and the Devil; after which he
> gave her to understand that, God having condemned the Devil to hell,
> to put him there was of all services the most acceptable to God. The
> girl asking him how it might be done, Rustico answered: 'Thou shalt
> know it in a trice; thou hast but to do that which thou sees me do.'
> Then, having divested himself of his scanty clothing, he threw him-
> self stark naked on his knees, as if he would pray; whereby he caused
> the girl, who had followed his example, to confront him in the same
> posture. E così stando, essendo Rustico più che mai nel suo disidéro

acceso per lo vederla così bella, venne la resurrezione della carne, la
quale riguardando Alibech e maravigliatasi, disse: "Rustico, quella
che cosa è, che io to veggio, che così si pigne in fuori, e non l'ho io?"
(Boccaccio 1903, I: 251-52).

The text continues in Italian for a page and half before it reverts to English.
The title page of this edition presents the *Decameron* as "faithfully translated",
and indeed it is: the Italian in the scene above has been translated into itself.
The Italian in the passage is obviously not just the original text, it is the Italian reinstated as part of the translation. The "faithfully translated" accolade
is repeated in subsequent editions of J.M. Rigg's translation (1905, 1921, and
so on), together with the footnote just before the Italian passage sets in: "No
apology is needed for leaving, in accordance with precedent, the subsequent
detail untranslated" (*ibid.*).

Rigg's reference to precedent is true enough. The anonymous 1806 edition,
"a new edition is which are restored many passages omitted in earlier editions",
left passages in Italian and French, while both the anonymous 1822 translation of this story and the 1855 version by W.D. Kelly, for example, retained
some parts in Italian and offered matching French versions at the foot of the
page. A prefatory note in the 1872 translation also says its rendering "will be
found to be COMPLETE, although a few passages are in French or Italian"
(McWilliam 1972: 28, 32; Stych 1995: 13). The French in these versions is
not contemporary but lifted from the sixteenth-century translation by Antoine
le Maçon, including its spelling. This also happens in an 1893 commercial
printing of John Payne's translation of the same passage from the story of
Rustico and Alibech:

Accordingly, having sounded her with sundry questions, he found that
she had never known man and was in truth as simple as she seemed;
wherefore he bethought him how, under colour of the service of God,
he might bring her to his pleasures. Et premierement lui monstra
auec plusieurs parolles combien le diable estoit ennemy de nostre
Seigneur: & apres lui donna à entẽdre que le seruice qui plus plaisoit
à Dieu, estoit de remettre le diable en enfer, auquel nostre Seigneur
l'auoit condemné. La ieunette lui demanda comment cecy se faisoit.
A laquelle Rusticque dist : Tu le sauras tantost : & par ce tu feras ce
que tu me verras faire. Si commença à despouiller ce peu d'abillemens
qu'il auoit vestuz, & demeura tout nud : & autant en fit la fillete ...
(Boccaccio 1893, 1: 249).

This version too features the usual explanatory footnote, here at the start of the chapter ("It being usual, for obvious reasons, to omit this story, it has been thought well, for sake of completeness, to substitute the French version from the fine sixteenth-century translation of Antoine Le Maçon, secretary to Marguerite de Navarre, authoress of the Heptameron"; Boccaccio 1893, I: 247), but at least one other edition slides into Le Maçon's French without warning (McWilliams 1972: 33).

Actually, the first printing of John Payne's translation of the *Decameron*, in 1886 and dedicated to Stéphane Mallarmé, had given the full story in English:

> Accordingly, having sounded her with sundry questions, he found that she had never known man and was in truth as simple as she seemed; wherefore he bethought him how, under colour of the service of God, he might bring her to his pleasures. In the first place, he showed her with many words how great an enemy the devil was of God the Lord and after gave her to understand that the most acceptable service that could be rendered to God was to put back the devil into hell, whereto He had condemned him. The girl asked how this might be done; and he, 'Thou shalt soon know that; do thou but as thou shalt see me do.' So saying, he proceeded to put off the few garments he had and abode stark naked, as likewise did the girl, whereupon he fell on his knees, as he would pray, and caused her abide over against himself.
>
> Matters standing thus, and Rustico being more than ever inflamed in his desires to see her so fair, there came the resurrection of the flesh, which Alibech observing and marvelling, 'Rustico,' quoth she, 'what is it that I see on thee which thrusteth forth thus and which I have not?' 'Faith, daughter mine,' answered he, 'this is the devil whereof I bespoke thee; and see now, he giveth me such sore annoy that I can scarce put up with it.' Then said the girl, 'Now praised be God! I see I fare better than thou, in that I have none of yonder devil.' 'True,' rejoined Rustico; 'but thou hast otherwhat that I have not, and thou hast it instead of this.' 'What is that?' asked Alibech; and he, 'Thou hast hell, and I tell thee methinketh God hath sent thee hither for my soul's health, for that, whenas this devil doth me this annoy, an it please thee have so much compassion on me as to suffer me put him back into hell, thou wilt give me the utmost solacement and wilt do God a very great pleasure and service, so indeed thou be come into these parts to do as thou sayst.' (Boccaccio 1886, II: 30-31)

Payne had built protective firewalls around this version. The title page confirmed that the volumes were not in the public domain but printed "by private subscription and for private circulation only". In addition, as the above passage shows, the translator used a peculiar, antiquated diction ("whenas this devil doth me this annoy," "otherwhat"). Even so, the 1893 printing, which was brought out by a commercial publisher, reverted to the old cautionary habit of sliding into French at the critical moment in the story, despite the fact that both the 1886 and the 1893 printings were limited editions. One reason for the caution in the 1893 edition may have been the outcry a few years earlier over the translations of Emile Zola's Naturalist novels by Henry Vizetelly, who was tried and found guilty of publishing obscene works in October 1888 and again in May 1889 (Fleming 2001: 47).

Rather obviously, all the editorial interventions stem from moral objections to perceived obscenity. The switch from English to Italian or French serves as an index of censure. Assuming the translations are aimed at audiences unfamiliar with Italian and put off by outdated French, readers are coyly being informed of the existence of material deemed unsuitable for them. They are actually shown this material in full, but in a veiled form beyond their reach. Since the run-up to the forbidden passage leaves little doubt as to its nature, readers can let their imagination run riot but must remain uncertain about the detail. The translators for their part have acquitted themselves of their duty, for they offer a complete version, without omission, addition or alteration. But by switching from one language to another they have marked the value conflict and imported into the text their own verdict on what can and cannot be shown. In this way the translator does more than merely reproduce words. A value judgement travels along with them.

There is a further, social aspect to this, bearing on what has become known as audience design. The antiquated diction, restricted distribution and hefty price of John Payne's *Decameron* were evidently aimed at an exclusive audience. His nine-volume 1882 version of the *Thousand and One Nights* too had been produced "by private subscription and for private circulation only" in an edition of just five hundred numbered copies (Payne 1882). Richard Francis Burton's even more outrageous *Book of the Thousand Nights and a Night*, "a plain and literal translation" in ten volumes (with six subsequently added), also "for private subscribers only", had employed a similar protective strategy of exorbitant price, limited circulation and outlandish idiom; this version, he declared in his 'Translator's Foreword', was definitely "not virginibus puerisque" (Burton 1885-88, I: 22). Even the *Decameron* translations that we saw occasionally slipping into Italian or Renaissance French would have remained accessible to that select coterie of readers with a knowledge of these languages. At the time of Henry Vizetelly's first trial for obscenity an editorial in the *Publishers' Circular* noted that especially "the unlettered classes" needed to be protected but that "the cultured man or woman" could read foreign novels in the original language "without harm resulting"; the fact that Vizetelly's company issued translations of Zola in cheap editions had been the main thorn in the side of the National Vigilance Association that brought the case against him (Fleming 2001: 47-48, 57).

The euphemistic recourse to an elite language to cover up licentious or otherwise sensitive passages is historically well documented. In Europe, Latin served this purpose until well into the twentieth century. Françoise Waquet's book on the use of Latin in the post-Classical world mentions, among a host of older examples, a 1953 German translation of tales from the *Arabian Nights* containing a passage in Latin preceded by a note explaining it was too obscene to be rendered in German (Waquet 2001: 250). The *Thousand and One Nights* translator Richard Burton had in 1856 published *First Footsteps in East Africa,* which featured an appendix on the practices of female circumcision printed in Latin (even so, in all but six or so copies the publishers withdrew it and inserted an apology; Woudhuysen 2004: 29). The conspicuously decorous *Thousand and One Nights* that Edward Lane published in three volumes in 1839 assumed an educated reader who, without so much as a line reference let alone a translation, "may remember the well-known line of Virgil – '*Nescio quis teneros oculus mihi fascinat agnos*'" (Lane 1839, I: 324). As early as the fourteenth century John Trevisa's English translation of a Latin encyclopedia could write of menstrual blood in general but was unwilling to discuss details of the menstrual cycle in English, making Aristotle speak Latin in the process:

> Þis blood is bred in wymmennes bodyes of superfluite of moisture and feblenes of hete [heat]. And for it schulde not greue [afflict] kinde, it is igedred [gathered] into þe modir as filþe into a goter. If it is iput out þerof in dwe maner, it clensith and releueþ al þe body, and clensiþ þe modir also, and disposiþ and makeþ able to conceyue.
>
> And *libro 9°* Aristotil seiþ: menstruum in fine mensis in mulieribus maxime viget, et ideo tunc vtiliter expellitur talis sanguis. Et libro 16° dixit quod sanguis menstrualis non habet cert*a*m temporis reuolucio- nem sed in maiori parte accidit in diminucione lune. [...] (Seymour 1975, I: 153-4)

The use of the device means, however, that social discrimination is written into translations along with the translator's value judgement. Some audiences are entitled to enjoy fruits forbidden to others, and the very wording of a translation can carry this message. At the same time, translators and editors who change languages in midstream or append cautionary prefaces and notes informing readers of omissions and doctored passages evidently anticipate their readers' accommodation in these interventions. The fact that their practices call on an existing tradition of screening and concealment suggests as much, even if we cannot know what individual readers actually thought of them. In this way too cultural affinities and ideological loyalties are being cemented and collective identities constructed. When Stuart Bates reviewed the sanitised Boccaccio versions by John Payne and J.M. Rigg in his 1936 monograph *Modern Translation*, he wholeheartedly approved, although he made allowance for integral translations of the classics if they were aimed at "special publics and students" (Bates 1936: 116-7).

The examples I have discussed illustrate conflicts of value being negotiated and processed in translations. If the values inscribed in a foreign text are felt to be reprehensible, the translation itself may attest to the translator's critical opinion of them even as those values are being reported word for word. This means the translation speaks with more than one voice and its words say more than what they say. The translator both speaks for the original author and signals reservations.

The model outlined in the following pages begins by positing translation as a form of quoting. I will suggest that translation can be viewed as direct speech mixed with elements of indirect speech. This impurity creates the space in which a translator's critical attitude towards what is being translated can be profiled and the concept of irony comes into its own. Viewing translation as reported speech is not new. Roman Jakobson mentioned the idea in his 1959 essay on linguistic aspects of translation (1959: 233), John Bigelow (1978) wrote about it in a way picked up by Anthony Pym (1992, 2004), Brian Mossop elaborated it in two substantial essays (1983 and 1998), Ernst-August Gutt briefly dealt with it (1991) and Barbara Folkart devoted a booklength study to it (Folkart 1991). My particular angle is informed by the kind of value conflicts sketched above. My starting point, the essay 'Quotations as Demonstrations' by the linguists Herbert Clark and Richard Gerrig (1990) also served Brian Mossop (1998) well.

Translation, quotation, demonstration

To convey the way in which someone walks one can describe this person's walk by means of words or show it by acting it out, walking a few steps in the way the other person walks. The difference between the two modes of representation, telling and showing, echoes the Aristotelian distinction between diegesis (telling) and mimesis (showing). Whereas diegesis provides a verbal account of an event and leaves it to the audience to visualise a scene, mimesis creates meaning by physically imitating certain gestures or actions, that is, by mimicking, simulating, aping, demonstrating them. The 'demonstration theory' that Clark and Gerrig (1990) outline in the opening pages of their essay invokes this distinction.

There is no need to go into every corner of Clark and Gerrig's demonstration theory here. It will be enough to recall the features that are most pertinent in view of the argument I want to present. Clark and Gerrig stress, for example, that demonstrations are sequences of actions that are parasitic with regard to one's normal behaviour. They are non-serious, playful, bracketed actions. While pretending to be someone else, the demonstrator temporarily suspends his or her normal behaviour. But simulating another's actions means dissimulating one's own self for the duration of the simulation. In the early seventeenth century Francis Bacon's essay 'Of Simulation and Dissimulation' (in his *Essays* of 1625) described these two aspects of the "hiding and veiling of a man's self" as "simulation, in the affirmative; when a man industriously and expressedly feigns and pretends to be that he is not" and "dissimulation, in the negative when a man lets fall signs and arguments, that he is not that he is" (Vickers 1996: 350), To avoid the risk of confusion between serious and non-serious behaviour, we tend to signpost demonstrations by announcing them in advance and signalling their end to ensure they are properly bracketed. In trying to capture the 'as if' nature of this kind of ostensive pretending, John Searle speaks of "nondeceptive pseudoperformance" (1979: 65).

Another point to note is that demonstrations represent their objects selectively. Not all aspects of the action being imitated are represented in the demonstration, and not all aspects of the demonstrative act have an exact counterpart in the original action. I can imitate the tantalisingly slow serve of a left-handed tennis player by pretending to serve a ball equally slowly but holding the imaginary racket in my right hand. Clark and Gerrig call an element like the imaginary racket, which is an essential but non-mimetic ingredient of the demonstration, a 'supportive' aspect (1990: 768). Finally, demonstrations depict their referents from a certain vantage point, and they contain a number of elements, such as the demonstrator's running commentary or the absence of a real racket, for example, which are not part of the demonstration itself and which the spectator is meant to be able to decouple from the demonstration (1990: 764-8).

Now, according to Clark and Gerrig, quotations can be regarded as demonstrations of pre-existing utterances. Like demonstrations, quotations are mimetic in nature, they "depict rather than describe" (1990: 774), and they are usually inserted into a discourse that is not itself a quotation. Quotations, that is, normally occur in a diegetic environment, and they are introduced by a verb like 'say' or 'tell' (1990: 771). As a rule, we encounter quotations as part of a sentence like:

(1) Yesterday Anna told me: "I'll get it translated by tomorrow"

The descriptive phrase 'Yesterday Anna told me' identifies Anna as the source of the original utterance and is followed by the quotation as object. The quotation itself, as an instance of direct speech, presents Anna's actual words. The reported discourse is clearly announced in the reporting discourse and set apart from it. It the context of the reporting discourse the quotation constitutes an embedded, second-order discourse. Although it is the object of the main verb, it retains the form of a syntactically autonomous sentence. The quotation mimics Anna's words, but it does so selectively. One could imagine tone, rhythm and pitch not being imitated. To the extent also that the quotation signals an earlier utterance it carries a deictic element that is not itself mimetic in nature; in his essay 'Some Questions Concerning Quotations' the philosopher Nelson Goodman says that a quotation "names" its referent (Goodman 1978: 42).

Quotations are enunciated by the reporting speaker but they report someone else's words and, as demonstrations, constitute non-serious actions. This raises questions of detachment and accountability. In normal, diegetic discourse, speakers are expected to accept responsibility for what they say. Clark and Gerrig however argue that the person who quotes is responsible only for the presentation of what is quoted, and then only, in fact, for the presentation of those aspects that were selected for simulation. Responsibility for that which is represented in the quotation rests with the original speaker (1990: 792). The American sociologist Erving Goffman (1981: 144ff., 226ff.) would say that the person mouthing a quotation assumes the role of 'animator', the soundbox that merely emits someone else's words; like a newsreader on radio or television, he or she is responsible neither for the script itself nor for the opinions or positions contained in it. I will return to this point.

Also worth exploring is the question of the point of view that the recipient is offered in a quotation. In example *(1)* the reporting speaker chooses Anna as the focaliser: in the quotation, Anna's words are presented to us as Anna spoke them and thus from Anna's point of view. In the next sentence,

(2) Yesterday Anna told me she would get it translated by today

Anna's words appear as indirect speech. Here it is the speaker of the sentence who serves as the point of orientation (or the 'focaliser') for Anna's words. As is well known, the shift from direct to indirect speech entails changes in pronouns and deixis. What was 'tomorrow' in *(1)* is now 'today', for example. In this formulation the representation of Anna's words tends towards description more than demonstration, diegesis rather than mimesis: the speaker is telling us about Anna's words rather than re-enacting them.

If in Erving Goffman's terms the person reporting someone else's words in direct speech could be characterised as an animator, a mere soundbox relaying words that were produced elsewhere, then indirect speech involves the reporter in more than just acting as a conduit. Now the reporter plays an active part in choosing the words that depict the words Anna spoke yesterday. The reporter now shares in the composition of the script. An increased share in writing the script also means increased responsibility for it. Next, consider the following:

(3) She would get it translated by today.
(4) She would get it translated by tomorrow.

The use of the third person and the conditional reminds us that in both cases Anna's words are relayed to us by a reporting speaker. Both are instances of free indirect speech, marked by the absence of a reporting discourse. This absence makes the sentences ambiguous when they occur in isolation. They require context to be interpreted as free indirect discourse; let us assume the context is the same as it was for *(1)* and *(2)*. The difference between sentences *(3)* and *(4)* is that *(3)* focalises through the reporter, hence the use of 'today', which is the reporter's here and now. Speaking yesterday however Anna would have used 'tomorrow', and in *(4)* Anna's perspective and the illocutionary force of her words – her making a promise – have been retained. In this sense *(4)* is closer to direct quotation as in *(1)*. This makes *(4)* more depictive, more like demonstration, than either *(2)* or *(3)*, which foreground the reporter's vantage point and hence reveal a more pronounced descriptive aspect.

Finally, when Clark and Gerrig stress that quotations, like demonstrations, are selective simulations of pre-existing utterances, they also draw the important consequence that quotations do not need to be restricted to verbatim repetitions of earlier utterances. Their claim that indirect discourse may contain both mimetic and diegetic elements already points in this direction. They also regard translations as quotations. In this they disagree with Nelson Goodman, who had considered the following three sentences:

(5) (a) Jean a dit: "Les triangles ont trois bords."
(b) John said: "Les triangles ont trois bords."
(c) Jean said: "Triangles have three sides."

and accepted only *(5b)*, but not *(5c)*, as a translation of *(5a)*. The reason, for Goodman, was that *(5c)* translated not only the reporting phrase ('Jean said') but also the words between the quotation marks, thus giving the impression that Jean had uttered English words where in fact he had been speaking French (Goodman 1978: 53; neither Goodman nor Clark and Gerrig, incidentally, ask whether 'John' is a translation of 'Jean'). Goodman insisted that quotations had to be verbatim repetitions containing what he termed "sameness of spelling" with the original words (1978: 43; Clark and Gerrig 1990: 798; we will meet Goodman's term again in the next chapter). He admitted that a French novel translated into English, for example, would put both the narrative and the dialogue into English but regarded this as "something between direct and indirect quotation" (*ibid.*).

Clark and Gerrig, in contrast to Goodman, accept both *(5b)* and *(5c)* as translations of *(5a)*. Both *(5b)* and *(5c)* report diegetically that Jean said something. The difference between them is that in *(5c)*, assuming the context indicates that John/Jean's language was French, the reference to John/Jean's language is treated as a 'supportive' and hence a non-mimetic aspect of the quotation. But *(5c)* does as good a job as *(5b)* in simulating the propositional expression (1990: 777-8, 783-5, 798-9). Clark and Gerrig would also agree that *(6)* and *(7)* are quotations:

> *(6) "Je le ferai traduire pour demain," Anna said.*
> *(7) "I'll get it translated by tomorrow," Anna said in French.*

Both sentences report in English on words that Anna spoke in French. Nelson Goodman would recognize the words in inverted commas in *(6)* as a quotation, but not those in *(7)*. Clark and Gerrig would argue that *(6)* describes or recounts that Anna said something and then demonstrates both what she said and that she spoke in French, while *(7)* recounts or describes that Anna said something and that she expressed herself in French, and then demonstrates the content and the illocutionary force of what she said.

Reported speech

The essay by Clark and Gerrig permits an understanding of translation as quotation, and of quotation as simulation and enactment. It highlights additional aspects of quotations that will prove useful, such as the ways in which quotations tend to be signalled and bracketed to distinguish them from the surrounding discourse, the fact that they offer selective representations, the question of focalisation and the issue of who is accountable for the words spoken.

Let me mention another two approaches that will help to shed light on the grey area between direct and indirect speech. My argument will be that just as quotations are more than verbatim repetitions of someone's words, translation is more than direct speech. It is a form of speaking that partakes of both direct and indirect speech. It is precisely to the extent that the translator is more than just a soundbox or mouthpiece or animator that the translator's subject-position becomes discernible in translations. This subject-position creates room for the expression of an attitude, a precondition for irony.

To develop that argument, I will first pick up Dan Sperber's essay 'Interpretive Ethnography and Theoretical Anthropology' (1985) and then Kristiina Taivalkoski-Shilov's book *La tierce main* (2006). Together with Deirdre Wilson, the anthropologist Dan Sperber invented Relevance Theory in the 1980s. His 1985 essay explores the nature of ethnographic representation, including the representation of an informant's words by the ethnographer. Sperber's terminology differs from that of Clark and Gerrig, but the approaches are compatible in some respects.

Sperber distinguishes, very broadly, between two kinds of representation, descriptive and non-descriptive, roughly in line with the distinction between diegesis and mimesis. I am concerned only with non-descriptive representations. They come in two kinds, which Sperber calls reproductions and interpretations. Reproductions, such as scale models and quotations, exhibit an "exterior resemblance" with their referents (1985: 12). Interpretations are defined, not altogether satisfactorily, as all other kinds of representations, "a vast and residual category" (1990: 13) comprising everything that is not either description or reproduction. Sperber regards direct speech, including quotations, as reproduction. Indirect speech he classifies as interpretation, presumably because it does not exhibit the "exterior resemblance" with a prototype in the way scale models and quotations match their respective objects. Sperber's distinctions and classifications seem debatable, but they are not the main issue in the present context.

Sperber also points out that reproductions, such as photographs or the diagram of a city's metro network, need a "descriptive comment" (1990: 12) which identifies the referent and specifies, explicitly or implicitly, what kind of representation is being displayed. The difference between the descriptive comment framing a representation and the representation itself, Sperber suggests, is clear enough when we are dealing with two distinct media, for instance a verbal caption explaining a picture. The difference however may become blurred when both the comment and the representation are verbal in nature, as is the case with reported discourse. As a rule, the framing comment will make up the main clause. It announces and contextualises the reported words. The representation appears either as an object clause in inverted commas, when we are dealing with direct speech, or, in the case of indirect speech, in a syntactically dependent *that*-clause. The main clause identifies the reporting speaker and specifies the reporting situation. The embedded clause contains the reported speech, that is, the quotation – which, as we know form Clark and Gerrig, includes translation.

Separating reporting from reported discourse is relatively straightforward in the case of direct speech. The transition from the main to the embedded clause is signalled by quotation marks. (Sperber does not consider free direct speech.) By contrast, Sperber argues (1990: 17-18), indirect speech does not always allow us to draw a sharp line between the diegetic and the mimetic, the framing and the embedded discourse, the reporting and the reported speech. They can become intermingled. The reported utterance may have been subjected to various kinds of condensation, expansion, affect or stylistic polish, and these would have to be attributed to the reporter. Indirect speech, in other words, grants the reporter substantial control over the reported utterance. Moreover, if the original utterance is not available for inspection, the reporter's interventions may be entirely impossible to identify. In an ethnographic account in English, say, the exact words as spoken by a local informant in Vietnamese may no longer be retrievable, even when Vietnamese words and phrases appear in the report.

Free indirect speech makes things are even messier. It dispenses with the framing discourse, and there is often considerable uncertainty as to whether an utterance is to be attributed to a reporting narrator or a reported character. As Sperber puts it, free indirect speech "allows the author to tell a story 'from the point of view of the actors,' and the reader to identify with them. The less an identification is conscious, the better it is accepted" (1985: 19).

It seems to me that translation, as a form of mimetic reporting that falls short of verbatim quotation but is not indirect speech either, partakes of several of these categories. It is normally framed as direct speech. The overwhelming majority of written translations adopt the person and vantage point of the original speaker. Conference and court interpreters are routinely urged to do the same. Only in community and informal interpreting is recourse to indirect speech relatively common ("He says he'll have it done by tomorrow"). Nevertheless, even when it is construed as direct quotation, translation gives the translator a degree of control over the choice of wording more like that found in indirect discourse. Perhaps we should anyway think of categories like direct and indirect speech not so much as discrete units but as forming a continuum in which one type shades into another and no type is pure.

Such a sliding scale of different forms of representing anterior speech by means of more or less manipulated, more or less constrained direct or indirect

discourse, is mapped in Kristiina Taivalkoski-Shilov's *La tierce main* (2006).
The book is primarily a detailed study of the translation of reported discourse
between English and French in the eighteenth century, but one more general
chapter is devoted to reported discourse as such – that is, without reference
to translation (2006: 35-73). Following a discussion of several proposals (by
Marguerite Lips, Brian McHale and Geoffrey Leech and Michael Short) for
the subdivision and classification of reported speech, Taivalkoski-Shilov offers
a continuum that integrates three variables:

(a)   the degree of control the reporter has over the reported utterance, stretch-
       ing from total to minimal control;
(b)   the syntactic relation between the embedded and the framing utterance,
       ranging from dependent (in indirect discourse) to autonomous (in direct
       discourse);
(c)   the shift from a diegetic to a more mimetic mode of representation of
       the anterior utterance, with an accompanying shift in person and vantage
       point from the reporter to the reported speaker.

The continuum set up on this basis comprises eight types, each type gradually
merging into the next (2006: 54). It is not hard to find or think up parallels in
the world of translation:

1   *Paraliptic résumé, or omission:* the reporter refers to the existence of
       someone's words but omits them. Applied to translation this might be
       a translator informing the audience that a passage has been suppressed.
       The audience is told of its existence but does not get to see it. Edward
       Lane's chaste version of the *Thousand and One Nights* is full of such
       messages: "The story here alluded to is inserted in the original; but, be-
       ing extremely objectionable, and too short and simple to be abridged, I
       have been compelled to omit it altogether"; "I here omit an explanation
       which is of a nature to disgust every person of good taste"; "Here, in
       the original, is introduced a character of a disgusting description, and
       unnecessary to the carrying on of the story"; "This story is followed by
       sixteen anecdotes [...]; eleven of which I translate, and here insert"; "A
       portion of my original I here omit"; "In the original are a few introduc-
       tory words, which I omit because they are inappropriate" (Lane 1839, I:
       517; II: 237, 320, 497, 637, 404; Borges 2004: 96)
2   *Diegetic résumé:* the reporter's summary of someone's discourse. Edward
       Lane again: "The foregoing is somewhat abridged" (1839, II: 223). In
       his Dutch translation of Justus Lipsius's Latin *De constantia*, published

in the same year as the original (1584), Jan Mourentorf summarises the content of three chapters ("het inhouden van ieghelijck Capittel int kort verhaelt", Lipsius 1948: 52) which he reckons the common reader will find too hard to read in full.

3   *Diegetic report:* a report of someone's words but using the reporter's vocabulary and register. A translator abbreviates a particular text or passage in his or her own words, and informs the audience of this. As mentioned above, this is not infrequent in dialogue interpreting. An interpreter may turn to a client and summarise several sentences by saying: "She says she will definitely deliver by tomorrow".

4   *Indirect discourse:* a full representation of someone's words but in largely diegetic form, that is, mostly using the reporter's vocabulary and tonality. Only some aspects of the reported discourse are depicted rather than described. An interpreter may turn to a client and report a single brief sentence as: "She says she will definitely deliver by tomorrow".

5   *Mimetic indirect discourse:* a form of indirect speech which retains the register and stylistic physiognomy of the reported discourse. In dialogue interpreting the interpreter might say: "She says she'll definitely deliver by tomorrow, that's a promise, hand on heart".

6   *Free indirect discourse:* a mimetic representation of someone's words but without a reporting discourse framing it. This would be a translation that is recognisable as a translation but is not announced or labelled as one. In dialogue interpreting, for example, a situation might arise in which it is not clear whether a sentence like "she'll definitely deliver by tomorrow, that's a promise" is in fact the interpreter's own diegetic statement of the import of the interlocutor's words or the interpreter issuing a more depictive but still third-person representation while leaving out the introductory "She says (that)…".

7   *Direct discourse:* the mimetic representation (in Clark and Gerrig's terminology: a demonstration; Dan Sperber would speak of a reproduction) of an anterior discourse, usually in quotation marks, and embedded in a reporter's framing diegetic discourse but syntactically autonomous. This is the standard form of a quotation. Following Clark and Gerrig in regarding translations as quotations, this would be the prototypical translation. It takes the form of a translator declaring that x said something in language y and then, shifting person and vantage point from translator to translated speaker, presenting the actual translation.

8   *Free direct discourse:* direct discourse but lacking the framing main clause. In literature, the best known example is interior monologue in

which words or thoughts are reported but there is no 'she said' or 'he thought'. In the world of translation this is a standard translation but without a frame identifying the text as a translation: in other words, a text that is a translation but conceals this fact. In the media and in some commercial translating this is not uncommon. Hope Inslow's novel *The Miser*, published in London in 1868, is a translation of Hendrik Conscience's *De gierigaard* of 1852, but the latter's authorship and the original title are not mentioned (as the online British Library catalogue will confirm). A variant on this would be a translation which plagiarises another translation: such a text advertises itself as a translation of a text in another language but omits to mention it is quoting an already existing translation.

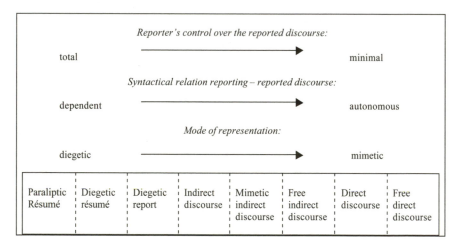

Table 1: Continuum of reported discourse
(based on Taivalkoski-Shilov 2006: 54)

A diagrammatic representation of Taivalkoski-Shilov's types of reported speech might look like *Table 1*. The partitions between the different types are porous to mark gradual transitions. The reporter's or the translator's control over the reported discourse may be total, as in the case of complete omission (paraliptic résumé), but at the other end of the scale it is not zero. As Clark and Gerrig stress, even verbatim repetition is selective and contains non-mimetic elements. Translation adds to this the change of language, which leaves the translator in charge of selecting the new wording.

Translation, as the retrieval and representation of an anterior discourse, can be viewed as a form of quotation. In this view the translator is a reporter who simulates, re-enacts, reproduces the reported discourse mimetically. That makes translation a form of direct speech, with, as a consequence, limited to minimal reporter control over the reported words. However even a simulation contains a deictic aspect, which we attribute to the simulator. The matter is complicated further, first, by the selectivity of the representation, which again reveals the simulator's agency, then by the problem of clearly telling the mimetic apart from the diegetic, and thirdly, and most importantly, by the fact that in interlingual translation the words we encounter are unmistakably those of the translating reporter. If translation were pure direct speech, the translator would be what Erving Goffman's 'production format' of utterances calls an 'animator', as we saw above. Responsibility for composing the script makes the translator into what Goffman terms an 'author'; the term is a little unfortunate in our context, but it indicates a larger measure of involvement and accountability (Goffman 1981: 144-5, 226).

The result of these complications is a degree of ambivalence as to exactly whose voice and viewpoint receive articulation in a translation. Perhaps translation is therefore best cast as a mimetic representation animated by the translator's vision and to a significant extent under the translator's control. Translation then becomes a form of direct speech affected, or infected, by indirect speech. The semiotician Susan Petrilli puts it the other way round, calling translation "*indirect discourse masked as direct discourse*" (2003: 22; her emphasis). The syntactic autonomy of translation in relation to the framing discourse and the ensuing shift in personal pronouns suggests to me the approach via direct speech is preferable. Either way the centre of gravity of translated discourse seems to lie between or across an impure direct and an equally impure indirect speech. The ambivalence of this speech situation creates the necessary room for irony.

Like translation, irony is an ambivalent type of speech, one which creates distance from itself and leaves the recipient unsure whether or to what degree the speaker assumes responsibility for the words he or she utters. Stable forms of irony are normally embedded in a framing co-text which signposts the irony and brackets the ironic utterance (Booth 1975). In the case of translation the phrase or label identifying the text as a translation is sufficient to put the translated words between inverted commas. As suggested in the previous chapter, a translator's preface will usually add to this by clarifying the speech situation. Whereas a translation which appears without the announcement that it is a translation may be read as free direct speech (for example, an unattributed translation, in other words a case of cross-lingual plagiarism) or not as a translation at all, the announcement framing a translation has essentially the form:

I say that x said in language y: "zzz"

The main clause provides the descriptive comment; it is the caption accompanying the reproduction, and is followed by the mimetic reproduction. The frame – the preface, the label 'translation' – is the main, contextualising clause. The actual translation is the quotation, an embedded if syntactically autonomous clause. As reported speech it cannot help being affected by the clause in which it is embedded, as indeed Mikhail Bakhtin already saw (1981: 340).

Insofar as the translator's preface continues to resonate in the translated discourse, it reminds us of the divided, impure, multivocal nature of translations. More voices than one thus make themselves heard in a translation, even if the ideology – that is, the social and historical construction – of translation strives to neutralise or silence this multiplicity. The standard admonitions to the effect that translators should not speak in their own name, should disappear behind their authors, should not interfere, should render the original, the whole original and nothing but the original, all seek to preserve translation as undifferentiated, monologic speech. To achieve this they reduce translation to direct discourse pure and simple, to verbatim quotation, casting the translator merely as mouthpiece, animator, ventriloquist. In contrast to this view I suggest an image of translation as direct speech contaminated by indirect speech, an impure mix of direct and indirect discourse in which several simultaneous voices have a stake. The margin between frame and enactment contains the potential for dissonance as well as consonance.

Echoic translation

Among the countless definitions of forms of irony that are in circulation, I have adopted the one offered by Relevance theory because it seems clear-cut, manageable and amenable to translation. In their book on *Relevance*, Dan Sperber and Deirdre Wilson describe irony as a second-order phenomenon, the interpretive representation of an existing representation. Irony plays when a speaker signals (a) that he is referring to an existing utterance or opinion, (b) that he has a certain attitude towards it, and (c) that this attitude is relevant (1986: 238-9). Irony is distinguished by the fact that the speaker distances himself from the opinion or words referred to. Appreciating irony requires that the hearer or reader recognise the reference and the speaker's critical attitude. Let us take a closer look at the Relevance view of irony.

In a series of essays and exchanges, Sperber and Wilson (1981, 1998; also Wilson and Sperber 1992) have characterised verbal irony as a form of 'echoic utterance'. An echoic utterance is a subcategory of interpretive utterances.

This latter term invokes a widely used distinction, that between interpretive and descriptive utterances. As already explained in Chapter One, the descriptive use of language means the deployment of language to make statements about the world. In contrast, language is used interpretively when it represents another utterance or thought which it resembles either in linguistic expression or in propositional content, as is the case with reported speech. Since an utterance is itself a representation (of a thought or a state of mind), an interpretive utterance offers a representation of a representation and is therefore a second-order or meta-representation (Noh 2000: 74; Sperber & Wilson 2004: 621). Translation, too, is metarepresentational to the extent that it is recognised as the interlingual representation of another utterance.

For Sperber and Wilson an echoic utterance is an interpretive utterance which derives most of its relevance from the dissociative attitude which the speaker tacitly signals with respect to the represented discourse. What makes an utterance echoic is the fact that the speaker indicates a belief about the represented utterance, and that this belief is dissociative, distancing, disapproving, mocking or skeptical in nature (Sperber & Wilson 2004: 621-2). The belief or attitude is not linguistically encoded, but left to the hearer to infer on the basis of various paralinguistic signals (Noh 2000: 94). The notion of 'echo' in this context is deliberately broad. It covers not only direct and immediate echoes as in reported speech, for instance, but also echoes of attributed thoughts and of norms or standard expectations (Sperber & Wilson 1998: 284).

For the hearer or reader it is important to recognise (a) that the utterance in question represents another utterance or thought, (b) that the speaker has a dissociative attitude towards the represented utterance or thought, and (c) that this distancing attitude is relevant. In Sperber and Wilson's words, "irony comprehension requires second-order metarepresentational abilities" (2004: 622). The advantage of thinking of irony as 'echoic' is that it emphasises the interplay of two discourses, one echoing and the other echoed, that is, a representing or reporting discourse on the one hand, and a represented or at least attributed discourse or thought on the other. This makes is easier to apply the concept to translation.

Like translation, all irony is intertextual. Ironic intertextuality always has a critical edge. Some translations, as we saw with reference to both the *Mein Kampf* and the *Decameron* translations, display a similar attitude. This means however that if translation is understood as reported speech, it is this critical edge that makes the translator rather more than either an 'animator' or (also in Goffman's terminology) an 'author'. An echoic translator, a translator with an attitude, assumes responsibility for the critical opinion he or she expresses and is therefore what Goffman calls a 'principal'. With responsibility come agency and accountability, and the ethical consequence that translators are accountable for the attitude they convey.

Most discussions of irony assume that irony begins with the ironist's intention to be ironic. They also tend to assume that irony consists in saying one thing and meaning the opposite. It is one of the merits of Linda Hutcheon's book *Irony's Edge* (1995) that it adds nuance to these views.

Hutcheon agrees that irony must be spotted if it is to work. If the recipient does not pick up what Sperber and Wilson call the echoic element in an utterance, the critical attitude being expressed will not register. At one point in his *Le Ton Beau de Marot* Douglas Hofstadter writes an innocent-looking passage which he reveals in the next chapter to have been written in what he calls 'Anglo-Saxon', a form of English that, in the style of the Oulipo group and Georges Perec, dispenses with the letter 'e'; when I first read the passage I failed to catch the oddity and hence both the joke and the allusion (Hofstadter 1997: 94-5, 105-6). However, Hutcheon argues that it is enough for a reader or hearer to attribute ironic intent to a speaker for irony to be activated, regardless of whether the intent is really present or not. We normally attribute irony to a speaker on the basis of certain signals, which may be textual, intertextual or contextual (Hutcheon 1995: 143ff.). The standard signal is a *pronunciatio*, an explicit announcement that irony is afoot. This could be a change in intonation, a facial expression, a cough or, in written texts, the use of typographical devices such as dashes or italics. The absence of a clear signal may run the risk of an ironic utterance being taken at face value and coming across as absurd or deceitful. In handbooks of classical rhetoric, irony is classified as a figure of both *simulatio* and *dissimulatio* (Plett 1979: 93-99), and, as we saw, both simulation and dissimulation have something in common with translating, quoting and demonstrating. Conversely, something may be taken as a signal of oncoming irony when no such signal was intended; or, in the absence of a signal, something may be read as ironic even though no irony was meant. When the Hong Kong-based journal *Renditions* was set up in 1973 to promote Chinese literature in English translation, the editors could not know that thirty years later the word 'renditions' would enter world news as the term for covert CIA operations translating terrorist suspects to a gulag of secret prisons. In February 1842 the young Karl Marx sent to a journal in Dresden a vigorous piece denouncing censorship. In his covering letter he already expressed concern that "the censor might censor my censure", and indeed the article was promptly banned (Mehring 1966: 33; Wheen 1999: 36). No doubt Marx appreciated the censor's unintended irony. The article appeared a year later in Switzerland.

Irony operates in a speech situation in which what is said evokes something that is left unspoken. This difference, the margin between the said and the unsaid, the spoken and the intimated, forms part of the ironic utterance. Hutcheon quotes Paul de Man in this context. For de Man, irony, like allegory, operates when "the sign points to something that differs from its literal meaning and has for its function the thematization of this difference" (Hutcheon 1995: 64; de Man 1983: 209). The editorial scaffolding Alvin Johnson's team built around Helmut Ripperger's translation of *Mein Kampf* in 1939 means that the translation itself, as reproduction of Hitler's words, points to something different from its literal meaning, namely to criticism of Hitler's ideas, and consequently the translation has for its function the thematisation of the difference between reproduction and criticism. The translation is echoic in that it both re-enacts Hitler's discourse and dissociates itself from the words being uttered. Irony allows the ironist – here: the translator – to resist the assimilation of his own and the ironised discourse and, in so doing, to contest the latter's authority and to undermine its persuasiveness – a non-harmonious relation prefigured in Bakhtin's 'Discourse in the Novel' of 1934-5 (Bakhtin 1981: 339ff.).

Just as Hutcheon regards the attribution of ironic intent as stemming from the receiver, she also stresses that irony consists less in saying the opposite of what one appears to be saying than in saying two things at the same time, both the said and the unsaid, while, crucially, highlighting the difference between them. Equally crucial is that the difference between the said and the unsaid reveals a particular attitude; here Hutcheon is entirely in agreement with Sperber and Wilson. In uttering words and signalling that they echo other words or opinions and that the difference between the two series is relevant, the speaker conveys an evaluative stance, a critical judgement about the words being uttered. Irony involves speakers dissociating themselves from what they are saying, and this act of distancing springs from a critical value judgement. Stacking an unspoken discourse on top of the ostensible discourse suggests a subject that does not coincide with the talking head. Irony plays precisely in the space between face and mask.

Irony, then, requires a knowing audience. It appeals to some, while others will just not get it or remain unaware of its operation, and their exclusion may well be intentional (Hutcheon 1995: 97). In this way irony sheds light on the relation between speakers and their audiences. As an example, Hutcheon mentions Robert Burton's *Anatomy of Melancholy* of 1621: the book is in English, but the sexual innuendoes in it are in Latin. Only the cultured elite, that is, would fully grasp the sexual references, readers without Latin could only see that something was being withheld from them and guess at what it might be (Hutcheon 1995: 97). Indeed in Part 3 Section 2 of the *Anatomy,* Member 1 Subsection 2, for example, on homosexual love, and Member 2 Subsection 1, on the effects of eating "lascivious meats", contain extended passages in Latin (Burton 1994, 3: 55-57, 63-5). This is, of course, the situation we encountered in the Boccaccio translations that shifted into Latin or Early Modern French when sexual overtures threatened to become graphic.

Devices like these ratify certain groups of recipients and exclude others. In that sense they actively engage in audience design. The addressees able to cope with the Latin passages in Burton's *Anatomy* or the English Boccaccio translations were the cultured elite who had done Latin at school and kept it alive. The more exquisite their enjoyment of the bawdy detail, the greater their appreciation of the good reasons why common readers should be denied access. Those common readers would be auditors at best, or more likely overhearers – while we, reading these passages today, are eavesdroppers on communicative exchanges not addressed to us.

These distinctions, and the terminology used to name the different types of audience, derive from the work of Alan Bell, who in turn builds on Erving Goffman (Bell 1984; Hatim & Mason 1997: 83; Mason 2000). Bell classifies receivers (hearer, readers) according to whether or not *(a)* their presence is known to the speaker, *(b)* the speaker acknowledges them as ratified participants in the speech event and *(c)* they are being directly addressed. Addressees are known to be present, they are ratified participants and directly addressed. Auditors are known to be present and ratified but not directly addressed. Overhearers are known to be present but neither ratified participants not addressed. Eavesdroppers are neither known to be present nor ratified nor addressed. *Table 2* lists these categories in diagrammatical form.

	Presence known to the speaker	Ratified participant	Directly addressed
addressee	+	+	+
auditor	+	+	-
overhearer	+	-	-
eavesdropper	-	-	-

Table 2: Audience design (after Bell 1984)

The identity construction engaged in by the *Decameron* translators who have recourse to Italian, Latin or French to veil objectionable scenes is socially selective. While overtly addressed to all who can read and purchase or borrow the books, the foreign-language passages speak to common readers only to deny them the status of ratified participants. At the same time the translator appeals to the common readers' understanding of this tactic: while lewd scenes can be unveiled for a morally robust élite, more often than not a moneyed intelligentsia, for everyone else it is sufficient to be alerted to the proximity of the lewd without being able to view it. This discriminating reticence is assumed to serve the common good. The consensus being sought in this way affirms not only shared values and narratives but, through these, a social order. And it is relevant to note that, in switching languages as a form of gatekeeping, translators (or editors, or whoever makes the relevant decision) align themselves with the social elite. They were evidently able to inspect the obscene close up; having done so, they made the decision to restrict access to the cultured class and expected the lower orders to accept being shut out.

The positioning that translators engage in is a dialogic, collaborative process in a differentiated social context. Just as the unfolding of a discourse entails the creation – and on the recipient's part the recognition – of a subject-position, the interaction between speakers and recipients locates participants in jointly produced story lines, shared narratives that shape collectives, maintain distinctions and secure values (Davies and Harré 1990: 48). When Pierre Letourneur translated Edward Young's *Night Thoughts* into French in 1769, he explained in his preface that he was offering his readers an integral version ("la traduction entière") but had nevertheless cut back some of Young's nauseous repetitions and omitted some passages that were no more than Protestant ravings against the Pope; as for a couple of other "fanatical lines," these, he said without any visible sign of ironic intent, he had actually crossed out in the original ("deux vers fanatiques [...] que j'ai rayés de l'original que je possède"; D'hulst 1990: 115). All of this he does as a writer who feels part of his nation and contributes to a national literature ("ma nation", "notre littérature", *ibid.*).

Translators position themselves as they convey attitudes through their translations. Irony conceived as echoic utterance provides a handle on this. Let me give one further example. In 1720 the Dutch writer Balthasar Huydecoper translated Pierre Corneille's *Oedipe.* In the preface (Schoneveld 1992: 76-81) he explained that he had followed the French closely except for a few minor alterations – which ones, and where, we are left to guess. One passage of eighteen lines, he went on, had been substantially modified. It concerned fate, free will and good works. Huydecoper's preface first translates the eighteen lines in full and then reduces them to six, adding that the reader will surely appreciate the reasons for the change. To Huydecoper's Dutch readers they will indeed have been obvious: Catholic dogma about free will and good works could not find a place in Calvinist Holland, and so, yes, those references had to be filtered out. The six lines duly reappeared in the actual translation of the play but by then the reader would have been aware that they contained a large dose of diegetic résumé. The reduced passage cannot help recalling the lines that might have been there but had, for obvious reasons, to be reshaped. However, different constituencies in the Dutch Republic may well have looked differently upon the obviousness of these reasons. The dominant Calvinist community could hail Huydecoper as one of theirs and a pillar of society; the Catholics who were excluded from public office were confirmed in their subsidiary role.

Six years later Huydecoper published a translation of the *Satires* of Horace. This was a version in prose. Had he used verse, he explained, he would have had to write Dutch satires and that would have meant targeting his own con-temporaries. Prose allowed him to let Horace himself speak. But Huydecoper realised that letting Horace himself speak in translation would mean adopt-ing Horace's viewpoint. He therefore added a general warning, drawing a parallel between a traveller to distant lands and the reader of a documentary translation:

> If someone who is not yet fully conversant with the traditional customs or with those things that are considered proper and necessary in his own country, travels to foreign lands, how often do we not see such a person adopting any and all customs that he comes across, to the extent even that, having returned to his native country, he may be regarded as a stranger among his own people? He who delves into Heathen Writings without first having armed himself with the knowledge of the pure truth is such a person. [*Begeeft zich iemand, die noch geen begrip heeft van zyne vaderlyke zeden, noch van datgeene, dat in zyn vaderland als welvoegelyk aangemerkt, en daarom noodzaakelyk ge-schat wordt, naar andere landen; hoe dikwils zienwe, dat zulk een alle zeden aanneemt, die hem voorkomen; zelfs zo, dat hy, in zyn vaderland wedergekeerd zynde, onder de zynen als een vreemdeling kan aangezien worden? Zodanig een is de onderzoeker van Heidensche Schriften, die zich niet eerst gewapend heeft met de kennisse der zuivere waarheid.*] (Huydecoper 1726: xix-xx)]

The danger Huydecoper perceives is that of going native among pagans. Because a strongly mimetic translation, being close to quotation and direct speech, assumes the original speaker's vantage point, impressionable readers could be enticed by the discourse they are reading. Huydecoper's preface urges detachment and adequate preparation on the part of readers who should not confuse the translator's persona with his personal stance. When in the transla-tion itself the translator speaks for Horace he is only enacting Horace and does not himself mean what he says. Readers are meant to realise this dichotomy and to appreciate the difference between the mimetic actor and the diegetic mediator. During the act the simulator leaves his own views unexpressed, but due to the diegetic frame these views constantly harass the translated words. This is what makes the words echoic. As a result, the actor's statements are transformed into quasi-statements, safely wrapped in quotation marks. The translation becomes self-reflexive and the translator Janus-like: the person observes the persona, and the persona knows. At the same time the construction contrives to project the translator as one whose faith is firm enough to withstand the confrontation with alien beliefs, and hence as a morally safe pair of hands and a trusty guide.

Approaching translation as a complex form of quoting makes it clear that translation matters, socially and historically, not only because it transmits cultural goods but because it transmits them under a certain angle, with evaluation attached.

Echoic speech is a slippery thing. It may be strongly or mildly critical, it may concern aesthetic as well as ideological or other issues, it may be more or less clearly announced, it may or may not be correctly ascribed or recognised. The critical or dissociative attitude may concern other translations and translators, or modes of translating, or certain aspects of modes of translating. This suggests that the line between a dissociative and a neutral attitude, and that between a neutral and an associative attitude, may sometimes be hard to draw. In fact, it may be better not to think of clear distinguishing lines between different kinds of attitude at all, but of gradations shading into one another. The attitude may not only be more or less pronounced, it may affect different aspects of the translated texts to different degrees. The total subjection of Barends's *Mein Kampf* and the wholesale rejection in evidence in the American *Mein Kampf* version edited by Alvin Johnson's team are points at opposite extremes; but then, *Mein Kampf* is hardly a typical book.

Working back in this way, and allowing the idea of echoic translation to reverberate back into the model, we can see that echoic translating, or translating with a dissociative attitude, is only a special case. The more general phenomenon is that of translating with an attitude. The translator's attitude frames and invades the performance of translation. The theoretical model creates room for it to the extent that it casts translation as not purely mimetic but as containing a diegetic element, as not purely direct speech but as containing elements of indirect speech as well. It is precisely to that extent that the translator is not a ventriloquist or a mouthpiece but an agent with views and opinions. In other words, if it is true that translation is not pure direct speech and that the translator is not purely an animator, it becomes possible to argue that echoic translation is merely one end of a cline that comprises different kinds of value judgement written into all translating.

The particular case of echoic translation conveys disapproval of and critical detachment from what is being translated. If the judgement is not critical, it can still range from neutral to supportive. Considered in this light, the reluctance to express a view also entails a view, just as neutrality is a position one can choose to take. In Francis Bacon's essay 'Of Simulation and Dissimulation' the first stage, before "simulation, in the affirmative" and "dissimulation, in the negative", is what he calls "Closeness, Reservation, and Secrecy", as when a person keeps his own counsel or plays his cards close to his chest, and thus "leaves himself without observation, or without hold to be taken, what he is" (Vickers 1996: 350). The non-interference routinely urged in translators' and interpreters' codes of conduct reflects this conscious choice. Still, the voice that chooses to keep silent communicates this choice through its silence. Equally, the reserved translator or interpreter who positions him- or herself on the sidelines of a communicative exchange takes a position, conveys this position to the participants and anticipates their understanding of the reasons why this position is being taken. As the Hainan Island incident that I mentioned in the previous chapter suggested, the translator's attitude may be directed at something in the original text but it may also concern his or her own role and responsibility as a translator. The Hainan Island interpreter may well have felt that, had he rendered the Americans' ambiguous " we are very sorry" in Chinese as either regret or apology, he would have been seen by his own side either as unnecessarily prolonging a conflict (if he had translated "sorry" as 'regret, for 'sorry' can after all be taken as apology as well) or as disloyally letting the Americans have the last laugh (by pretending to ignore the ambiguity in their statement and giving it as 'apology' when he knew perfectly well they were not really apologising). By leaving the American "sorry" in English, he also kept his distance from the statement and allowed ambiguity to continue to colour the relations between the two countries. In the same way, endorsement of what is translated, whether expressly stated or left to be pieced together from paratexts and extraneous evidence, also springs from a value judgement, as Steven Barends's loyal rendering of *Mein Kampf* showed.

In all these cases the attitudes frame but also inform and subtend the actual translation. Attitude, then, applies across the board, to routine professional as well as to ideologically motivated translating. In accepting a request or a commission translators may indicate that they agree with the import of what they are about to translate, that they remain indifferent to it, or indeed that financial gain or pressure overrides other considerations. This attitude is written into the resulting product and remains separate from the translation's representational aspect. For this reason, attitude and position-taking cannot be written out of the picture of what translators do. All translating is translating with an attitude. It could not be anything else, since all translations contain the translator's subject-position.

Formally, then, translation has the structure of ironic discourse. It has an evaluative attitude built into it, this attitude is inscribed in and comments on the actual translation, and the difference between comment and translation, diegesis and mimesis, is relevant. Establishing the difference may be an analytical procedure, and in that sense the model can be made operational, as the present chapter will hopefully have shown. Perceiving the difference is also a matter of recognising the translator's ethical and social responsibility. While translators may disclaim responsibility for the re-enactment of someone else's discourse in the form of direct speech, they can be held accountable for the diegetic aspect of their mimesis. The decision to translate, the presentation of the enactment and the value judgements that inform the performance are theirs.

4. Real Presence

A translation 'stands for', 'represents' or 'mediates' its original. But how, exactly? Is the relation one of identity, of figuration, of symbolisation? In what sense or in what form is the original 'present' in a translation? How should we understand the claim that a translation is still, substantially or essentially, the same work as the original – ontologically, epistemologically, transcendentally? How do we overcome the accident of linguistic difference to reclaim an identity of substance between translation and original? How to think the double identity of the translated text, as an individual text in its own language and as still the work of the original writer?

We normally think of translation as involving the transformation of an original text, the donor, into something new, the host. The process suggests a genetic link: the original gives rise to, or spawns, a translation. In this chapter I propose to invert this perspective. I will claim that, if there is conversion, it is not the donor which undergoes it but the host. I will suggest, in other words, that it is possible to think of a new text springing up alongside a pre-existing text and then being converted into and recognised as a translation of that pre-existing text. The conversion means that the new text, upon becoming a translation, is brought into convergence with the pre-existing text.

The particular approach I want to develop can be put in a nutshell as follows. In the most sacred part of the traditional Latin mass the priest echoes the words that Jesus Christ spoke when, during the Last Supper, he pointed to the bread on the table and declared, in the Vulgate version: "*hoc est corpus meum*" ('this is my body'). Can a writer point to a translation of his or her work and say 'This is my work' in the way that Christ said 'This is my body'? How similar is the writer's '*hoc est opus meum*' ('this is my work') to Christ's and the modern priest's or celebrant's '*hoc est corpus meum*'?

Copyright law and the French literry theorist Gérard Genette – a daunting combination – would probably answer that they are very similar indeed. Copyright law, as I understand it, regards translations as derivative works. Authors own the copyright in their work because it is the fruit of their labour. When a work is translated, the translator may claim copyright in the actual words chosen in the new language, but this claim in no way diminishes the author's right to continue to be regarded as the author of the work. Copyright law as laid down in the Convention of Berne enshrines the idea that, despite their different form and outlook, original and translation remain essentially and substantially the same work. A translated work is still the author's work. A writer can point to a translation and say '*hoc est opus meum*'.

Speaking of the various "modes of existence" of artworks in his two-volume *The Work of Art. Immanence and Transcendence* (1997), Genette distinguishes between three modes that are relevant in the case of written texts and books. There is first the "material object", which would be the individual copies I have on my desk, some of which show signs of wear while one is cheerfully dog-eared. Each material object is unique. Secondly there is the "text", which is defined by "literal identity" or "sameness of spelling". All copies of *Moby Dick* in the library contain the same words in the same order, even though some may be hardback and others may be paperback editions and they may use different fonts ("sameness of spelling" does not have to be understood in any rigid sense; for one thing, it ignores the differences between British and American spelling). Finally there is the "work", which for Genette is the ideational object we construct in our heads as we read a text (1997: 177). With respect to translations Genette argues under the heading 'Plural Immanences' that

> if a *text* is surely defined by literal identity (sameness of spelling), a literary *work* is defined, from one text to the next, by semantic identity (sameness of meaning, as one might put it), which the passage from one language to another is supposed to preserve – not totally, to be sure, but sufficiently well and accurately enough for the reader to have a legitimate sense of operal identity (*ibid.*).

"Sameness of meaning" is meant to be preserved in the passage from one language into another by means of translation. No doubt the phrase "sameness of meaning" does not have to be taken literally either; we can read it as comprising the kind of semantic or functional similarity normally associated with translation. Although two texts may then be quite different in language and script, "sameness of meaning" guarantees operal identity and for this reason the two texts are the same work. For Genette, as for copyright law, a writer can look at a translation of his or her work and declare: '*hoc est opus meum*', 'this is my work'.

Let us return to our initial questions. How can we think the relation between two texts that are different but are nevertheless, somehow, believed to constitute the same work? The perspective on this issue that I want to explore in the following pages takes its inspiration from the doctrine of the Real Presence in Christian liturgical doctrine. It is a very particular doctrine, and its application to translation will make certain aspects of translation appear in a different light. At the end of the chapter I will try to push the perspective as far as it will go.

The Real Presence is closely connected with the central part of the Eucharist, the ritual that celebrates and commemorates the Last Supper, Christ's farewell dinner with his disciples. During the Eucharist the priest or minister consecrates a piece of bread (the host) by imitating Christ's words and actions during the Last Supper. For believers, something happens as a result. Christ's Real Presence is established. Exactly what happens to the bread and exactly how Christ comes to be 'really present' among the congregation of believers, is a matter of debate. In pre-Reformation doctrine, and in Catholic doctrine since the Reformation of the sixteenth century, the Real Presence is tied to the concept of transubstantiation. I will explain these terms as we go along.

A word of caution is in order before we proceed. The Eucharist concerns the central dogma in Christian doctrine and is Christianity's most sacred rite. The topic is very large and the literature on it correspondingly huge. I have consulted only a very small part of it. I am not a theologian, not even a believer. I will deal with only a few historical aspects of the disputes about the Real Presence in the medieval and Reformation periods in the Catholic and Protestant churches (that is, excluding the Greek and Russian Orthodox churches, out of ignorance). While these historical debates are fascinating in their own right, I cover them here only insofar as I can see an application to translation.

The starting point is the Last Supper, the meal that Jesus Christ shared with his disciples on the eve of his arrest, trial and execution. The episode is related in three of the four gospels (Matthew 26: 26-28; Mark 14: 22-24; and Luke 22: 19-20), and there are related passages in John 6: 48-58 and in Paul's epistle 1 Corinthians 11: 24-25. During the Last Supper Christ broke the bread that was on the table and handed it to his disciples, saying: "Take this and eat, this is my body." He likewise poured the wine, shared it out and said: "Take this and drink, this is my blood." He then added, "Do this in remembrance of me." These words – probably spoken originally in Aramaic, but the gospels record them in Greek – are known as the 'words of institution'. They instituted the lasting covenant between Christ and his followers, the community of believers that would continue to exist after his death. It is at this moment, and by means of the words of institution, that Christ is deemed to have founded his Church.

The Eucharist (the word means 'thanksgiving') is that part of the liturgical service which, in commemorating the Last Supper, celebrates and renews the covenant between Christ and those who believe in him. During the Eucharist the priest or minister echoes the words of institution that Christ spoke at the Last Supper, and in so doing he consecrates both the host (that is, the bread) and the wine as he repeats Christ's actions of breaking bread and pouring wine. The words that are spoken during the Eucharist recall the Last Supper and bring about Christ's Real Presence for the faithful.

The words play a crucial role. When Christ at the Last Supper said "This is my body," the utterance was not just descriptive or constative, it was also an injunction with the meaning 'take this, accept this as my body, agree to take this as my body.' Obeying the injunction means accepting Christ's authority and joining the community of believers in Christ. When a priest utters the words of institution after Christ, the words not only echo and thus recall Christ, they also make something happen. They are performative, and their effect extends to the physical world. They transmute or convert the bread and the wine on the altar into something else. Exactly what kind of change is brought about is again a matter of dispute, and we will trace some of these different opinions. Catholic doctrine holds that the bread and wine undergo a real change of substance: at the moment of consecration they become literally the flesh and blood of Jesus Christ. In the medieval period the Catholic Church coined the term 'transubstantiation' for this unique and miraculous phenomenon (one would expect the spelling 'transsubstantiation', but one 's' appears to have been spirited away). Other Christian denominations reckon the change is more symbolic in nature, but they are particular about the meaning of 'symbolic.'

Uccello's predella

Before we address these debates, here is a visual illustration of the late-medieval, pre-Reformation doctrine. It incorporates the notion of transubstantiation. Paolo Uccello (1397-1475) was a fifteenth-century Italian painter with a keen interest in perspective. Among his works is *The Profanation of the Host*, a large narrative painting in six panels, now in the Palazzo Ducale in Urbino, Italy. The painting is a predella, a long rectangular panel forming part of an altarpiece. Its six scenes tell the story of a miracle that is supposed to have happened in different parts of Europe in the later Middle Ages. The story, which appears designed to reinforce a point of Christian belief, is that of a malicious test. It typically involves a non-believer who steals a consecrated host, takes it home, stabs it with a knife to see if it really is the body and blood of Christ as the Christians claim, and is astonished to find real red blood flowing from it. The story usually ends with the sacrilege being discovered and the perpetrators duly punished.

The second of Uccello's six panels is of particular interest (see *Figure 6*). It shows, on the right, soldiers battering down the door of a house from the outside while, inside the house, blood flows from what looks like a three-legged frying pan across the tiled floor of a room, squirting into the street through a crack in the wall. The source of the blood, the host, is an ordinary piece of bread which, however, when consecrated, becomes the body and blood of Christ. When enemies of Christianity desecrate such a host, the blood miraculously flowing from it constitutes visible proof that it really is Christ's flesh and blood.

Figure 6: Paolo Uccello, The Profanation of the Host, second panel (Courtesy Soprintendenza per il Patrimonio Storico Artistico ed Etnoantropologico delle Marche, Urbino)

The literature on Uccello's painting includes an essay by the New Historicist Stephen Greenblatt, 'The Wound in the Wall' (Greenblatt 2000). Discussing Uccello's second panel, Greenblatt highlights the rather extraordinary pictorial illusion used in it. Uccello's presentation of the scene is reminiscent of a stage: the panel lets the viewer see both the inside and the outside of the house because, as often happens in stage productions, the 'fourth wall' nearest to the viewer has been removed and the wall holding the front door is shown almost perpendicular to the viewer's angle of vision. This allows us to see the blood streaming out of the profaned host at the back of the room and running first across the floor inside the house and then into the street through the 'wound' in the wall. The blood leaves the privacy of the house and enters the public sphere of the street. Its vivid redness is visible proof that the bread is Christ's body. In order to show the blood as real, there for all to see, the painter has resorted to the deliberate 'unreality' of the pictorial convention of the cutaway fourth wall. As Greenblatt explains, the convention marshals the spectator's suspension of disbelief in order to make the doctrinal point that in matters of faith we should not require visible proof to believe: the consecrated host *is*

Christ's body and blood even though outwardly it continues to look like any other piece of white bread. Believers should have no need to test the reality of transubstantiation. The eyes of faith should not be deceived by physical appearances. Christ's Real Presence in the consecrated host defies representation but is nevertheless real (Greenblatt 2000: 107-8).

Uccello's *Profanation of the Host* illustrates the pre-Reformation doctrine of the Real Presence of Christ in the consecrated host. But Greenblatt's reading of its use of a pictorial illusion to make a doctrinal point about the belief structure underpinning the sacrament of the Eucharist has a relevance that extends to translation. The parallel can be formulated as follows. To be effective, translation too requires a leap of faith, a suspension of disbelief. Entering into the compact demanded by translation means accepting a given text as a translation of another, pre-existing text and therefore as bodying forth, embodying and actually 'being' that pre-existing text in one way or another. Whether individual readers or communities of readers are prepared to make this leap of faith depends on their following the injunction 'take this as a translation, this *is* the original work, even though it appears here under a different guise'.

The view I am putting forward here is that a translation comes into being when a text that has been written alongside another text is declared to be a translation of that other text. The declaration is an illocutionary speech act. If it is heeded, that is, if the speech act has its intended perlocutionary effect, it changes a text into a translation, and thereby converts it into that other 'work' (in Genette's sense) which is the original. A text that is converted into a translation does not change outwardly, but inwardly. Its words remain the same, but it is now, in essence, another 'work'. The approach I am taking starts not from the original but from the translation, and I regard a translation as initially being merely another text until it is declared to be a translation. At that moment, provided the speech act succeeds, a change takes place: the translation continues to look as it did before, but its nature has altered because somehow it is now another work. The 'somehow' will need to be specified below, and different readings will be possible, just as the doctrine of the Real Presence allows for different interpretations of the exact relation between the consecrated host and the body of Christ.

To return to the parallel with Uccello's painting: just as in the painting the red blood is proof that the consecrated host really is the body of Christ, so dissecting a translation will show the original hidden inside it. The important thing to note however is that this reality is real only for believers. For all its claims to universality (and 'catholic' means 'universal'), the doctrine that Uccello portrays is universal only within its own confines. That is why viewed from within the doctrine the proof furnished by the red blood is objective and incontrovertible – but also unneccesary. Once we have accepted a text as a translation we will find the original inhabiting it and rest assured in the conviction that doubters too will recognise this manifest proof that both texts are the same work even though they are made of different words. But then, a believer should have no need to put the proof to the test.

In what follows I want to trace some of the historical debates around the Real Presence to see what may be gleaned from them about translation and the way in which the relation between translation and original could be thought. We will need to follow up on several aspects. What kind of transmutation or conversion is occasioned by the words spoken over the bread and wine in the Eucharist? If the change that happens comes about through the performative use of words, what are the 'felicity conditions' governing this speech act? If the bread is somehow altered, is there a leftover, a residue, a material remainder, in other words, is the bread still bread even though it simultaneously is or comes to figure the body of Christ?

Despite the prolonged and fierce debates about the Real Presence there is common ground between them, just as there is broad agreement about its importance. All sides agree that the Real Presence of Christ in the Eucharist constitutes the sacramental – that is, the mysterious and ritual – point of intersection between two realities and two levels of reality, the visible and the invisible, the material and the immaterial, the human and the divine, the temporal and the eternal, the world of matter and the realm of God. Mystery and sacrament are intertwined: in the early Christian church the Latin *sacramentum* translated the Greek μυστηριον (*musterion*) (Heron 1983: 69; Pelikan 1984: 178). The connection between the two orders is made by means of the spoken words uttered by the priest over the bread and wine. In this respect consecration resembles other sacraments, which always involve spoken words. In Augustine's influential phrase, "the word comes to the element and it becomes a sacrament, itself a kind of visible word" (*Accedit verbum ad elementum et fit sacramentum etiam ipsum tanquam visibile verbum*; Heron 1983: 71). Augustine specifies that the sacrament must resemble that which it symbolises, and that it is the word spoken about the material element that makes the latter into the visible sign of an invisible reality (Heron 1983: 70-1).

During the service, 'holy communion' follows the consecration of the bread and wine, when the faithful follow the priest or minister in partaking of the host. In doing so, "the communicant swallows the divine Word translated into human flesh" (McNees 1992: 20). Communion therefore also signifies a profession of faith and signals membership of a community: "Communion in the body of Christ implies community in the body of Christ" (Crockett

1989: 31), and indeed the term 'the body of Christ' also stands for the community of believers united in their Christian faith.

In addition, there is the commemorative element. The priest who consecrates the bread commemorates the Last Supper and thus performs an act of *anamnesis* (McNees 1992: 18) as well as, performatively, bringing about Christ's Real Presence. How exactly Christ is then made present is the subject of the debates we will be exploring.

Before delving into the historical controversies it will be good to remember that they were as much about grammar and the meaning of words as they were about theology, and that they were fierce. By 1577 Christoph Rasperger could catalogue no fewer than two hundred different interpretations of the words of institution in a handy little book (Raspergerus 1577). "What words can be more plain than to say 'This is my body'?", Henry VIII's archbishop Thomas Cranmer asked, but he went on: "Truth it is indeed, that the words be as plain as they may be spoken; but that the sense is not so plain" (Pelikan 1984: 194). According to the seventeenth-century Catholic grammarians of Port-Royal, the word '*est*' in '*Hoc est corpus meum*' "transforms the thing that '*hoc*' designates from bread into body, the body which is that of the subject who originally pronounces the words" (in Greenblatt 2000a: 141-2), but for the modern Anglican H.E.W. Turner, "[t]he copulative 'is' is a more complicated word than appears at first sight" (1972: 102). "Most of the world's squabbles are occasioned by grammar! [...] How many quarrels, momentous quarrels, have arisen in this world because of doubts about the meaning of that single syllable *Hoc*", Michel de Montaigne noted with some exasperation in his *Apology for Raymond Sebond* (Montaigne 1987: 99; "*La plus part des occasions des troubles du monde sont Grammairiennes. [...] Combien de querelles et combien importantes a produit au monde le doubte du sens de cette syllabe:* hoc!", 1969, 2: 192).

Grammar and semantics apart, the relative weight of the act of consecration itself compared with the good faith of those involved was also an issue. There was controversy, for example, about the question whether the sacrament of the Eucharist was effective because of the right words being spoken, that is, *ex opere operato*, 'through the enacted act', or *sola fide*, 'through faith alone,' that is, because the believers believed in the miracle (Turner 1972: 104). For Uccello, it will be remembered, the bread was Christ's body even to unbelievers. Small wonder someone like Erasmus referred contemptuously to the ritual observance of ceremonies as the surest way to degrade them to *cerimoniolae*, "trivial little ritual nonsenses", as M.A. Screech aptly rendered the word (Screech 1980: 119).

I will concentrate on the debates between Catholic and several Protestant positions in the sixteenth century, during the period of the Reformation. Apart from the Catholic position we will be reviewing the opinions of John Wycliff, Huldrych Zwingli, Martin Luther and John (Jean) Calvin. But since these debates are foreshadowed in the medieval era, that is where we need to begin.

Transubstantiation

While the Eucharist was the central Christian ritual from an early date, the exact nature of the Real Presence was not from the beginning a matter of doctrine or an article of faith. There appear to have been different views about how the Real Presence could be understood. They hinged on the question whether the bread and wine *in reality* or only *symbolically* changed into the body and blood of Christ during the Eucharist. For some, the consecrated bread and wine merely *signified* Christ's body and blood. For others they *were* literally and truly his body and blood.

Different emphases appear to have existed among the early Christian thinkers and theologians known as the Church Fathers. Around the beginning of the fifth century Augustine, as we saw, held that the visible reality, the bread and wine, became a sign of an inner, immaterial reality when the 'element' was activated by the spoken word as part of a sacramental act. This meant that after the sacrament the bread and wine stood for or symbolised Christ's flesh and blood (Schillebeeckx 1963: 92; Crockett 1989: 92). His slightly older contemporary Ambrose took what has variously been called a 'conversionist', 'transformationist', 'metabolic' or 'realist' view according to which the words of consecration actually changed the bread and wine, inwardly though not outwardly. He argued that if the word of Christ was able to perform miracles and to create something out of nothing, it also had the power to make things undergo change; the sacramental word inherited this power (Crockett 1989: 97). Both views coexisted, but in the course of the Middle Ages the 'realist' position came to predominate and eventually hardened into doctrine.

One of the earliest attested conflicts of opinion on the matter emerged as two monks, Ratramnus and Paschasius Radbertus, clashed in the ninth century in the monastery of Corbie in France. Both apparently agreed that some kind of 'mutation' took place in the Eucharist. For Ratramnus this meant that after consecration Christ's spiritual rather than his actual body was present among the believers and the bread and wine were the signs of this presence, whereas Paschasius asserted a factual change in the material elements, so that Christ's flesh and blood were truly rendered present (Heron 1983: 93; Rubin 1991: 15-16).

The most famous early challenge to the conversionist view was launched by Berengar of Tours in the eleventh century. It introduced an important philosophical distinction and provoked a debate that threw up the new term 'transubstantiation'. Berengar's view was similar to that of Ratramnus but he put it by drawing on Aristotle's distinction between 'accidents' and 'substance'. The terms are important. In somewhat simplified form we can understand 'substance' as meaning the durable essence or identity of a thing or a person, and 'accidents' as an entity's outwardly visible qualities and attributes. Individuals remain the same persons (in 'substance') even though they change in appearance (in their 'accidents') as they grow older. For Berengar, the bread could entertain only a 'figural' relation to Christ's body because accidents, the appearances of natural objects, cannot be separated from the essence or substance to which they belong. If something looks and tastes like bread, then it is bread, both before and after consecration. Following consecration the bread sacramentally *signifies* Christ's body, but as this body is of a different order from that of the bread, the bread is still bread.

Berengar was opposed by Lanfranc of Bec, abbot of Caen and later to become Archbishop of Canterbury under William the Conqueror. Lanfranc argued that in the sentence '*Hoc est corpus meum*' not only must the subject and predicate be fully equal, but it is the noun which possesses enduring signifying power. Since 'hoc' refers to bread, the bread must become body, in substance though not in appearance.

Lanfranc's view prevailed. Berengar was forced to recant, publicly and repeatedly, first in 1059 and again in 1079 (Rubin 1991: 16-20). The recantation of 1079 was insistent on the real and substantial rather than any figurative or symbolic change of bread into body:

> I Berengar believe in my heart and confess with my mouth that the bread and wine which are laid on the altar are, through the mystery of the sacred prayer and the words of our Redeemer, converted in their substance into the real and truly life-giving flesh and blood of Jesus Christ our Lord, and that after consecration they are the real body of Christ that was born of the Virgin and died on the cross for the salvation of the world and sits at the Father's right hand, and the real blood of Christ which spilt from his side, and that they are flesh and blood not merely in the form of a sign through the power of the sacrament but in their actual nature through the power of the sacrament. [*Ego Berengarius corde credo et ore confiteor panem et vinum, que ponuntur in altari, per mysterium sacre orationis et verba nostri Redemptoris substantialiter converti in veram et propriam vivificatricem carnem et sanguinem Iesu Christi domini nostri et post consecrationem esse*

> *verum Christi corpus quod natum est de Virgine et quod pro salute*
> *mundi oblatum in cruce pependit et quod sedet ad dexteram Patris, et*
> *verum sanguinem Christi, qui de latere eius effusus est, non tamen per*
> *signum et virtutem sacramenti, sed in proprietate nature et virtutem*
> *sacramenti*] (Rubin 1991: 20; Heron 1983: 94-95).

Berengar's 1059 confession had also stated that after consecration Christ's body and blood "are physically taken up and broken in the hands of the priest and crushed by the teeth of the faithful, not only sacramentally, but in truth" (*sensualiter non solum sacramento sed in veritate manibus sacerdotum tractari frangi et fidelium dentibus atteri*; *ibid.*), an idea the Reformer John Calvin would later describe as "monstrous" (Pelikan 1984: 199).

The term 'transubstantiation' began to be used around the time or shortly after these debates to indicate the real and substantial change that according to Berengar's opponents took place in the Eucharist. The doctrine was endorsed by the Church at the Fourth Lateran Council which Pope Innocent III convened in 1215 and would be emphatically reaffirmed as Catholic dogma during the Council of Trent. Berengar's views are unambiguously called 'heretical' in the online *Catholic Encyclopedia* (Scannell 2003)

In the thirteenth century the *Summa Theologica* of Thomas Aquinas, the major theological digest of the medieval era, summed up the doctrine in terms that recalled Berengar's recantation:

> The complete substance of the bread is converted into the complete
> substance of Christ's body and the complete substance of the wine
> into the complete substance of Christ's blood. Hence this change is
> not a formal change, but a substantial one. It does not belong to the
> natural kinds of change, and it can be called by a name proper to itself:
> transubstantiation (section III, 75, 4: Kelly 2001: 61).

At around the same time the felicity conditions of the consecrating speech act were defined. Robert Grosseteste's *Templum dei* of *ca.* 1220-35, for example, prescribed wheaten bread, pure water, uncorrupted wine, clearly pronounced words, a male priest and good intentions (Rubin 1991, 37).

As we saw in Chapter One, the Catholic Church countered the growing Reformation tide by reaffirming its basic tenets during the Council of Trent, which was held from 1545 till 1563. The Council emphatically asserted the doctrine of transubstantiation during its thirteenth session of 11 October 1551. The first chapter of the decree issuing from this session declared that by the consecration of the bread and wine a change is brought about of the whole substance of the bread into the substance of the body of Christ our Lord, and of the whole substance of the wine into the substance of his blood. This change the holy Catholic Church properly and appropriately calls transubstantiation (Noll 1991: 195; Pelikan 1984: 299).

As a result, the decree's fourth chapter concluded, "Jesus Christ, true God and true man, is truly, really and substantially contained in the august sacrament of the holy Eucharist under the appearance of those sensible things" (Noll 1991: 193). Because the change affecting the bread was miraculous and beyond human comprehension, the Council argued, the unique word 'transubstantiation' to label it was justified. The Council dismissed as "satanical untruths" the Protestant opinion that Christ's words at the Last Supper should be understood figuratively rather than literally, and upheld the view that Christ could be in two places at the same time, in the bread and in heaven, "by a manner of existence which, although we can scarcely express in words, yet with our understanding illumined by faith, we can conceive and ought most firmly to believe is possible to God" (*ibid.*).

A year after the Council of Trent ended, Pope Pius IV issued a bull which yet again reaffirmed the doctrine of transubstantiation (Heron 1983: 107). Three years later, in 1567, Thomas Aquinas was elevated to the status of Doctor of the Church. In the seventeenth century no less a thinker than René Descartes found a way of coming to terms with the doctrine. In the replies to objections raised against his philosophy by Antoine Arnauld and incorporated in his *Meditations on First Philosophy* (1641), and in a letter to the Jesuit Denis Mesland of 9 February 1645, Descartes even sought to modify the Aristotelian notion of 'accidents' so as to make the mystery of transubstantiation more acceptable (1984, II: 172-8; III: 241-4; Dear 1991: 130-33); he reckoned he deserved thanks from the theologians "for putting forward opinions in physics which are far more in accord with theology than those commonly accepted" (1984, II: 175).

The reality of transubstantiation was affirmed again as recently as 1965, in Pope Pius VI's encyclical letter *Mysterium fidei* ('The mystery of faith'), which declared: "Nor is it right to treat of the mystery of transubstantiation without mentioning the marvellous change of the whole of the bread's substance into Christ's body and the whole of the wine's substance into his blood, of which the Council of Trent speaks, and thereby to make these changes consist of nothing but a 'trans-signification' or a 'trans-finalization', to use these terms" (Douglas 1973: 69).

Figuration

The Reformed interpretations all deny transubstantiation. To the Protestant reformers who broke away from Rome in the sixteenth century the doctrine of transubstantiation lacked a basis in scripture and was merely the fantastical invention of Pope Innocent III and his Fourth Lateran Council; it led, in their view, to the idolatrous worship of a piece of bread and to the presumptuous idea that reciting Christ's words had the power to call him down from heaven or change bread into his body (Pelikan 1984: 190, 200). Their views of the change happening in the Eucharist are perhaps rightly typified as consisting of nothing but 'trans-signification'. In the 'diffusive' and purportedly non-sectarian translation of the New Testament that Edward Harwood produced in 1768 (we met Harwood in Chapter Two), the verses Mark 14:22 and Luke 22:19 are rendered not as 'This is my body' but as "This figuratively represents my body" (1768, I: 156, 266). Still, the Reformed reading of the change as primarily symbolic leaves room for different nuances. Luther, for one, continued to insist that the Eucharistic event was more than symbolic.

Well before the Reformation proper, John Wycliff (died 1384), the 'morning star' of the Reformation as he would later be called, was expelled from Oxford University following his attack on transubstantiation (Daniell 2003: 72-3). Wycliff appears to have taken the view – as far as we know, since most of his own writings were destroyed as heretical – that the sacrament brings about a change in the bread, not however in its accidents or substance but in its signifying quality. After consecration Christ was present in the bread "in some manner or other" (*quodammodo*, Pelikan 1984: 58), rather like a token or an image, or like a keepsake serving a memorial function (Rubin 1991: 324-5). Materially the consecrated bread remained bread, Wycliff argued, however it now symbolised Christ, who was present figurally, in other words, as a figure or a sign (*"sacramentum eucharistiae est in figura corpus Christi et sanguis"*, in Hudson 1985: 112). The body of Christ was present in the bread not physically or according to its dimensions but "according to its power" (*virtualiter*, Pelikan 1984: 58). The church formally condemned Wycliff's views at the Council of Constance in 1414-18 (Pohle 2003).

The opinions of the Swiss reformer Huldrych Zwingli (1484-1531) were similar to those of Wycliff. For Zwingli, the *'est'* in *'hoc est corpus meum'* was to be taken as meaning 'signifies' (Crockett 1989: 136-7). Just as he regarded the mass not as re-enacting Christ's sacrifice but as a mere commemoration of it, Zwingli, in a letter of 1526 addressed to the Nuremberg town council, gave as his view that "the bread and wine in the [Lord's] supper are merely a sign" (Plöse and Vogler 1989: 308, 436). Rasperger's 1577 catalogue of interpretations of '*hoc est corpus meum*' firmly placed Zwingli's reading of '*est*' as '*significat*' among the wicked depravations.

Wycliff's and Zwingli's understanding of the Real Presence leaves the relation between the bread and wine and the body of Christ underdetermined. The material elements point to the immaterial realm in the way that in C.S. Peirce's sign theory a symbol acts as a sign of what it symbolises primarily on the strength of a relation established by convention. The sign, that is, is motivated neither by similarity, as is the case with what Peirce calls an icon, nor by causality, as with an index. As Wycliff and Zwingli appear to read the matter, Christ willed the bread into standing for his body, and the church that he established follows him in reading the same symbolic relation into the element.

When Martin Luther heard of Zwingli's view, he is said to have been horrified by it (Heron 1983: 117). Of all the reformers, Luther remained perhaps closest to the Catholic position. He was willing to take the words of institution literally, and although he passed over the issue of transubstantiation, he stressed the Real Presence as an actual and true presence. The 'is' in 'this is my body' meant exactly what it said, he would insist. As he saw it, after consecration the bread and wine became imbued with the invisible, glorified body of Christ. Consecration meant therefore that the bread and wine acquired the qualities of Christ's body. Luther used the parallel of heated iron to illustrate his point: an iron heated in the fire retains all the qualities of iron, but also possesses all the qualities of heat (Higman in Calvin 1970: 18). Christ, he wrote in a celebrated formula, was present "in, with and under" the consecrated bread and wine, which however did not change in substance (*"in, mit und unter dem der Substanz nach unveränderten Brote und Weine"*, Pelikan 1984: 200). The bread remained bread but Christ, who could unite both human and divine natures in his person, was present in every particle of it (Heron 1983: 118). Opponents referred to Luther's view as 'consubstantiation', a term that is however not accepted by Lutherans (Pelikan 1984: 201).

A representative statement of the Lutheran position may be found in the Wittenberg Articles of 1536, prepared jointly by Lutherans and an English delegation sent by Henry VIII and Archbishop Cranmer to forge links. The talks broke down but a draft confession had been drawn up by then, in Latin and German, which declared:

> we firmly believe and teach that in the sacrament of the Lord's body and blood, Christ's body and blood are truly, substantially and really present (*vere substantialiter et realiter adsint corpus et sanguis Christi*) under the species of bread and wine (*sub speciebus panis et*

vini), and the under the same species they are truly and bodily (*vere et corporaliter*) presented and distributed (*exhibeantur et distribuantur*) to all those who receive the sacrament." (Bray 1994:137)

No mention is made of any actual change in substance; hence there is no transubstantiation, only 'presence'. The formulation is similar to that devised earlier by Philip Melanchthon, the author of the Augsburg Confession of 1530 (revised version), Article X of which declared that "with the bread and wine the body and blood of Christ are truly presented (*exhibeantur*) to those who eat the Lord's Supper" (Pelikan 1984: 186). In both the Wittenberg Articles and the Augsburg Confession the Latin word translated into English as "presented" is "*exhibeantur*", 'are exhibited'. The bread and wine 'exhibit' the body of Christ and in so doing render it present. This version proved acceptable also to other protestants including the Genevan Reformer John Calvin. Later however Calvin distanced himself from the Lutheran view.

For Calvin, too, the bread and wine in the Eucharist were primarily signs, the 'visible words' – the term harks back to Augustine – which signified Christ's presence (Pelikan 1984: 190). The Genevan Confession of 1536, drawn up by Calvin or his colleague Guillaume Farel or both, declared: "The supper of our Lord is a sign by which under bread and wine he represents the true spiritual communion which we have in his body and blood" (Noll 1991: 130). In the treatise on the Last Supper he published in 1542 Calvin consequently rejected transubstantiation as a "diabolical invention" ("*ceste transsubstantiation est invention forgée du diable*"; 1970: 120). He read the Eucharistic formula 'this is my body' as a figure of speech, more particularly a metonymy in which "the sign borrows the name of the truth which it figures" ("*par une figure qu'on dit métonymie, le signe emprunte le nom de vérité qu'il figure*", in the 1551 French translation of the Latin *Consensus Tigurinus* of 1549; Greenblatt 2000a: 146, 225). This "manner of speaking", Calvin argued, could be discerned in all the sacraments (Calvin 1957: 401, 405; Pelikan 1984: 194).

Similarly, in his main work, the *Institutes of the Christian Religion* which he continued to rewrite for most of his adult life and translated from his own Latin into French (first edition 1539, definitive edition 1560), Calvin argued that the relationship between the sign and the thing signified is more than merely linguistic. It is one of both representation and presence. The sign not only represents the thing signified but also makes it present by calling it forth. In paragraph 4.17.10 of the *Institutes* he urged the faithful to "hold above all to this rule, that every time they see the signs ordained by God, they understand with equal certainty that the truth of the matter represented is conjoined with it" ("*les fidèles ont du tout à tenir ceste reigle, que toutes fois et quantes qu'ils voyent les signes ordonnez de Dieu, ils conçoyvent pareillement pour certain la vérité de la chose représentée y estre coniointe"*; Calvin 1957: 385; my translation). Through the visible signs a spiritual truth is "figured and exhibited" (*"figurée par iceux, et pareillement exhibée"*, *ibid.*).

A few paragraphs further on he indicated the ground on which this signifying quality is based, stressing "the affinity which the things signified have with their symbols" (*"l'affinité qu'ont les choses signifiées avec leurs figures"*, 1957: 401). As a result, the name of the thing signified can pass to the sign signifying it in a movement which he calls by its rhetorical name "translation" (French *"translation"*, the corresponding Latin term is *"metonymia"*, 1957: 401, 402; the standard rhetorical term in Latin would be *transmutatio*, Plett 1979: 77; Vickers 1988: 496). The bread can stand for the body and vice versa, and this mutual 'translation' is possible due to the "affinity and similitude" between them (*"il a telle affinité et similitude de l'un à l'autre, que telle translation mutuelle ne doit pas estre trouvée estrange ne rude"*, 1957: 402). This ground enables the sign to present the object and transfer its own name to it even though in the case of the Real Presence the physical bread and Christ's body belong to radically different and unequal orders of reality. Speaking with C.S. Peirce in 1906 we could say that the ground compels the sign: "a sign, in order to fulfil its office, to actualize its potency, must be compelled by its object" (Peirce 1991: 255). Due to this compulsion the sign is true because it is in conformity with its object. Or, using a different terminology, that suggested by Gilles Deleuze commenting on Plato's distinction between copies and simulacra (Deleuze 2001: 294ff.): the host becomes a true copy of the body of Christ because it is endowed with an internal, spiritual and essential resemblance; without this, it would be a mere simulacrum.

Calvin's 1542 treatise on the Last Supper rehearsed more or less the same points as his *Institutes*. It stressed that the bread and wine were the "visible signs" representing Christ's body and added that they are called his flesh and blood because they are like the instruments Christ uses to make his body manifest to us (*"ce sont comme instrumens par lesquelz le Seigneur Jesus nous les distribue"*, Calvin 1970 : 106). In the same way John the Baptist saw the Holy Spirit in the shape of a dove. The event illustrated God's way of making visible to human eyes what is in fact invisible, and thus accommodated limited human capabilities. The vision therefore "was not a empty figure but a sure sign" of the Spirit (*"ceste vision n'estoit pas une vaine figure, mais un signe certain de la presence du S. Esprit"*, 1970: 107). So it was also with the Eucharist, hence "it is right that the bread should be called body because it not only represents it for us but also presents it to us" (*"C'est donc à bon droict que le pain est nommé corps, puis que non seulement il le nous represente, mais aussi nous le presente*", *ibid.*). And just as actual water was needed in baptism to serve as material witness to the spiritual cleansing which the ritual performed, so the bread of the Eucharist testified to Christ's body serving as nourishment of the soul ("*aussie faut-il qu'en la Cene il y ayt du pain materiel, pour nous testifier que le corps de Christ est nostre viande*" (1970: 120). Exactly how the flesh and blood of Christ were communicated to the congregation, however, remained beyond human understanding ("*Ainsi en est il de la communication que nous avons au corps et au sang du Seigneur JESUS. C'est un mystere spirituel, lequel ne se peult veoir à l'œil, ne comprendre en l'entendement humain*", 1970: 107).

By thus insisting that the sign was grounded in similitude and that the operation of the Real Presence remained unfathomable, the Reformers could also refute the Catholic charge that their conception of the Eucharist held no mystery and reduced the bread and wine to a lifeless sign, a simulacrum, "a bare representation … as dead men are represented through statues or other images", "something like a painted fire, which gave neither light nor heat" (Pelikan 1984: 192) – images reminiscent, incidentally, of the objections sometimes raised to the way translations represent original texts.

Conversion

Let us retrace our steps and consider where this exploration of the historical divisions over the doctrine of the Real Presence leaves us with respect to translation. We began by wondering whether an author could point to a translation of his or her work and say 'this is my work' in the way a minister or priest says, in imitation of Christ picking up the bread during the Last Supper, 'this is my body'. The elaboration of the parallel took us into the Real Presence and a consequent shift of emphasis. The focus of attention moved from the original text to the translation, more particularly to the text that, through the power of words, is made into a translation. Before consecration, the bread is just bread. Consecration changes the bread into something else or something more. Depending on which theological reading one prefers, the bread is either transubstantiated into the body of Christ or its signifying quality is altered to make it figure the body of Christ. A given text that has sprung up alongside other texts in the way intertextuality governs the production of all texts, is picked out, consecrated and thereby converted into a translation of one of these other texts. It is altered as a result. Although it has not changed outwardly, it is now another work or, alternatively, it now represents, figures and/or exhibits another work.

Understanding translation through the prism of the doctrine of the Real

Presence provides us with a novel perspective and puts translation in a new light. We can try to assess the implications of such a move.

1.   It focuses on the host text – that is, the translation – and its relation to the anterior text. This means inverting the standard approach, which starts from the original and casts every translation as deriving from it. The Real Presence perspective affords the spectacle of a new text being created alongside and contiguous with a pre-existing text. About this new text the claim is subsequently made that it is a translation of the pre-text. If the claim finds acceptance among a particular community – if, that is, the speech act does its work and the new text is consecrated – several things happen. Firstly, the pre-text remains what it always was, a text among other texts, except that it now enjoys the added distinction of being an original – an accidental change. Secondly, a particular relation between translation and original is instituted. Thirdly, as soon as a text becomes a translation, it acquires dual status: it is both text and translation, in other words, its accidental nature remains unaffected but its substance has altered; alternatively, in line with the idea of transubstantiation, the translation continues to look like a text in its own right but it is now entirely that other work of which also the pre-text is a manifestation.

2.   It supplies a ground for burying the idea of translation as involving the transformation of an original text. In other words, it foregoes the notion of an original that gives rise to a derivative, transmogrified product called translation. Transformation assumes there is an invariant, an essence or identity that remains the same despite different manifestations and changes in form and language. Identifying such an invariant has proved problematic in translation studies. If there is alteration in a Real Presence perspective it is the conversion of a text into a translation by means of a speech act which declares this text to be a translation and in so doing changes either its substance or its signifying quality.

3.   It dispenses with the idea that in translation something – a content, meaning – is transferred from an original to the translation. In other words, it discards the idea of translation as consisting of the transport of meaning from original to translation. The notion of an invariant that is kept intact as it travels from one language to another, can also be jettisoned.

4.   It claims instead that another process is at work. It is this: when a text is successfully declared to be a translation of a pre-existing text, the pre-text comes to inhabit the translation. The original's body or substance is now somehow present and manifested in the translation. The decisive moment in this chain of events is neither that of the original secreting a

translation nor that of the translation being materially constituted, but that of the consecrating speech act which converts a text into a translation. The speech act cleaves the host in two; it separates substance from accident, reduces the host's linguistic appearance to accident and infuses its substance with the substance of the original.

5.   It stresses the idea of communities of believers and, in the same breath, that of the institutional context of the consecrating speech act. As the word 'successfully' in the previous paragraph already indicated, translations function as translations – that is, they are accepted and recognised as translations – only for believers, communities of readers or text users who are willing to suspend their disbelief and to consume translations as either being or representing an underlying original. But as we also saw before, in Chapter One, the effectiveness of a speech act depends on institutional factors. What counts as translation in one environment will not necessarily be accepted in another. And as the controversies surrounding the Real Presence showed, even when a text is recognised as translation there is still plenty of room for different opinions about the precise nature of the relation between a translation and its pre-text.

6.   It highlights the commemorative function of translation. Just as the Eucharistic ritual commemorates the Last Supper and serves anamnesis, translations counteract forgetting by bringing back and revitalising anterior texts. Such translative commemoration takes place continuously and in any number of locations. An original may be simultaneously exhibited in numerous translations in different languages across the globe.

Depending on the position one adopts regarding the Real Presence, following conversion a translation 'is' its pre-text, that is, an allographic token of it, or it is 'inhabited by' it, or it 'signifies' and 'recalls' it and in so doing 'renders it present' or 'presents' it in an active and effective sense. Let us try to see how each of the main theological stances sketched in the previous pages might reflect on the way a translation relates to its pre-text.

Transubstantiation may be understood as the opposite of transformation, as indeed Cornelis de Waal points out in his little book on Peirce (de Waal 2001: 25-6). De Waal draws on the Aristotelian distinction between accidents and substance to clarify the difference. In transformation, the substance – that is, the object, an invariant – remains the same while the accidental qualities change. Even Proteus, through all his protean transformations, remains himself; he just looks different with every change. In transubstantiation, the opposite occurs. The attributes remain as they are but the object, the inner reality, changes.

This is what happens when a text becomes a translation as viewed in the light of the transubstantiation paradigm. It is transmuted into the original from the moment it is converted into a translation. On the surface, nothing happens. The words remain as they are. The change affects what Genette called the operal identity of the object. Declaring a text to be a translation brings it into convergence with another text such that both works are now the same work. The convergence is total. It also exceeds what Genette termed "sameness of meaning". Similarity or convergence of meaning is likely to aid the acceptance of a text as a translation of another text (I will return to this point), but the decisive shift is the alignment of the two texts in such a way that they now stand as the same work. In other words, operal identity is not preserved despite translation, as the traditional perspective which casts translation as transformation has it, but exactly the opposite happens: recognising a text as a translation creates operal identity with another text.

Adopting a Lutheran perspective would mean leaving transubstantiation aside but still assuming that the pre-text is present "in, with and under" the translation, which therefore will have changed in status if not in substance. Just as for Luther the bread must remain bread even as after consecration the body of Christ inhabits it, so a translation remains a text in its own right while at the same time, as a translation, it also 'exhibits' another text. The term sometimes employed to label the Lutheran position, consubstantiation, even though Lutherans reject it, has the advantage of drawing attention to this dual nature of a translation, an aspect which the transubstantiation perspective covers under the blanket of a radical change that leaves only the accidents but nothing of the old substance of the text converted into a translation. Consubstantiation points to a translation's two bodies, its simultaneous and analogical articulation of two orders of meaning, as incarnation of another text and as a text *per se*. In other words, and phrased in Relevance theory terminology, translations can be read both interpretively as texts representing other texts, and descriptively as texts speaking about the world in their own right.

Both the Roman Catholic and the Lutheran positions can readily be accommodated by the Berne Convention on copyright. If a translation in effect changes into another work the moment it becomes a translation, then at that instant it is appropriated by whoever owns this other work. In contrast, the semiotic stance that looks to Wycliff, Zwingli and Calvin for inspiration has nothing to say about ownership. It posits a different signifying quality in texts declared to be translations but it does not foresee a change in their operal identity.

The view Wycliff and Zwingli take of the Real Presence is probably the most rationalist of all those we have surveyed. They too grant that a change takes place during the sacrament, but it concerns only the signifying quality of the bread and wine. In this perspective, converting a text into a translation of a pre-text would imply that the translation, while it remains a text in its own right, additionally comes to stand for the pre-text. A translation can act as a substitute but should not be taken for the pre-text, however. The ground on which the translation acts as a sign of the pre-text is not specified here – and neither is it in the Catholic or the Lutheran perspective.

Seen from this angle, Calvin's position may be the most amenable to translation. Calvin captures the change that the sacrament of the Eucharist brings about with the rhetorical concept of metonymy. Before consecration the bread is identical with itself, afterwards it is a sign which calls forth the body of Christ, which 'presents' it in the full sense of the word: causes it to be seen and to be present. As a result the name for the thing signified can be transferred to the sign, and this transfer Calvin calls metonymy. In this view metonymy would be the figure of speech I use when I point to *War and Peace* in English and say: 'This is *War and Peace*'. The same name can be used to designate either the translation or the original. The two are not to be confused, and they remain of different orders, but the close link between them allows for the shifting designation. And the link is close because Calvin insists on 'affinity', 'similitude' and relations of contiguity as the cement holding the sign and its object together so that the former is 'true' to the latter, its image rather than its simulacrum.

This is important because it allows us to see how far the perspective on translation sketched in this chapter can go beyond illuminating the relation between translation and original. My account so far has stressed the speech act that makes a text into a translation of another text. Can *any* text be converted into a translation? On the strength of most of what has been said above, yes. In practice, no. Much depends, in the model that I have presented, on the speech act that brings about the conversion of a text into a translation. Who is authorised to utter such a speech act with any prospect of perlocutionary effect? In the religious ritual the minister's authority derives from Christ, whose words of institution are echoed in the institutional ritual that is the Eucharist. In the secular world, only the author of the original is entitled to say '*hoc est opus meum*' about a translation, a text whose words the author manifestly did not write. As we saw, copyright law stipulates that even though a translator can claim ownership of the form of words of a translation, this claim does not in any way diminish the author's claim to be regarded as the owner of the work. It follows that strictly speaking only an author can change a text X in another language into a translation of his own work A.

However, as we also saw before, copyright law is a tool of limited reach. It is restricted to texts circulating in the public domain and it expires seventy years after the author's death. After that, what? Perhaps Calvin can help here. Calvin argued that Christ took bread and wine to stand as signs of his flesh and blood because of the affinity and similitude between the solidity of the bread and his body and the fluidity of the wine and his blood, and because the foodstuffs on the table and his own future spiritual presence among his followers shared the idea of sustenance. These parallels provide the signs with their ground. In the same way, it could be argued, history and tradition, convention and consensus have seen to it that 'relevant similarity' with an original (Chesterman 1997: 69) conditions the acceptability of a text's claim to be regarded as a translation. If the sign shows the right affinity with its object so that it can be seen, in Peirce's terms, as being compelled by it and therefore true to it, then chances are that the conversion comes into being and the sign can legitimately stand for the object – in our case, a text X will be recognised as a translation of work A. The implication is that the claim for recognition may be made by the translator or indeed by anyone, provided there is a tradition that supplies models and samples of the kind of affinity that satisfies the condition for recognition as translation.

This also means that authors and other copyright holders cannot escape the force of precedent and tradition. While they can, for whatever reason, or even for no reason, prevent a translation of their work from entering the public domain, they cannot elevate just any random text to a translation of their work. On the contrary, conventions and consensus ratify translations. They see to it that communities accept that if X is offered as a translation of A, and X shows an acceptable level and kind of resemblance with other instances of authorised translations, then X has a fair chance of being accepted as a translation of A. Who decides what is acceptable? In a world of professional and specialised translating, which as a result shows a degree of institutionalisation, the words of the recognised practitioners and their organisations will carry most weight, as indeed Andrew Chesterman has suggested with reference to professional translation norms (1993; 1997: 64-70). In less well-organised and less institutionalised parts of the world of translating, things will be more fuzzy. Here sectarianism has ample scope, as partial agreements and disagreements proliferate and different poetics compete. But then, the expectations about translation in these areas and genres may also be more diffuse, so that conventions rather than norms structure the field (Hermans 1999: 79-85). In all these cases, however, history has the last word.

This leaves a further issue to be resolved. Does not translation presuppose a genetic link that starts with the original as the source of translation? What happens to this link and to the original's logical and chronological primacy?

The question of primacy is not in doubt. Just as theology would have no hesitation in assigning primacy by invoking the gravitas, omnipresence and supra-temporality of the divine, so there must be a pre-text before a new text can be aligned with it as its translation. But viewing translation through a Real Presence prism reorients the idea of a genetic link and the associated notion of derivation by foregrounding intertextuality and subsequent convergence. All texts feed on other texts. In this sense intertextuality describes the general condition of text production. But not all intertextually produced texts are translations. Some may be intended as translations but fail to be ratified as such and end up having another label attached to them. The particular align-ment called translation requires a valid speech act resulting in recognition by a congregation. What matters in this perspective is not the derivation, since all texts derive from other texts, but the alignment and the way it comes about.

To end on a textual note: perhaps the alignment that translation brings about with a pre-text can be understood in anagrammatic terms. If the Real Presence means recognising the body of Christ in a piece of bread, a translation might be read as an anagram of a pre-text, which is contained, as it were, beneath the translation's verbal arrangement. Once we have been handed the key, we can read the surface text as a sign manifesting a different corpus. The triumphal *Imago primi saeculi Societatis Jesu* (1640), the collection of emblems that celebrated the one hundredth anniversary of the founding of the Jesuit order in the Low Countries, featured a programmatic anagram in which '*Societas Iesv*' (Society of Jesus) was transmuted into a militant '*Vitiosa seces*' ('cut off wicked things'); in the same way Orpheus' lyre was first christianised into a '*cithara Iesu*' and then anagrammatically elevated into '*Eucharistia*' (Manning 2002: 195-7).

5. Connecting Systems

In a now famous essay first published in 1979, 'The Conduit Metaphor', Michael Reddy (1993) showed how pervasive the standard way of thinking about language and communication in English is. The essay featured a long list of common turns of phrase associated with the transmission and exchange of information. The image of communication that English usage projects, almost invariably casts language as first packaging and then conveying a speaker's thoughts, intentions and meanings. Communication, in this view, consist in transferring messages from one person to another as if along a channel or conduit called language. The metaphors of encoding a message at one end, transmitting it by means of some kind of vehicle, and then decoding it at the other end, are so common we hardly notice them. They have become, in the words of Lakoff and Johnson's classic study, *Metaphors We Live By* (1980). We take them for granted when we conceptualise language and communication – and, by extension, translation. Because they are so ingrained, it is very hard to liberate oneself from these routine modes of thinking.

As an alternative to the conduit metaphor, Reddy proposed a thought experiment which he called the toolmaker's paradigm. Imagine, he suggested, different individuals who live in complete isolation from one other, each inhabiting an environment that is physically quite distinct from the other environments. Each individual has devised tools to work their own habitat. The individuals can communicate with one another about their tools in rudimentary ways only, by passing through a hatch bits of paper with marks and crude drawings on them. Being dependent on this type of communication, each inhabitant could see the others' drawings but would be able to make only very limited sense of them. Only very slowly, by trial and error and by making tentative inferences, would they manage to reach even a basic understanding of their neighbours' living conditions and of the nature and use of the tools the neighbours had devised. Moreover, they would never be in a position to verify their understanding of how the others had organised their respective worlds.

If we read the physical habitat in the thought experiment as standing for a person's mental furnishings, Reddy proposed, we have an idea of how communication might function in this alternative model. Communication is here primarily a matter of emitting signals that a receiver has to make sense of in their own world as best they can. The key image is not that of a message travelling along a transmission belt and reaching its destination more or less intact, but that of stimulus and inference.

The consequences of adopting a frame like this are significant. Among other things, as Reddy pointed out, in the toolmaker's paradigm successful communication cannot be taken for granted: "Partial miscommunication, or divergence of readings from a single text, are not aberrations. They are tendencies inherent in the system" (Reddy 1993: 175). What needs to be explained in this paradigm is not that communication may go wrong once in a while, but that it can succeed against the odds. Successful communication is not only improbable, checking its success can be done only by producing more communication, while forever deferring the possibility of any final check.

The different view of communication that arises from the toolmaker's paradigm is not the result of initial fieldwork investigating the nature of language, followed by the design of a theoretical model to account for the findings of this investigation. On the contrary, it privileges the bold new perspective and exploits the vocabulary that comes with it. In this sense it demonstrates the heuristic power of a theoretical approach. We can think of the role of theory in research in at least two ways. The more empirical line stresses the need to start from observation. It casts theory as coming after a fact-finding mission and as seeking to offer a cogent explanation of whatever has been found to be the case. First we observe, then we explain. This view assumes that there is a world to be observed, and perhaps it can even be observed more or less objectively. The other view of the role of theory claims that theory enables observation. In this view, theory plays a heuristic part as a particular way of looking. Adopting a new theoretical framework amounts to more than an inconsequential redescription of the same reality. The new perspective and vocabulary afforded by the theory remind us that things only were what they were because they had routinely been described that way. As a result, familiar contours shift and different aspects and issues leap to the fore. A world seen differently becomes a different world. The more one puts the emphasis on the formative role of theory and moves towards a constructivist vision, the more one will be incliend to say that a theory creates its own world.

The previous chapter explored a theologically inspired perspective on translation that sought to think translation without invoking the idea of transformation. In the following pages I will again be using theory in this heuristic sense as a tool to reconsider and redescribe translation, and I will again be calling on another discipline. The perspective I have adopted here, the theory of social systems as developed by the German sociologist Niklas Luhmann (1927-1998), will, I hope, be sufficiently new to defamiliarise translation at least in some respects and to raise new issues, perhaps prompt new questions and, who knows, suggest a certain potential for future research.

Luhmann's social systems theory possesses considerable range and depth. It has been applied, by Luhmann himself and others, to a variety of social domains including politics, the economy, law, religion, education, intimate relations, environmental debates, protest movements, art and literature. As far as I know, its application to the world of translation has barely begun. Andreas Poltermann worked with it in the 1980s and early 1990s (Poltermann 1992) and I devoted a few pages to it in *Translation in Systems* (Hermans 1999: 137-50). More recently Hans Vermeer (2006, 2006a) incorporated parts of it into his comprehensive 'intertheory' of translaton. But whereas Vermeer effectively built his own theory mixing in Luhmann together with quite a number of other ideas, my exploration seeks to determine what social systems theory, or elements from it, might mean for the world of translation.

I am not interested in demonstrating that translation *is* a social system. Such a demonstration would be misguided. The constructivist outlook of social systems theory means that the theory assumes that there are systems. My intention is to redescribe translation using the terms and perspective of social systems theory. In other words, the aim of describing translation as a social system is not ontological proof but the deployment of a conceptual apparatus, so as to see what we can see when we decide to see things from this vantage point. The vantage point is tied to a location in space and time, and although its reach is broad, it is not limitless. The theory is most at home when it deals with the modern and postmodern context of Western societies. Luhmann has written about other parts of the world too, and about other historical periods, but the bulk of his work concerns the industrial and postindustrial West, whose prime form of social organisation he describes as functional differentiation, in contrast to the segmented and stratified societies that preceded it. He is aware that his own brand of sociology is a product of the contemporary world it seeks to describe. How it will fare when it engages in detail with other societies remains to be seen. All the same, some of the theoretical reflections are very general and abstract, and may be applied to a variety of contexts.

Social systems theory, like most theories, was developed using elements from other theories. It harks back to earlier sociology, notably the work of Talcott Parsons, but it also borrows liberally from general systems theory, the cybernetics of Heinz von Foerster, the biology of Humberto Maturana and Francisco Varela, the theory of evolution, and the differential calculus of George Spencer Brown. Language and communication occupy a prominent place in Luhmann's work, and his ideas in this respect build on Saussure and Karl Bühler. With deconstruction social systems theory shares the emphasis on difference.

A frequently repeated anecdote about Luhmann has it that, shortly before he was appointed professor of sociology at Bielefeld in 1968, he was asked about the likely duration and cost of his research project; his reply was: "Duration: thirty years. Costs: none" (in Luhmann 2005: vii). Over the next thirty years the project was carried out more or less as planned, resulting in an imposing oeuvre. The key ideas of Luhmann's social systems theory are to be found in all his major books. *Social Systems* (Luhmann 1995; first published in German in 1984) lays out the foundation for the mature work. Luhmann went on to devote substantial volumes to each of the major 'functionally differentiated' systems he discerned in modern society. For our purposes, the main texts in this respect are a book on the sciences as a social system (*Die Wissenschaft der Gesellschaf*, 1990, not yet available in English) and on *Art as a Social System* (2000; *Die Kunst der Gesellschaft*, 1995). Shortly before his death Luhmann summed up his work in the two volumes devoted to 'society as a social system' (*Die Gesellschaft der Gesellschaft*, 1997, as yet untranslated into English). Not all these weighty tomes make light reading. Accessible introductions in English may be had from collections of essays (Luhmann 1998, 2002), from shorter works like those on the social codification of love, on ecological communication, on the mass media or on risk (Luhmann 1986, 1989, 2000a, 2005), or, in German, from the course of lectures introducing students to systems theory (Luhmann 2004).

System

As a sociological theory, social systems theory should help us understand translation in its social dimension. It may therefore come as a surprise right at the start that translators are not part of the social system of translation. Translators are out of it, as are their professional associations, their printed texts, their dictionaries, their mailboxes, even their memories, computerised or not. All of these are presupposed by the system, but they do not belong to it. They belong to its environment. The distinction between system and environment is fundamental. Computers, dictionaries and the like are part of the physical environment of the social system of translation, the bodies of translators are organic systems and their thoughts are psychic systems. All these systems are enclosed within themselves and they do not communicate with one another. Systems can operate only within their own boundaries, not beyond them. Thoughts can trigger further thoughts but they cannot move mountains and neither can they communicate. The living organism exists within the skin that encloses it. When a body becomes indistinguishable from inert matter and worms start eating into it, this means it is dead and no longer a living organism.

Nevertheless all these systems are interdependent. The body requires food and air, the mind needs a body, and bodies rely on minds. Each takes from its environment and remains 'open' in this sense, but it then processes in its own way what it takes, and in this sense it is closed. Our organs of perception supply stimuli to the mind, which the mind interprets in the only way it can, by means of mental operations.

Luhmann thinks of systems in terms of events and operations, that is, in 'operative' (or operational) terms. Like signs in C.S. Peirce's semiotics, systems happen. The key metaphors making up the theory are temporal rather than spatial in nature. Systems as Luhmann conceives of them do not consist of fixed elements and the relations between them, and not of centres and peripheries either, but of operations that happen momentarily and have to be connected over time to form a recognisable sequence. The system exists for as long as the sequence continues. It dies when no connecting operations ensue. To put it another way: systems only ever exist on the spur of the moment, as the events that keep the system going light up and fade away, and new events must follow.

The perspective is both fluid and posthumanist. As in the theory of the selfish gene or that of the nimble meme, man is not the centre of things. Social systems consist neither of individuals or groups nor of their thoughts and instruments, but of *communications*. Social systems are communication systems in that they are made up of communications, and *only* of communications. Particular social systems consist of communications of a certain kind. Think of them as discourse communities if you will, provided the emphasis is put on the to and fro of discursive exchanges rather than on communities of bodies and minds. Yury Lotman's notion of a semiosphere might be another parallel. Discursive formations or regimes, another. For Luhmann it is not humans who communicate, however much they may think they do and however much their minds participate in communication through language; only communication communicates (2002: 168; Schwanitz 1996). In terms of social systems theory, human persons are ciphers or identity markers constructed in the course of communication. Communicative events, that is, may be construed as actions and attributed to subjects or agents by an observer, but these observations are themselves communicative events (Luhmann 1997: 620). Different systems incessantly construe subjects in their own terms. Put differently: individuals constantly weave their way through different systems and social roles as family members, employees, consumers, taxpayers, citizens, and so on; if we shift the perspective away from the identity of the individuals and towards the communicative networks that they participate in and that constitute them as subjects, we gain an impression of social systems in action.

The social system of translation consists of communications perceived as translations or as pertaining to translation. The most basic operation in the system is not the composition of a new translation – I can do that in my head as a mental operation – but its articulation and recognition as a translation, and the ensuing response. Only then does a translation acquire a communicative dimension, the only dimension a social systems perspective will consider.

A translative communication, like any other communication, comprises the coincidence of three aspects: enunciation, information and understanding. *Enunciation* refers to the performative or self-referential aspect of a communication, the presentation of something, the communicative act of presenting something. In the case of translation this means the presentation of something as a translation, that is, as the representation of something else. What is presented is *information*. Information indicates what the utterance is about, as distinct from the communicative act itself. In the case of translation this means primarily the reference to another text, typically one that exists in another language. *Understanding* observes enunciation and information together and involves the inference that something is being said by someone to someone.

This model of communication is not new. It derives from Karl Bühler and is very much the stimulus and inference model that Michael Reddy illustrated with his toolmaker's paradigm and that also underpins, for example, skopos theory and, in linguistics, Relevance theory. In their book *Relevance,* Dan Sperber and Deirdre Wilson dispense with the conduit model in the opening paragraph and move swiftly to replace the idea of understanding as decoding with that of inference, invoking Michael Reddy in their very first footnote (1986: 1, 9-15). Luhmann, too, explicitly rejects the idea of communication as transfer (1997: 194; 1999a: 147) and stresses that understanding a message includes misunderstanding whatever a speaker may have intended; understanding, that is, is always selective (1995: 157ff; 2002: 158-9).

The model's most important aspect, for our purposes, is its inferential nature. This entails that communication, and hence translation, is not thought of as the transmission of pre-given content via some linguistic conduit. The model chafes against all the common images that visualise translation as transference, transport, ferrying or shipping across, in short against all the traditional metaphors rooted in the etymology of the English word 'translation' and its cognates in related languages. We will need to remain wary of these metaphors and the mental picture of translation they promote.

Communications are fleeting events. The mind participates in communication because it processes information and stimulates response, but only communications can trigger further communications. This means communications have to connect and keep connecting if a system is to come into being and continue. Social systems achieve connectivity by processing meaning selectively and then redeploying that selection to create new sets of connective possibilities in the next communication. Of all the meanings a communication offers, only some are selected and reinserted into the communicative chain.

A system of translation needs to recognise communications in their translative aspect, make sense of the particular selection this communication represents, and then reinvest that knowledge to produce new translations or comments about translation, in the expectation that those fresh productions will in turn be accepted as translations or as valid comments about translation. Put differently: we can translate because there are translations; and if we know a translation when we see one, it is for this same reason. Individual translations look backward and forward at the same time, and the combination of recursive and anticipatory movements enables the system to exist in time. In this sense the translation system is a *self-reproducing* or *autopoietic* system (the term 'autopoietic' is Maturana's). It continually produces the building blocks – that is, the operations – of which it consists and by means of which it reproduces itself. The building blocks are translative communications, that is, translations recognised as translations and statements taken as pertinent to translation. The latter include translation studies, which I take to engage in a form of translating translation: the study of translation translates its object into its own metalanguage (Hermans 1999: 146-8). To an extent however this is a matter of choosing a system reference, since translation studies as an academic discipline could also be regarded as part of the sciences.

Over time, as the system reproduces itself through the recursive circularity of its own operations (its autopoiesis), it builds up regularities, patterns of expectation, in other words: structures. Social structures are structures of expectation, taking expectation in a de-psychologised sense as the anticipatory projection inherent in every communication. With respect to translation, three things are important here.

Firstly, as translations and discourses about translation cluster and multiply, discursive identities are established. In this way translators and their clients re-enter the scene, not as individuals of flesh and blood – they are organic, not social systems – but as points of reference, ciphers in the ongoing discourse of and around translation. In the same way, social roles may be understood as bundles of expectations formed by and in turn informing communicative exchanges.

Secondly, since a translation system will emerge only if translations are recognised and redeployed as communications of a certain kind, we can see how, through this process of recycling, the translation system generates a dynamic of its own – acquires a certain individuality if you like – and differentiates itself from other discursive practices, other social systems. This differentiation between system and environment is rehearsed within the system as the distinction between self-reference and external reference (or other-reference). Using Cecilia Wadensjö's terms from Chapter Two, we might associate self-reference with display, presentation or enunciation, and external reference with replay, which ties the system to the function it fulfils for the outside world, its client systems.

Thirdly, the expectations that grow within the system facilitate the recognition of certain communications as translations and the exclusion of others that do not fit the mould. In this way the system draws its own boundary as it becomes distinct from its environment. Systems create their own environment as they differentiate themselves from everything that they read as external to them, including other systems. A system that draws its own boundary also observes itself.

I will address the historical form of this differentiation later. Let me suggest here that, as translation differentiates itself, it organises itself around a basic value, a guiding difference that allows it to distinguish discourses that pertain to it from those that do not. This matrix – Luhmann speaks of a 'code' – I take to be the notion of *representation*. I understand representation here in the double sense of *proxy* and *resemblance*. Translations are texts that speak for other texts and they do so by virtue of some relevant resemblance to those other texts. They typically appear in the shape of interlingual re-enactments. Because translations re-enact other texts, they are *metarepresentations*, that is, representations of representations. And because the medium involved is not necessarily lingual but could in principle be any semiotic medium, it might be prudent to speak of the code of translation as being *intersemiotic metarepresentation*.

Metarepresentation, in the double sense of proxy and portrayal, is the translation system's backbone. It endows the system with its basic orientation and renders it distinct. This distinctiveness allows the system to fulfil a specific *function*, which I take to be that of extending the communicative range of society across individual languages while simultaneously reminding society of the limitations of its linguistic – or, more broadly, semiotic – media. Discourses that cannot in the final analysis be reduced to discourses about metarepresentation are not part of the translation system. In this way the code or matrix provides the system with a means to distinguish between what belongs to the sysem and what does not.

Representation is a broad category and can take a number of shapes. In practice, translation, like other social systems, is built around a series of more concrete and both geographically and historically specific *programmes*. These are the diverse sets of rules, norms, conventions, preferences and prohibitions that govern translation, the locally grown poetics that spill out of and in turn inform and legitimate particular modes of translative representation. Their very diversity and, more often than not, the friction between different poetics equip the system with its adaptive potential. They also articulate the system's internal differentiation.

Ultimately however the programmes all revolve around the issue of cross-lingual (or cross-medial) representation. This convergence allows translative communications to be recognised, produced and continually reproduced as communications of a certain kind. It provides the system with its unique self-propelling momentum, its principle of autonomy, what Luhmann calls its *operative* (or: operational) *closure*. The term does not mean autarchy or solip-sism, it means merely that the system cannot operate outside its own boundaries but draws on its own resources and its own past to create the conditions for its continued existence. In this way the translation system determines its own course and creates its own time even as it supplies other systems with texts that represent existing texts in other languages. As translations come and go, and conventions take shape and wane, the system develops a degree of stabil-ity by crystallising structures of expectation around individual programmes. These structures make some occurrences – that is, some modes of translating – more likely than others and allow a more effective use of the memory of the past and of projection into the future. In this way structures reduce uncertainty and bind time. Translation norms, for example, emerge and are consolidated as the system, or certain parts of it, observe the success of existing translations and accordingly build the anticipation of a particular audience response into the production of appropriate new translations, reducing the risk of failure in the process.

Through all this the system remains operatively locked in itself and reads its environment in its own self-centred manner. The environment contains all the other systems that together make up the world, but each system constructs its own world in its own image. The translation system perceives the world through a translative lens. It reads utterances less for their use value as such than for their potential to be re-used in other linguistic contexts. It also sees a large number of other social systems, including institutions and organisations, all with their own rules and preferences as regards the kinds of communica-tions that can circulate in their own sphere. The demands that are formulated in these client systems regarding the well-formedness of texts cannot deter-mine the structure of the translation system. This is because systems do not communicate with their environments and because, being operatively closed, systems determine their own structures on the basis of their own operations. However, the system may pick up these demands as it scans its environment, and they may find resonance in the system.

When this happens, the system may or may not take much notice. If it does, and if it allows itself to be sufficiently *perturbed* or *irritated* by what it registers in another system, it can adjust its own structures to take account of this. When that happens – and it happens routinely in professional translation – the result is what Luhmann calls *structural coupling*. One part of the translation system then correlates its resources with those of another system so they form a close fit. The concept of structural coupling captures the fact that we distinguish between financial, medical, technical, literary and other kinds of translation, each attuned to a particular sphere of activity outside the translation system. This form of internal differentiation ensures that the system remains compatible with its environment. Structural coupling also suggests a degree of mutuality between system and environment. Localisation is the illustration *par excellence*: as a type of translation it is adjusted to the particular requirements of certain organisations and media, and the organisation assists the localisers by ensuring that the texts to be translated lend themselves to deployment in different languages and different locales.

As the translation system adjusts its structures in response to being irritated by particular sections of the environment, it gains in complexity and adaptability. Because it caters for a variety of client systems, it now accommodates a corresponding variety of programmes. In other words, the system's internal differentiation mirrors its differentiated environment. The match is not perfect. While a certain correspondence is necessarily there, it is never one to one. A system is always already adjusted to its environment; it could not exist if its environment did not tolerate it. But because each system has its own momentum and temporal horizon, mismatches will occur.

This is a consequence of systems being open and closed at the same time: open to their environment, but operatively closed as self-reproducng, autopoietic systems. Indeed Luhmann thinks of modern society as consisting essentially of an assemblage of *functionally differentiated* social systems. Among the main ones are politics, the economy, the legal system, the worlds of education, of the arts, the mass media, the sciences and religion, but there are others, large and small, and most are highly differentiated internally. And they are all there is, socially speaking. Society as a whole is not more than the sum of these parts; it has no centre and no overarching rationale or narrative. Individual systems, self-centred as they are, have only themselves and what they make of other systems to determine their course. The total picture is closer to chaos theory than to clockwork, and it is governed by a Darwinian type of evolution, not teleology. For all that, the constructivism of social systems theory does not deny that there is a world; it claims merely that the world cannot be known in its entirety or 'as it is', for each system constructs it in its own image.

If these are the rudiments of translation as a social system, let me sketch four aspects of translation that could acquire a different hue when viewed through a system-theoretic lens. They are: the form of translation, translator training, second-order observation and finally the history of translation. In each case I want to suggest that social systems theory has the potential to point up aspects of translation that look different under its gaze.

Form

Translations are distinct kinds of communication. They are metacommunications, as a rule of the interlingual sort. Rather than speaking directly about the world, they represent other communications. As mentioned several times before, Relevance theory, too, treats translations as instances of interpretive as opposed to descriptive use of language (Gutt 1991). Still other approaches cast translation as reported speech, as we saw in Chapter Three.

As communications, translations invoke the difference between enunciation and information, self-reference and external reference. External reference here concerns what a translation speaks about, what it points to outside itself. This includes the 'relevant similarity' (Chesterman 1996) or 'interpretive resemblance' (Gutt 1991) that enables a translation to substitute for another text. It takes account of the demands of client systems to establish the appropriate kind of resemblance in accordance with internally created programmes.

The self-reference of a translative communication entails, as we also saw before, the actual display of that resemblance, the dramatisation of the quotation marks that frame the performance of translation. In this way the self-reference of translation draws attention to the particular character of its re-enactment of the original. It exhibits the fact that this and no other kind of resemblance has been chosen to do the work of representation. It is this reference to the particularity of the resemblance that I call the *form* of translation.

Form, as Luhmann describes it (1990: 79) following Spencer Brown (1969), means indicating one side of a distinction and not the other. Form is two-sided. It has an inside and an outside. Recall Michelangelo, for whom the statue he wanted to carve was already there in the block of marble before him; all he had to do was liberate it by chipping away the redundant stone around it. Every form has a boundary that profiles it against its surroundings. It becomes discernible as a form only when it is distinguished from what is not it, when the real is separated out from the virtual. The inside of a form is what is marked or visible. It is only when we cross its boundary and indicate its outside that we can appreciate how the significance of a given form changes depending on what the form is profiled against. For example, we conventionally regard a translation as profiled against its original and we then discuss the type and measure of resemblance it displays. But it is equally possible to see translations as profiled against non-translated texts in the receptor language (that is, texts in client systems), or, as suggested in Chapter Two, against other translations.

Form is also to be distinguished from medium. For Luhmann, *medium* means a fairly loose collection of elements leaving "an open-ended multiplicity of possible connections" (2000: 104). Language is a medium in this sense, it is not a system (1997: 112). Sentences and discourses however are forms, because form is generated in a medium via a tight coupling of its elements. Form is always form in a medium.

This last point matters for the self-reference of translation. Norm theory can help us see what is at stake here. Viewing the translator's work through a norm-theoretic lens casts it as a series of choices of particular translative options from an array of alternative but equally available options. The actual selections that are made will be attributed to the normative pressure governing the process. Since the resulting translation is the outcome of these selections, its meaning stems not only from the words that have been chosen but just as much from recognising what might have been there but is not. The exclusions gain significance as the counterform to what is there. If we think of the medium of translation as the set of modes of representations that are acceptable in certain circles at a given time, then individual translations are forms generated in this medium. This also shows that media are not visible (sentences and texts are visible, language as such is not) but that they are more constant and more durable than forms. At the same time, the medium becomes visible only through forms. We can read sentences but we cannot view language as such. We can peruse individual translations but we cannot put our finger on modes of translative representation. While the medium enables form, the medium itself is reproduced through the ongoing generation of forms, just as in Saussurian linguistics *parole* would not be possible without an underlying and invisible *langue*, but conversely *langue* needs *parole* or it dies.

If form means selection and hence also exclusion, the excluded alternatives can be said to provide a strong link with the past, since the alternatives are alternatives only because translators working in comparable contexts must have had some use for them before. In this way the choices individual translators make build complex intertextual relations by both aligning themselves with and distancing themselves from existing translations and styles of translating. Here we meet the translation-specific intertextual network from Chapter Two again. As explained there, it covers a wide range. It can comprise particular translations, as when one translator translates in opposition to – or indeed paying homage to – a predecessor. It refers, more generically, to a certain style or mode of translating. Beyond that, it appeals, architextually, to an historically sedimented notion of what a particular culture or community has come to regard as translation per se. As, over time, translations intertextually fall in or out with one another, the form of translation is condensed and confirmed into a series of patterns for further use. It is condensed in that a particular mode of representation can be applied again at a later moment and it will still be recognised as being the same mode. It is confirmed in that the same mode can be applied in different circumstances and thus extend its range while still remaining the same mode. Both condensation and confirmation are aspects of repetition (Luhmann 2002: 120, following Spencer Brown).

Every choice, then, potentialises and temporalises alternatives. It pushes the excluded others into obscurity, nevertheless these exclusions continue to shadow individual translations. By thus potentialising alternatives, translations also signal their own contingency and provisionality in a temporal sequence. A translation of a particular original could have been different from what it is and still claim legitimacy, it can always be attempted again at a later date, and those new attempts will be able to draw on the reservoir of currently excluded options. Re-translations of canonical texts routinely tap into this store of rejects, without ever exhausting it.

Hence, while a translation shows the underlying original to have been translatable, the provisionality of the rendering suggests the impossibility of arriving at a definitive version. Translation remains forever open-ended. Translations may represent their originals, but the iterability of translation sees to it that no individual rendering can claim to be an original's *sole* representative. Considered in a different light, the repeatability of translation may simply be another way of filling out the notion of the *untranslatable*, understood here as the impossibility of exhausting the store of possible alternative renderings and of reaching a definitive translation. Every translation gestures to a multitude of alternative translations. In doing so it affirms its own contingency and opens the prospect of an unresolvable indeterminacy (Spencer Brown 1969).

As far as I can see, there are only two ways of providing closure in this respect. We rehearsed both of them before; both are institutional and therefore restricted in their scope, which means the closure they provide is incomplete.

The first is authentication as discussed in Chapter One. As we saw, it operates in strongly institutional contexts and entails a proclamation which makes a translation equivalent to its original. Authenticating a translation alters this translation's status, as a consequence of which translation and original become authentic versions and are presumed to have the same meaning. When this happens the translation ceases to be a translation: with the metarepresentational function gone, we no longer have a translation. But because authenticaton depends on a speech act, it succeeds only when there is agreement that the speech act's felicity conditions have been met. A translation that no longer functions as a translation may have transmogrified into an authentic texts in a legal sense, that is, as far as the legal system is concerned. Challenging the authenticity of authenticated texts is rare there, and indeed such a challenge would have to be articulated in a court of law. In other words, conflicts over authentication belong in the legal system. The translation system is at liberty to indulge in revisionism, recall the document's origin as a translation, treat it as a translation and perhaps produce new translations, but the legal system is unlikely to take much notice and even less likely to authenticate them.

The other instrument to halt the proliferation of translations is called copyright law, and we came across it in several earlier chapters. It cannot stop translations being produced privately, but it can prevent them, temporarily, from entering the public domain. It can do this because a translation, which the Berne Convention defines as a derivative product, needs the copyright holder's authorisation before it can be published. The copyright holder may forbid all translations of his or her work, or may restrict them to just one in any particular language. But copyright law applies only up to seventy years after the author's death, a very short time if we adopt a broad historical perspective. When it expires, the free flow of translation is ready to resume. Copyright law can delay but it cannot arrest the repeatability of translation.

It may be useful to think of the particular choices that make up individual translations as constructing both a *past* and a *future*. The past contains not only the virtual store of possible options and potential alternatives but also, concretely, the archive of successful choices, modes of representation that were found to be apposite on particular occasions. These earlier choices make connectivity more likely in comparable situations in future, as new translations harking back to previous and current forms of translating have a better chance of being accepted as translations themselves. The archive, too, is selective, for it sustains itself by forgetting as well as remembering. We deselect once valid but now outmoded ways of translating and retain only a conveniently foreshortened canon that serves present needs. This canon feeds the translation system's autopoiesis. It nourishes the medium, the set of available translative modes, out of which forms, as individual translations, are fashioned. Still, nothing prevents us from occasionally reinstating previously decommissioned forms. They normally require a legitimating discourse to justify their being brought back from oblivion. This is what Lawrence Venuti did in *The Translator's Invisibility* (1995), for example, when he extracted an historical genealogy of non-fluent translation as a way of buying credit for his own programme of 'minoritising' translation. Put differently: the past is that selection of forms which the present holds available for future use. The future belongs to the deferrals of the present.

Training

Considering translator training from a system-theoretic viewpoint does not lead to practical advice to trainers. Rather, it provides a perspective on how training relates to the world of translation. The question is how to phrase this relation in terms of social systems theory. We can do so from at least two perspectives. We can view translator training either as part of the system of education or as part of the translation system. This is a matter of choosing a system reference, as we saw above. I will treat translator training here as part of translation.

Generally speaking, the school system, from kindergarten to university, complements natural socialisation by combining the acquisition of general knowledge and social skills with the inculcation of specific competences. Translator training is almost exclusively concerned with specific competences, and offered mostly in further and higher education. This is not to say that schools are unimportant for translation. They transmit core ideas about it through language learning, for example. But in speaking of translator training I am thinking primarily of specialised courses leading to professional or semi-professional qualifications. This is a recent arrival on the education scene, as indeed it is on the translation scene.

Most translator training is strongly vocational, reflecting the closeness of modern translation to its client systems. Rephrased in social systems terminology: training repeats the structural coupling between an internally dif-ferentiated translation system and its various client systems that characterises the contemporary translation scene as a whole. It is no doubt symptomatic that much translator training today comes in the form of in-house training within client organisations such as multinational companies and institutions like the European Union or the United Nations. Often even the physical location where the training is dispensed has shifted to the relevant organisation. At the other end of the spectrum, when translator training does not take place in-house or in a specialised institute but is embedded in a higher education institute, there tends to be only limited cross-over from research to teaching, even though the intimate relation between teaching and research is meant to be the hallmark of university education. In most specialised translator training institutes, research tends to be of the applied kind. All of this is symptomatic of the vocational nature of translator training.

The role of the translator training institute, then, is the inculcation and certi-fication of a particular competence. The institute cannot guarantee its graduates success in the profession but it can equip students with an entry visa. It seeks to ensure that the visa is valid by implementing curricula that are attuned to the criteria prevalent in the world of professional translating. Coursework and tests will often simulate professional conditions and standards. In some cases degrees may even be accredited by professional organisations, to seal the correlation between training and the profession. To enable the transition from training to workplace, the institute interiorises the relevant expectations and rules of translation as they exist in the world outside. It recreates, selectively, within its own walls, the working conditions that prevail in professional trans-lating. In this way the institute copies into itself and then constantly rehearses and reproduces a model of the social system of translation, including all or part of the system's internal differentiation.

The model is necessarily a foreshortened and refracted projection, but the institute can shore up its adequacy by employing teachers who are or have recently been professional translators themselves and therefore possess relevant first-hand experience of the job. Such a teacher acts as a *theōros* in the ancient Greek sense (even though they may be horrified by the term), as an eye-witness who has been out of town – abroad, or to the Olympic games – and can report back authoritatively on what they have seen there (Maier 2006; Luhmann 1999: 140). Very often the teacher-cum-translator is the most visible link between the world of training and the profession.

Another and rather obvious symptom of the weight of vocational factors in training is the privileging of modes of representation that will allow transla-tions to meet the criteria of textual well-formedness and 'relevant resemblance' prevalent in the market-place. This requires that the training institute adopt those criteria and organise its curricula and pedagogical programmes accord-ingly. It will do so, but to a limited extent only. Too close an association with very particular market sectors would lead to over-specialisation and hence reduced employability for the training institute's graduates. Also, today's markets change rapidly, and the inculcation of generic and transferable rather than narrowly specialised skills will enable students to slot more adroitly into different and dynamic environments (Pym 1993). The institute monitors the professional world and may track the career paths of its alumni to this end, but reaches its own conclusions as to which sectors to correlate its own activities with.

The students' progress through the curriculum then reveals the improb-able emergence of order out of chaos. Students may enter the institute with a range of ideas about what translative representation entails, and they may be uncertain as to what mode to apply in what circumstances. The training sees to it that students develop the skills to select and apply the appropriate modes. This process too involves condensation and confirmation. Condensation here means that repetition cements certain solutions into place and fixes their identity as they are applied again and again. Subsequent operations are then seen as the same operation repeated. Confirmation means that solutions that have proved successful once can be applied to new texts and contexts and thus increase their range. In this way routines and structures are formed – a *habitus*, to use a term from a different glossary. The other side of this process is that discarded options are forgotten or end up on a scrapheap of spare parts, retrievable in principle but unlikely to be of real use given the streamlined nature of much professional translating. The process itself constantly looks both backwards and forwards. For the student, each individual translation exercise or assignment integrates an increasingly selectively remembered past with an equally selectively projected future. This is how their translations acquire forms capable of entering the recursive network of professional translation. Students able to produce these forms as and when required enjoy good career prospects.

The decisions regarding which options are to be retained and which to be rejected to arrive at valid translations rests ultimately with the instructors. Teachers and students occupy different institutional positions. However much teachers may cast themselves as advisers or facilitators, at the end of the day, or at the end of the course, they appropriate the criteria they have imported from the outside world and arbitrate, from case to case, on their application by individual students. This is what entitles the institute not just to inculcate but also to certify competence. The fact that, during the learning process, the teacher already knows while the learner finds out, means that negotiating translation options in the training institute is a normative business as far as the trainer is concerned and a cognitive process in the learner's case. By and large, trainers keep their notions of what makes acceptable translations intact despite the learners' frequently aberrant behaviour, whereas learners adapt and change their mental habits.

This division points to a key difference between the training institute and the world of professional translating. The institute simulates the professional workplace, but only up to a point. It constitutes an artificial bubble, a suspended state of virtual reality insulated against professional working conditions. As a result, mistakes made by students do not have the consequences they have in the world outside. Indeed the learning situation not only makes allowance for errors but actually needs them to as to be able to make the underlying norms and rules of translation the subject of observation and reflection. Errors and the comments they trigger are essential to get students to develop the necessary insight into requisite options and procedures of translation, and to build the structures of remembering and forgetting that underpin the practice of translation.

These options and structures are not visible. The training institute's insulation however creates the space that enables talk about them. It allows the invisible to be made visible, norms and expectations of translation to be the subject of extensive discussion between staff and students. Nowhere else in the world of translation do we find actual translating and discourse about translation yoked so tightly and so consistently together, and so interdependent. Hardly anywhere outside the training institute, for that matter, do we see originals and translations staying together for so long, and being checked so exhaustively against each other.

The combination, as part of translation teaching, of practice and explication, of doing and discussing, of procedural and declarative knowledge, means that the training institute lingers on that which professional routines will eventually cast aside or push into a parasitic margin, namely explicit reflection on translation options and decisions, the exploration of different possible solutions by way of inconsequential experimentation. In this way training cannot help foregrounding and thematising the contingency of translation choices, and by implication its own ambivalent relation to the professional workplace. To the extent that the institute seeks to deliver competent translators, it imports the profession's criteria and delivers certification on this basis. But to the extent that learning involves reflection and self-observation, it also inspects and probes those criteria.

Observation

There is a further dimension to this. In deliberating at length on individual acts of translation and their relative merit, the teaching and learning situation resembles those translations which are reluctant to commit themselves to a single rendering and thus highlight the problematic nature of translation without resolving it. Some years ago Kwame Anthony Appiah called for heavily footnoted translations that would highlight the difficulty and inappropriateness of a seemingly straightforward linear rendering (Appiah 2004). Vladimir Nabokov, too, championed the use of towering footnotes, footnotes reaching to the top of the page. Erasmus's *New Testament*, several hundred years before Nabokov, offers a good illustration. The opening of his Gospel according to John, set out on a large page in two columns of small print, features a single wispy line of original Greek and Latin translation drowning in a swirling mass of footnotes.

These translations advertise their self-doubt and question the very possibility of translating even as they perform their task. In questioning the adequacy of any particular rendering, they bring about a re-entry of the form of translation into the act of translating. *Re-entry* (the term is Spencer Brown's) means that the distinction which created the form in the first place is re-introduced into the form. The effect is like that of watching a play within a play. In a play, the characters are not normally meant to be aware of the audience watching them. When a play is enacted within a play, the characters in the embedded play are equally meant to be unaware of the characters in the framing play who are watching them. The audience in the theatre however can appreciate the drama convention being laid out in front of them. Because the play within the play is a form within a form, it draws attention to the enclosing form. This allows the convention sustaining the dramatic illusion, the formality of the form, to be observed (Roberts 1992). The examples of self-reference reviewed in Chapter Two all involved the idea of re-entry.

Translations which draw deliberate attention to their form by presenting it as problematical, raise the inherent self-reference of translation to self-reflection. As I suggested in Chapter Two, every translation carries a self-referential aspect as the selection of a particular kind of representation distinct from other kinds. Drawing attention to this selectivity by raising the issue of representation in an actual translation will lift self-reference to the level of self-reflection. That is what the abundance of metadiscourse about translation in the translator training institute achieves.The metadiscourse comes not only in the shape of critical paratexts accompanying translation exercises but also in that of the display character, the metadiscursive dimension, of student translations intended to demonstrate ability and skill. In this way the training institute continually generates reflection on the range and relative merits of translation options and choices, on what is prescribed, proscribed, permitted and preferred under the heading 'translation', and on the contingency of norms, rules, expectations and criteria. In other words, the training institute is that part of the social system of translation where the system looks into itself, observes its own structures and, in doing so, issues self-descriptions. The training institute is uniquely equipped to do this and it is unique in the intensity with which it does it. There are other areas where self-descriptions are generated, but spread over longer periods of time, as when successive re-translations of canonical texts also allow the system to observe itself. I will come back to this below.

Most of the self-descriptions generated by translator training institutes are conditioned by the institutes' vocational nature and their normative orientation, both of which reflect the structural coupling and the internal differentiation that tie the translation system to its client systems. This helps us understand a division of labour in translation studies. If the more speculative reflection theories tend to issue from less vocational places like universities, training institutes prefer the solidity and practical relevance of self-descriptions. Both have their uses.

Self-reflection, as an intense form of self-observation, is not restricted to educational contexts. Moreover, it involves the distinction between first-order and second-order observation. In social systems terminology, observation is understood in a very broad sense as the use of a distinction to indicate something – the side that is named, in contrast to whatever is not indicated, the other side of what is named. Observation in this sense is first-order observation. We do it all the time when we talk about the everyday things around us, when we indicate a table and distinguish it from everything that is not a table, or when we name tables in contradistinction to chairs. In contrast to first-order observation, second-order observation observes how first-order observers observe. That is, it wants to know not *that* something is being observed or *what* is observed, but *how* other observers observe, by means of what distinctions. Scientists, for instance, may publish papers about a particular topic; their fellows will peruse these papers not just for what they say about the topic but for their theoretical soundness and methodological finesse, for how questions are framed, arguments constructed and conclusions drawn. Critics and researchers may read cultural artefacts, social practices or individual behaviour as symptomatic of something larger and hidden. Karl Marx and Sigmund Freud are the towering models of this kind of symptomatic reading. Works of art may be viewed not only as the objects they are but also as displaying an individual kind of structure or order, as flaunting stylistic affinities, or as trapping the spectator's attention in a certain way.

Because second-order observation is interested in the way observers observe, it generates uncertainty. What seems self-evident to a first-order observer appears as the outcome of a particular presupposition when viewed from another angle. Second-order observation thus seeks to reveal what Hans-Georg Gadamer called "the tyranny of hidden prejudices" (1989: 270), the ideas and categories one takes for granted as a child of one's age. By observing first-order observers from a position different from theirs, second-order observation constructs a different rationale for the actions and distinctions made by first-order observers. It may also distinguish statement from meaning – distinguish, that is, between what someone's words ostensibly say and what the observer construes as the unspoken assumptions undergirding those words (Esposito 1996: 600). Deconstruction, for Luhmann (2002: 94-112), is a particular brand of second-order observation.

Translations cannot help engaging in second-order observation, as I hope Chapter Three has shown. But a translation informs not merely about what an original means but also about how that original construes meaning. Saying that translation requires or embodies an interpretation of the original is another way of saying that a translation contains observational directives that tell the reader how to imagine the original. Translations observe their own observation of their originals and account for it in prefaces, footnotes or epilogues, by creating ironic distance towards an original's ideas, values or style, or through the differential choices that set a translation apart from its predecessors. We saw examples in Chapters Two and Three.

The difference between first-order and second-order observation is neatly captured in the story 'Averroes' Search' by Jorge Luis Borges (1981: 180-88). The story portrays the medieval Muslim philosopher Ibn Rushd (also known in the West as Averroes) translating Aristotle from Greek into Arabic. Pondering some key terms in Aristotle's *Poetics* the translator looks out of his window to see children play-acting in the yard below, but as his culture does not have a concept of theatre he remains incapable of grasping what Aristotle means by tragedy. He eventually renders the term, incongruously, as panegyric, praise-poem. For Ibn Rushd and those around him this was a perfectly adequate rendering, the best possible. The incongruity is a construction of a second-order observer who observes Ibn Rushd observing Aristotle. Ibn Rushd could not see his own blind spot, but the narrator of Borges' story, who occupies a viewpoint different from Ibn Rushd's, can see it.

The narrator could also have seen, if Borges had cared to fictionalise it, that Ibn Rushd was translating in line with a tradition. The operation, that is, concerns not only the relation with originals, translation's external reference; it extends to the relation with other translations, that is, the system's self-referential dimension. In following or opposing other translations, individual renderings comment intertextually on the form of these other translations. Translation reviewers, critics and researchers extend the practice still further. In this way the system's constitutive difference, that between itself and its environment, a difference that results from an operatively accomplished differentiation, re-enters the system as the distinction between self-reference and external reference, translation pointing back to itself while offering metarepresentations of other texts.

Because second-order observation engages with the modality and orchestration of translative representations, it renders their form contingent. It locates each form in a nexus of forms, a conceptual and historical continuum. If individual translations fix particular ways of looking at originals and at other translations, second-order observation unmasks these ways as selections that are neither inevitable nor impossible. Needless to say, these critical observations can in turn be observed and unhinged by other observers.

Translation understood in these terms does not log existing correspondences between languages. It creates them. Nowhere is this more clearly demonstrated than in those historical instances when two utterly different cultures first encounter each other. Lydia Fossa has documented the way in which the sixteenth-century Spanish translator Juan de Betanzos, who worked in Peru, struggled to make Spanish somehow match the Quechua words and concepts he had learned (Fossa 2005). He translated by projecting his own foreshortened understanding of the Inca world into Spanish terms and by fixing passing intersections in meaning between the two languages into glossaries and colloquies. In the texts he produced Betanzos left evidence of the labour of translating in the shape of multiple glosses, explications and untranslated Quechua words, metatextual observations on the arduousness of the task. The forcible matchings he and others created eventually resulted in dictionaries whose neat columnar layout would suggest semantic correspondence and perhaps even equivalence. It takes a second-order observer – Fossa, for example – to unpick the discrepancies and asymmetries, the over- and undertranslations, and the ideological filter in the shape of the hispanicising and christianising perspective which Betanzos and his fellow translators, actors in a political as well as linguistic and conceptual universe, brought to their task and which constituted their blind spot.

History

This has led us into history. As I said at the beginning of this chapter, Luhmann's social systems theory is mostly concerned with Western modernity, including forays into the early modern era. This is the period when Western society reshaped the form of its social organisation from a primarily rank-based stratified society into its present complex amalgam of functionally differentiated systems. The change took place over several hundred years, roughly from the sixteenth to the nineteenth century. As Luhmann was at pains to point out, it concerned the primary *form* of system differentiation in Western society (1997: 610ff.); it did not, for example, annul the perception of the relevance of social class in the modern world.

Is it possible to sketch the evolution of translation in this context as the development of a self-reproducing or autopoietic system? The guiding idea would be that, in line with the evolution and functional differentiation of Western society, translation grows in both complexity and autonomy. The growth in autonomy will mean that translation develops a memory of its own and becomes more self-reflexive. Increased complexity implies that the emergent system differentiates internally and generates self-descriptions in the process.

The changes are not a matter of a linear development or a series of causes and effects. Systems theory suggests, in contrast, that we look for variation, selection and relative stabilisation. Bearing this in mind, it seems to me that we can discern two crucial moments in the history of translation in the West that contributed decisively to the emergence of a system of translation. These moments are not starting points. There are no beginnings in history, only re-orientations of existing constellations resulting from the interplay of changing environments and an internal dynamic. The first of these moments occurs in the sixteenth and seventeenth centuries, the second in the Romantic period.

The momentous changes affecting early modern Europe involve such things as increases in urbanisation, trade and literacy, scientific and technological breakthroughs, the fissure of Western Christianity and the rise of nation states. As regards language and culture we begin to see national language policies, the extended reach of vernaculars, and renewed interest in the origins of Western culture. Among the factors of immediate import for translation are the spread of print culture and the rediscovery of the ancients.

Print culture matters mainly but not only because of the rapid expansion in the number and availability of books from the late fifteenth century onwards (an estimated twenty million books were printed in the half-century before 1500 alone; Febvre and Martin 1976: 248). It also, for example, fixed multiple copies of virtually identical texts ('sameness of spelling', if only very approximately in the early days of print), enabling the idea of an authentic 'text' transcending the errors and whims of copyists and directly reflecting an author's intention (Eisenstein 1980: 80ff.; Chartier 1994: 55). But sheer volume had its own effects. Print both satisfied and stimulated the demand for practical knowledge. Translation from and into various vernaculars as well as into the international language of the time, Latin, proved an effective means of increasing the volume of reading material for different types of readers. For the first time, therefore, multiple translations of key texts arrived more or less simultaneously on a highly competitive market for books. As a result, translators and publishers intently watched the market and each other, and translations attempted to outdo and outsell one another. In other words, translation began to observe itself and to cater deliberately for particular markets.

In the competitive context of commercial publishing, rival versions polemicised with one another and with earlier renderings not only in the differential choices of the translations themselves but also in the numerous prefaces and dedications of the period. These legitimated particular modes of translating and enumerated criteria that translators were supposed to meet, providing translation with a coherent body of self-descriptions and creating common points of reference in the process. As early as the sixteenth century we find translators speaking of 'laws' of translation (Hermans 1997). At the same time, competing versions and rival renderings also furnished proof of a plurality of possible translations for any one original and thus exhibited their own provisionality as part of a series that was unfolding over time. All of this suggests a emergent system defining its boundaries and structures. The new terms for 'translation' and 'translating' appearing in several languages in the fifteenth and sixteenth centuries (Folena 1991; Norton 1984) confirm the sense of a culural practice reshaping itself.

The market, for all that, was not the only force driving the process, as the prevalence of dedications shows. The patronage system characteristic of a stratified social structure remained in place for a long time, especially as the elites that ran the new nation states invested in the new national languages and enlisted translation in this cause, as happened in France in the first half of the sixteenth century under François I. The result was not necessarily favourable to translation. The pre-Reformation church banned Bible translations into most vernacular languages at one time or another. Post-Reformation churches sought to control them by combining with the political powers that be, so as to produce unique, authenticated versions like the English King James Bible of 1611 and the Dutch *Statenbijbel* of 1637.

The rediscovery of the Latin and Greek classics generated high-prestige and therefore self-conscious translation, helped no doubt by the recognition that the admired Latin models had themselves been copying the Greeks. The canonical status of the originals promoted frequent re-translation and hence an awareness of different representational modes to suit changing circumstances and purposes. Since the church remained suspicious of the pagan ancients, translation had to be selective, and translators would reflect on their selections. Translators at home in the classics noted the rhetorical qualities and historical remoteness of these texts and demanded that translation engage with these issues, forcing distinctions between learned and vulgar translating (as did Etienne Dolet in 1540). Similar divisions were to follow, notably those between literary and other kinds of translating, again introducing internal differentiation. In the 1630s John Denham, Abraham Cowley and Nicolas Perrot d'Ablancourt insisted on compensatory stylisation and were doubtful whether their renderings could even be called 'translation'. The ensuing debates (as in the polemics of Pierre-Daniel Huet and Anne Dacier with the libertine translators, or Dryden's threefold subdivision of translation) concerned the boundaries of the concept. The debates helped to establish precisely these boundaries and made them visible. The numerous pseudo-translations appearing in eighteenth-century Italy, for instance, are possible only against this background (Rambelli 2006): pseudotranslations presuppose a clearly delineated concept of translation. At the same time, translation shows growing internal differentiation. A flamboyantly literary translation of the Bible like Edward Harwood's New Testament of 1768, as discussed in Chapter Two, would have been hard to imagine before the eighteenth century.

In addition, and crucially, the return of the ancients installed models for imitation and restored imitation as the core principle of writing. Translation could consequently be regarded as a species of imitation, just as, beyond this, language, knowledge and the arts imitated nature (all were 'mirrors of nature'). Translations were imitations of imitations (hence, meta-imitations) and, at least in literature, not always strictly separated from other imitative modes. And since imitation might seek to improve its model, some translations claimed such latitude. It is not until the demise of imitation as a formative principle in the course of the seventeenth and eighteenth centuries that translation will need to redefine itself against the new concept, originality.

Throughout this period translation remained predicated on the assumption of translatability. This is a given in the Christian West. Its most foundational text, the Bible, was read in translation and, with Europe's overseas expansion, exported in translation. An anonymous writer from John Wycliff's circle had put it very clearly: "however diverse languages may be, the evangelical truths remain invariant. Therefore the gospel can be written and spoken in Latin and Greek, in French, in English and in any other language" (*quamuis lingue sunt diuerse, tamen veritates euangelice non variantur. Ideo euangelium potest scribi et pronunciari in Latinis et Grecis, in Gallicis, in Anglicis et in omni lingua articulata*, in Hudson 1985: 153). Luther's Germanisation of the Bible took it for granted that, once properly understood, the Word could find a voice in any tongue.

The notion of translatability was correlated with a conception of language that separated meaning from expression, substance from accident. As different views of the nature of language emerged in the late eighteenth and early nineteenth centuries, these ideas became problematical. As far as I can see, the very possibility of translation was not seriously called into doubt until the Romantic era. The crisis forced translation to look inward in ways it had never done before. It did so primarily by replacing imitation by hermeneutics as a guiding principle and by repositioning itself with reference to the concept of originality.

The questioning of translatability was a decisive moment in the emergence of translation as a functionally differentiated social system in that it signalled the re-entry of the foundation of translation into translation itself. Wilhelm von Humboldt used the preface to a translation – his 1816 version of Aeschylus' *Agamemnon* – to deny that the original was translatable; this he ascribed to the lack of synonymy between languages, yet he asserted in the same breath that we must translate precisely because of the enormity of the challenge (Lefevere 1977: 40-41; Robinson 1997: 239). His contemporary Jean Paul remarked that if a text was translatable it was not worth translating in the first place (Schmitz-Emans 2001: 564).

It is no coincidence that paradoxes like these were aired with reference to literary translation. Literature was by now a differentiated domain where self-reflection had been instrumental in affirming the field's autonomy (Werber 1992). Both the involuted plot and the countless digressions in Laurence Sterne's novel *Tristram Shandy* are symptomatic in this respect and show a literary text dissecting its own conventions. Literary translation offered a niche for similar self-reflexive demonstrations, designed to dramatise untranslatability while translating.

The most spectacular of these demonstrations are Friedrich Hölderlin's forbiddingly literal versions of Greek poetry and drama, but Chateaubriand in France and later Robert Browning and William Morris in England produced similar (though very much tamer) calques. Their artificiality is rendered functional by stressing that translation puts the language through its paces – quite literally: Hölderlin compares translation to gymnastics (Louth 1998: 58). At the same time, they are barely comprehensible texts (we saw one critic's bewildered response to them in Chapter Two) and as such do not slot comfortably into any one of translation's client systems, not even that of literature. They become intelligible however as acute if wayward reflections on modes of translative representation. Whereas the eighteenth century had conditioned translation through norms of good taste that echoed bourgeois social and ethical values, Hölderlin's Sophocles heightens its self-reference as a translation in that it draws attention to its own particular mode of representation by virtually cancelling out external reference. This is translation scrutinising its own constitutive difference in a gesture of self-observation.

What this difference consists in will be articulated in Friedrich Schleiermacher's well-known lecture 'On the Different Methods of Translating' of 1813 (Lefevere 1977: 67-89). Schleiermacher, too, wonders if translation of what he would regard as 'cultured' texts is not a fundamentally impossible task, but he approaches the question from the vantage point of hermeneutics. Schleiermacher is the founding father of modern hermeneutics, the discipline that seeks to understand how we understand others. For Schleiermacher the problem of translation is the problem of understanding, and the latter is serious because "the talent for misunderstanding is infinite" (in Ellison 1990: 78). Understanding others is problematic, and the hermeneutic task infinite, because linguistic usage and thought are interdependent but also highly individual. It takes a refined kind of reading between the lines to construe the meaning of a text. Reading between the lines amounts to putting oneself 'inside' an author and becoming aware of meanings even the author himself may have remained unaware of, hence Schleiermacher's well-known dictum that the hermeneuticist endeavours to understand an author better than he understood himself (*ibid.;* Schleiermacher 1978: 9-10). Differences between languages and cultural distance compound the problem; as Johann Gottfried Herder had noted as early as 1774, all cross-cultural comparison is problematic because cultures inhabit their own linguistic and conceptual worlds (Herder 2002: 196-7). In his *Dialectic* of 1814-15 Schleiermacher phrased it with unsettling force: "No knowledge in two languages can be regarded as completely the same; not even ... A=A" (Schleiermacher 1998: xxi).

Even though the elaborate machinery of what Schleiermacher calls grammatical and technical interpretation with their additional operations of divination and comparison is not foregrounded in the essay on translation, it informs it nevertheless. The significance of Schleiermacher's essay, that is, does not lie in the trite preference for 'taking the reader to the author' rather than the other way round. It lies in the vision of translation as a daunting hermeneutic challenge. The challenge is that of articulating a specific understanding in mimetic form in a different medium. Indeed Schleiermacher's hermeneutic ideas grew out of his own translation of Plato in the years 1799 to 1805 (Lamm 2000: 222, 231), a project he had undertaken not just to make Plato available to German readers, but primarily, as he explained in the General Introduction to the first volume in 1804, to discover the inner coherence and unique invididuality of Plato's thought, which in turn would, in due course, enable interpreters "to understand Plato better than he understood himself" (Schleiermacher 1836: 5; Zhang 1992: 10-11).

The Romantic scrutiny of translation, closely correlated with the emergent system of literature, was intense. It responded to society's ongoing reorganisation along lines of functional differentiation by making translation turn inward and aligning it with a sublime idea of culture (Lianeri 2002). Disconnecting translation from external compulsion in this way created room for forms of radical experimentation that allowed the issue of representation to be raised again and again, both in actual translations and in criticism.

Ironically, when at the beginning of his 1813 lecture Schleiermacher dismissed commercial translation as routine and not worthy of serious attention, he nevertheless surveyed the field of translation in its entirety and marked it as an internally differentiated unity. The extent of the differentiation was becoming evident even as Schleiermacher was delivering his lecture. In the following decades, the demand for popular translations led to the so-called 'translation factories', conveyer-belt professional translating on an industrial scale. Whereas between 1820 and 1845 the total number of novels published in Germany increased threefold, the number of translated novels in the same period grew fourteenfold and by 1850 reached fifty per cent of the overall production of novels (Bachleitner 1989: 4-5). Other languages and other genres would see comparable if less dramatic increases in commercial and technical translating. The huge output, which remained as yet unchecked by any effective copyright legislation, was helped by industrial-style production and distribution, making use of mechanical presses, well-organised postal services, and networks of lending libraries. In France, Auguste-Jean-Baptiste Defauconpret (1767-1843) translated over 600 volmes, most of it popular fiction ; we know of one translator in Germany who employed four scribes to take down his dictation, while the two most prolific German translators churned out around 150 titles each, may of them multi-volume works (Pickford 2007; Bachleitner 1989). The translation system adjusted to the pressure by creating structures – that is, programmes – which allowed translators to interact with publishers and audiences, and translations to respond to one another and to their client systems.

Romantic translation liberated itself from market conditions and, following the example of the arts, affirmed its autonomy and created comprehensive theories to reflect on itself. In the same period other sectors of the system adjusted to changing conditions by organising the industrial production of translations for mass consumption. These sectors would introduce professional training on a large scale in the twentieth century, thus completing the picture of the social system of translation in its current, diversified form.

6. The Thickness of Translation Studies

"Our ordinary conceptual system, in terms of which we both think and act, is fundamentally metaphorical in nature", George Lakoff and Mark Johnson argued in *Metaphors We Live By* (1980: 3). Michael Reddy exposed the conduit metaphor as one of these deeply ingrained ways in which, in the West, language and translation are conceptualised, as we saw at the beginning of the previous chapter. As Reddy also showed in devising his alternative paradigm, different metaphors can change our perception, and hence the thing itself. "New metaphors have the power to create a new reality", Lakoff and Johnson proclaimed (1980: 145).

In the previous two chapters I adopted certain angles on translation in an effort to shift the metaphorical ground. They may not quite have created a new reality but, with luck, they have suggested that, in principle at least, the ground can be shifted and new perspectives gained. In this final chapter I want to try a different tack. Its direction stems from the rapid expansion of translation studies, as novel kinds of translation emerge, new research tools provoke new questions, historical inquiry deepens and the discipline becomes increasingly international. These developments have momentous implications for the entire field. Some of them have been mapped in Maria Tymoczko's 2005 article 'Trajectories of Research in Translation Studies' in the fiftieth anniversary issue of the journal *Meta*. As regards the challenge of internationalisation in particular, Tymoczko points up various adjustments that Western researchers need to make. They include "interrogating the pretheoretical assumptions about translation" that are currently prevalent, and "becoming much more self-reflexive in understanding the subject positions and the places of enunciation that characterize Western discourses about translation" (Tymoczko 2005: 1094).

It may be worth wondering in this context how the the exploration of translation across divides of time, place and culture can be harnessed to a self-reflexive project. In what follows I will suggest that such an exploration calls not only for acts of translation but also for critical reflection on the vocabulary and orientation of translation studies in the West. The encounter with different concepts and traditions invites examination of the categories that are available to describe them. By opting for thicker descriptions, the study of translation can learn from these encounters. Let me begin by offering three examples to illustrate the kind of issue I am trying to address.

Domestic representations

The first example concerns the *Poetics* of Aristotle, and more particularly the revisionist reading of some of its key concepts and terms in John Jones's *On Aristotle and Greek Tragedy* of 1962 (Jones 1971). Jones's book is widely regarded as having altered the modern perception of the way in which Aristotle conceived of the nature of Greek tragedy. Among other things, Jones demonstrated that, contrary to received opinion, Aristotle did not operate with a concept of a 'tragic hero' in an individualised or romantic or Hamlet-like sense. Instead, Jones argued, Aristotle thought of tragedy in 'situational' terms, as concerning interpersonal relations in a set of social roles or between individuals and the metaphysical realm. A notion like the 'peripetia' or 'change of fortune' in a tragic play should therefore be understood not in a 'personal' but in a 'situational' sense. Jones pointed out, for instance, that Aristotle does not speak of 'the change in the hero's fortune' as some translations have it, but simply of 'the change of fortune', the reference being to "a state of affairs" rather than to "the stage-portrayal of one man's vicissitude" (1971: 14-16).

A different understanding of Aristotle's meaning means a different translation of his words. Successive re-interpretations of a text bring about not just new descriptions but also differentials in translation. An account of Artistotle in English, for example, will need to wrap itself around the quality of the Greek words as understood – or understood anew – by the modern commentator; at the same time it needs to mark the departure from earlier understandings. The particular crux I have picked concerns the concept of the 'recognition' (*anagnorisis*) of the fatal error in a tragedy, the moment when the protagonist's eyes are opened and the causes of the disaster that has befallen him or her become clear.

Traditional Englishings of the *Poetics* described Aristotle's idea of *anagnorisis* as

> ... a change from ignorance to knowledge, producing love or hate between the persons destined by the poet for good or bad fortune. (Butler 1907: 35)

> ... a change from ignorance to knowledge, and thus to either love or hate, in the personages marked for good or evil fortune. (Bywater 1909: 31; Hamilton Fyfe 1940: 30)

> ... a change from ignorance to knowledge, [which] leads either to love or to hatred between persons. (Dorsch 1965: 46)

It is the word 'love' in all these renderings that I want to focus on. John Jones translated Aristotle's definition as

> ... a change from ignorance to knowledge, and thus to a state of near-
> ness and dearness [*philia*] or to a state of enmity, on the part of those
> ... (Jones 1971: 58)

Now, "state of nearness and dearness" is a decidedly awkward mouthful
compared with "love", as Jones knew perfectly well. His comment homes in
on the Greek term *philia*, which, he says,

> I render, hideously, 'state of nearness and dearness' in my determination
> to avoid 'love', the word favoured by English translators (*ibid.*).

The reason why Jones so emphatically declines to render *philia* as 'love' becomes apparent when he quotes a fellow classicist, Gerard Else (*Aristotle's
Poetics: the Argument*, 1957), who explains why, in the context, 'love' will
not do as a translation:

> ... φιλία [*philia*] is not 'friendship' or 'love' or any other feeling, but
> *the objective state of being φίλοι [philoi]*, 'dear ones', by virtue of
> blood ties. When Oedipus 'recognizes' Laius – that is, realizes who
> it was he killed at the crossroads – he changes from ignorance to
> knowledge, and at the same moment, since Laius was his father, he
> moves into the status of [*philia*]. 'Love', not to mention 'friendship,'
> is much too puling a word for his feelings at that moment, and anyhow
> his feelings do not count so much as the new *situation* into which he
> has moved with his shift from ignorance to awareness. (Else 1957:
> 349, in Jones 1971: 58).

Another, more recent translator of the *Poetics* speaks of *anagnorisis* as

> ...a change from ignorance to knowledge, and so to either *friendship*
> or enmity... (Janko 1987: 14; my emphasis,TH)

– opting for 'friendship' despite Else's strictures. However, in his annotations,
which run to more than twice the length of the actual translation of the *Poetics*, this translator points out that the Greek *philia* is not only "much stronger"
than the English 'friendship' but also "has connotations of kinship by blood,
marriage or ties of hospitality" (Janko 1987: 95-6). The annotations qualify
the choice of "friendship" almost to the point of disqualifying it as a translation. The gloss makes us appreciate why Jones felt he had to put the dictionary
aside in favour of the differential hideousness of his "state of nearness and
dearness". It also reminds us that we cannot read translations like these without

the elaborate notes and critical apparatus that accompany them, if only because the latter invalidate the glib linearity of one-to-one lexical matchings naively aligning *philia* with 'love' or with 'friendship'.

I did not discover Jones's book by myself. I was put on its trail by Lawrence Venuti's *The Scandals of Translation* (1998). In the course of his discussion of Jones's book, Venuti also speculates about the reasons why it became such a landmark. As he sees it, Jones's reading of Aristotle appealed to the scholarly community because it chimed with the spirit of the times; it contained what Venuti calls a "domestic representation" (1998: 70), a useful phrase, meaning the inevitable inscription of an observer's partial and localised values and modes of thought into the object of observation. Uncovering first-order observations as "domestic representations" is, of course, the work of second-order observers.

Checking through reviews of Jones's book from the 1960s, Venuti indeed found several that traced Jones's perception of Aristotle to the prevailing philosophical climate of existentialism, and he concurs with them, observing that

> As reviewers suggested, Jones's concept of determinate subjectivity
> reveals an "existentialist manner of thinking" that enabled him both
> to question the individualism of classical scholarship and to develop
> an interdisciplinary method of reading, not psychological but "socio
> logical" and "anthropological" (1998: 70).

He concludes that both the nature of Jones's reading of Aristotle and its ready acceptance by fellow scholars were due at least in part to the fact that "it reflected the rise of existentialism as a powerful current in post-World War II culture" (1998: 71). This may well be true, although it does not explain why Jones's emphasis on "determinate subjectivity" survived the subsequent demise of existentialism. If it is true, it is worrying. Why should an approach to Aristotle inspired by a particular twentieth-century intellectual fashion result in a more adequate understanding of Aristotle's ideas than any other approach? Yet how could the perception of the past not be conditioned by the intellectual climate of the present?

I am not in a position to judge whether the reviewers at the time were right to posit a link between Jones and existentialism, or for that matter whether Venuti's explanation of why Jones's view was able to establish a new orthodoxy hits the mark or constitutes simply another domestic representation, this time on Venuti's part. His speculation is of interest here primarily because it shows that each reading creates a perspective not only on the object in question but also on existing interpretations of it. This process of reading other people's readings of individual texts can create long threads: Jones reading his predecessors' readings of Aristotle, the reviewers reading Jones, Venuti reading both the reviewers and Jones, myself now reading Jones and Venuti – a chain of second-order observation, as if to illustrate Montaigne's comment that "we do nothing but write comments on one another" ("nous ne faisons que nous entregloser", Montaigne 1969, 3: 279). With each re-reading the potential for revision is there, and the process has no end. Each re-reading is also conditioned by its presuppositions, and they are its blind spot.

There is no need to stay with this particular example. The brief glimpse of different readings of Aristotle's *anagnorisis* is intended to highlight a few simple points: firstly, the difficulty and complexity of interpreting texts and concepts across time and place, even, perhaps especially, when the exercise is applied to canonical texts like the *Poetics*; secondly, the fact that this re-visionary enterprise is an ongoing process reaching into the here and now and extending into the future; thirdly, the inevitability of translation as the companion and instrument of cross-temporal, cross-lingual and cross-cultural interpretation; fourthly, the pertinence of what Venuti terms "domestic representations" and what hermeneuticists might call the interpreter's historicity, or the particular position from which one views and makes sense of a phenomenon; and fifthly, the close correlation between differential translations like Jones's and changing contexts and agendas.

The assumptions and presumptions which inform domestic representations also allow us to recognise – perhaps we should say: to construe – similarity in what is different. At the same time, like all forms of second-order observation, they generate their own dyslexia, enlarging certain aspects or kinds of similarity and contrast while creating blind spots elsewhere. In addition, the readings and re-readings they produce are self-referential to the extent that they fold back on the tradition that enabled them and the vocabularies supplied as part of this tradition. If we are to engage with cultural concepts and practices lying beyond the range of the familiar, we need to consider the terms on which, and the means by which, the engagement is played out.

The concepts and practices I have in mind are concepts and practices of translation in other cultures. We can ask ourselves how we gain access to the meaning of terms used in discourses on translation in cultural environments we are not familiar with. Let us approach the issue through two further, very brief examples. From where I am writing – London – and for someone with my West-European background, the first example is not that distant; the second is significantly more so.

Pierre-Daniel Huet's Latin treatise 'On the best kind of translating', *De optimo genere interpretandi,* first appeared in 1661; the expanded, definitive edition is from 1683. It is a carefully crafted and structured work. Just how different it is from modern handbooks and their categorisations of translation may be apparent from the way Huet homes in on his subject (DeLater 2002: 43-45, 140-42). He begins by distinguishing three meanings of *interpretatio*. Only one of these, interlingual *conversio*, will be the topic of his treatise. *Conversio* comes in two species, corresponding to two different purposes: to develop one's own style, or to represent an unknown discourse. Huet will elaborate only the latter. This latter species in turn comes in two kinds, according to whether the translator adheres exclusively to the original author, or whether he also indulges either the reader or himself. The latter kind includes verse translation, free translation, epitome, paraphrase, periphrase and metaphrase, but Huet's treatise will restrict itself to outlining the principles of the former. The central part of the treatise goes on to outline the principles of this particular type of *conversio*.

There is only one complete translation into English of Huet's treatise, by James Albert DeLater (2002), but we have a couple of partial renderings, by Edwin Dolin (in Robinson 1997: 163-9) and André Lefevere (1992: 86-102). Comparing the use of keywords in the passages where the three renderings overlap, it is striking to see Lefevere consistently reducing Huet's terminology to the standard vocabulary of literary and translation studies today. For example, whereas Dolin and DeLater work hard to convey in their versions that the distinctions being made pertain to Huet's Latin terms *interpretatio* and *conversio*, Lefevere consistently but confusingly gives *interpretatio* as either "interpretation" or "translation" and *conversio* as "translation". Huet's term *sermo*, which Dolin and DeLater both render as "discourse", becomes "text" in Lefevere. The Latin *sententia*, which both Dolin and DeLater render variously as "meaning", "idea" or "thought", depending on context and nuance, is for Lefevere always "meaning". Huet's *ingenium*, translated as "personality" or "innate talent" in the others, is "creativity" in Lefevere's rendering.

Lefevere makes Huet's concepts easy enough to understand, in that Huet is made to speak our modern critical idiom. But it is precisely the use of this familiar idiom that makes it hard to appreciate where and how Huet differs from modern thinking. One way of gauging that difference is to consider the provenance of Huet's terms. All are rooted in the Humanist culture of Early Modern Europe, none more so than *sermo*, which recalls the most famous crux in perhaps the most controversial translation ever, Erasmus's Latin version of the New Testament first published in 1516 and revised four times until his death in 1536. Erasmus's daring choice of *sermo* in preference to the Vulgate's *verbum* for the Greek word *logos* at the start of the gospel of John ('In the beginning was the word') occasioned a lengthy – eventually a book-length – defence, in the course of which Erasmus combed through every aspect of meaning and use of *logos* and its possible counterparts in Latin. Among the arguments he adduced in favour of *sermo* was its sense of a speaker's active deployment of linguistic resources, language in action as an effective, dynamic force and hence a concept closer to rhetorical practice than to dull grammatical classification. The very care that Erasmus took over the translation of what Thomas More (in *Letter to a Monk*, 1519) thought might well be an untranslatable Greek word sprang not only from the need to cover himself against attacks from theologians but also from the kind of Humanist concern with stylistic adequacy that had led earlier translators like Leonardo Bruni and Gianozzo Manetti to stress how formidable a task translation was (Kinney 1986: 237-51; Botley 2004). Huet echoes his predecessors in his insistence on the translator as a protean figure who subordinates his own expressive preferences to mirror his author's thought and style.

Bearing intertextual filiations like these in mind, translating Huet's *sermo* as "discourse" is fine, but "text" is lame. So is "creativity" for *ingenium*. Historically, as C.S. Lewis has pointed out, 'wit' was chosen as a translation for *ingenium* and subsequently became its recognised equivalent, entering into the same traditional antitheses as *ingenium* (Lewis 1960: 88ff.). Lefevere's assimilating and very domestic representations overcome historical distance, but at the cost of erasing it. As Aristotle remarked in his *Rhetoric*, familiar words allow us to see only the familiar things we know already (Freese 2000: 395-7).

My third example involves Chinese, a language and tradition I am wholly ignorant of. The case concerns the celebrated set of three terms occurring right at the start of the 'General Remarks on Translation' with which Yan Fu prefaced his Chinese rendering, in 1898, of Thomas Huxley's *Evolution and Ethics*. The terms have been translated into English in a number of ways. I am not interested in what the best rendering might be, but in what would be needed to give me, as an outsider obliged to rely on translation, access to the terms' meanings and operational range.

The terms, in transcription, are *xin*, *da* and *ya*. A fairly random sampling of translations into English, several of them from one and the same encyclopedia of translation, can be tabulated as in *Table 3*.

xin	**da**	**ya**	Source:
faithfulness	comprehensibility	elegance	Hsiu 1973: 4
faithfulness	communicability	elegance	Hung and Pollard 1998: 371
faithfulness	expressiveness	elegance	Wang Nin 1996: 43
faithfulness	expressiveness	gracefulness	Liu Miqing 1995a: 3

trueness	intelligibility	elegancy	Huang 1995: 278
faithfulness	expressiveness	elegance	Ma 1995: 382
faithfulness	comprehensibility	elegance	Fong 1995: 582
faithfulness	comprehensibility	elegance of style	Sinn 1995: 441
fidelity	intelligibility	elegance	Wu 1995: 529
faithfulness	intelligibility	elegance	Wang Zongyan 1995: 560
'to be faithful,	expressive, and	elegant'	Wang Zuoliang 1995: 999
faithfulness	readability	refinement	Fan 1994: 152
fidelity	fluency	elegance	Yuen Ren Chao (in Fan 1994: 171)
faithfulness	comprehensibility	elegance	Xing 1998: 10
fidelity	clarity or comprehensibility	elegance or fluency	Venuti 1998: 182

Table 3: English translations of Yan Fu's terms

At first blush there appears to be a reassuring amount of agreement between the renderings on offer, with 'faithfulness' and 'fidelity' the most common choices for *xin*, 'elegance' the most frequent choice for *ya,* and 'comprehensibility', 'expressiveness' and 'intelligibility' vying to cover the middle term, *da*. However, the remark by one Chinese critic that for Yan Fu's terms *da* and *ya,* "so far at least eight and fifteen interpretations are on record respectively" (Liu Miqing1995b: 1034), makes me wonder how much the apparent agreement among the translations conceals. This skepticism only increases when Yan Fu himself rehearses his key terms later in his preface and evokes both Confucius and the *Book of Changes* in the process:

> The *Book of Changes* says that rhetoric should uphold truthfulness [*xin*]. Confucius says that expressiveness [*da*] is all that matters in language. He adds that if one's language lacks grace [*ya*], it will not travel far. These qualities, then, are the criterion of good writing and, I believe, of good translation too. (Yan Fu in Wang Zuoliang 1995: 999)

Yan Fu's terms carry intertextual echoes taking us back two thousand years and more. In overwriting the terms with English labels these echoes and networks are obliterated. Venuti, for example, equates Yan Fu's third term, *ya,* with "fluency". In view of the particular resonances audible in Yan Fu's term on the one hand, and, on the other, the specific sense of assimilationist and domesticating conversion with which Venuti has charged the word 'fluency' in his own critical work (especially Venuti 1995), this translation seems limiting at best. The fact that at least one critic (Yuen Ren Chao) saw fit to render Yan Fu's *second* term, *da*, as "fluency" does not help matters either.

But the question remains: where do we locate Yan Fu's concepts in the web of English terms that offer themselves as potential candidates, and what would be an appropriate vocabulary to convey a sense of their specificity to someone without access to Chinese? A recent comparative study of ancient Greek and Chinese rhetoric (Xing Lu 1998) pits Yan Fu against Walter Benjamin. Its author claims that Benjamin's 'The Task of the Translator' argues for

> ... a revised theory of translation based upon the notion that trans-
> lation is a process of interpretation rather than a mere reproduction
> of the original meaning. Accordingly, translation is not a one-to-one
> correspondence or mere substitution of words and sentences from one
> language into another. Therefore, a translator should be primarily con-
> cerned with 'appropriation' as opposed to fidelity. (Xing Lu 1998: 10)

Benjamin's essay has been read in a number of ways, and Harry Zohn's standard but notoriously problematic English translation of it, which Xing Lu refers to, may or may not open up a range of readings similar to that of Benjamin's German text. Personally I do not think Benjamin, in German or in English, argues for anything like the revised theory of translation as de-scribed in the quotation above, and so for me at least this attempt to place Yan Fu contrastively in the grid of Western thinking misfires as badly as Venuti's appropriation of *ya* as "fluency".

Perhaps, then, the question of how to represent Yan Fu's or Pierre-Daniel Huet's concepts in the terminology currently available to Anglophone trans-lation studies is not quite so simple. Assuming these concepts can in principle be explicated, should we perhaps take a leaf out of Jones's book, shun the standard vocabulary and embrace something altogether more hideous?

The thick of it

Let us leave the examples for what they are and try to formulate the more general issue at stake. I think it is at least twofold. First, there is the problem of grasping and gaining access to concepts and discursive practices, in our case those pertaining to translation, in languages and cultures other than our own; this is primarily a problem of hermeneutics, of understanding and interpretation.

Secondly, the cross-lingual and cross-cultural study of concepts and discursive practices involves recourse to translation if we want to articulate in our own language what we have understood as happening in another language. We need to translate in order to study translation across languages and cultures. My assumption in all this is that the problems posed by diachronic study and by the synchronic investigation of other cultures are similar in that both reach beyond the investigator's here and now.

Both issues are familiar territory for anthropologists and historians, and for comparatists in a number of other disciplines. Both also carry an element of latent or overt self-reflection on the terms on which and the contexts in which the representation of otherness is acted out. But while these problems have been debated anxiously and extensively by ethnographers and historiographers, they have remained largely and surprisingly absent from the study of translation.

The absence is not inevitable, as becomes clear when we recall some earlier attempts to create a methodology for the cross-cultural study and representation of concepts. In 1932, for example, in his book *Mencius on the Mind*, I.A. Richards developed what he called a "technique of multiple definition" as a way of negotiating alien meaning. The technique involved an insistent probing of the various uses to which certain terms in a particular language had been put and of the diverse and always provisional ways those meanings might be represented interlingually. He applied the technique to the writings of the ancient Chinese thinker Meng Tzu (Mencius), presenting the reader with a mixture of interlinear cribs and lengthy glosses which demonstratively refrained from proposing fixed English equivalents. The very peculiar set of 'Specialized Quotation Marks' (later renamed 'Meta-Semantic Markers') which he developed elsewhere (in *How To Read a Page*, Richards 1943), served the same end of signalling, in the language of description, the lack of interlingual semantic correspondence.

Twenty years after *Mencius*, in *Speculative Instruments* (1955), Richards reviewed his cross-cultural mapping tool in the essay 'Toward a Theory of Comprehending', which, interestingly, had first appeared under the title 'Toward a Theory of Translating' (Richards 1955: 17-38). This is the essay, incidentally, in which Richards famously claimed that translating between languages like Chinese and English "may very probably be the most complex type of event yet produced in the evolution of the cosmos" (1955: 22). As regards the cross-cultural study of concepts, he observed, we compare things in certain respects, and we select those respects that will serve our purpose. How effective these respects are will emerge only in the act of comparing; or, as he disarmingly put it: "we make an instrument and try it out" (1955: 21). Trying out the instrument means that the comparison also continually inspects its own terms and procedures. It is only by trying out an instrument that we can "develop our comprehending of what it is with which we seek to explore comprehending" (Richards 1955: 22; also Richards 1932: 12). Any similarity thus established between two entities is a function of the respects that were selected as the ground for comparison in the first place. Comprehending, as the perception and positing of similarities and differences, is continually thrown back on an examination of the instrument which enables the similarities and differences to be established. A cross-cultural comprehending that ensues from comparison must remind itself of the contingent nature of comparing. As Ann Berthoff put it in a discussion of Richards' endeavour, "the language we use about language must itself be included in the audit of meaning" (1982: 70).

This was also a conclusion Rodney Needham reached in his *Belief, Language and Experience* (1971), a long reflection on anthropological representation triggered by the Oxford ethnographer Edward Evans-Pritchard's studies of the Nuer in Southern Sudan. Needham recognised that there is no metalanguage to hold or represent the invariant of translingual and transcultural comparison. Because there is no such metalanguage or invariant, we cannot establish what Richard Rorty calls "unwobbling pivots" (1999: 15) enabling firm or objective comparison. All we can do is constantly reconsider the language that serves as our probing tool. This means that cross-cultural mapping, comparison and translation can hardly avoid being self-reflexive. Or, as Lydia Liu has it in the introduction to her *Translingual Practice*, because a cross-cultural study is itself a translingual act, "it enters, rather than sits above" its object (Liu 1995: 20). In the absence of a fixed external point from which to ascertain the adequacy of our renderings of other worlds, we must, pragmatically, deploy certain instruments, certain terminologies and angles of vision, and try to see what they allow us to see – and where, as instruments of reading, they leave us dyslexic.

Support and comfort for such an approach may be found in the constructivism we encountered in social systems theory, or indeed in the anti-essentialism of philosophical pragmatism. Constructivism holds that systems see the environment in their own terms. Since every observation has a blind spot, second-order observation leads to different views but not to an ultimate truth, since every second-order observation will have its own blind spot. For a pragmatist like Richard Rorty it is pointless to speak of statements as being 'true' in the sense that there would be a matching or mirroring between the relevant sentences and the external world. Language does not reflect the world more or less accurately. It does not give us access to the essence of things. We can never know whether our formulas have wrapped themselves 'correctly' around phenomena or not. All we can say is that certain vocabularies allow us to handle certain aspects of the world more or less effectively, and effectiveness depends on purpose. In Rorty's words: "the fact that Newton's vocabulary lets us predict the world more easily than Aristotle's does not mean that the world speaks Newtonian" (Rorty 1989: 6). If predicting the world is the aim, then it pays to work with Newton rather than Aristotle; it does not follow that Newton is necessarily more 'true to nature' than Aristotle.

For a cross-cultural study of translation the implication of this kind of constructivism or pragmatism would be to drop the idea that the aim of the exercise is a full or accurate representation of foreign concepts of translation, that the accuracy of this representation could be measured in a way that would allow available representations to be compared and the best one selected, and that once we have arrived at the best available representation we might consider the matter closed. Once that idea is dropped, the path lies open to the creation of vocabularies that will enable us to do certain things, such as mapping concepts of translation across cultures in particular institutional contexts, while at the same time re-examining the vocabulary we use as a tool to perform these mappings.

The issue is not only methodological or philosophical, it also has an institutional and perhaps a political side. As a pragmatic translingual act, the study of translation across cultures obliges us to reflect not just on the instrument but on the aim of the exercise. What do we want to achieve by studying translation in other cultures, who are we speaking to or for? At the start of her study of modernisation in China, Lydia Liu asks: "In whose terms, for which linguistic constituency, and in the name of what kinds of knowledge or intellectual authority does one perform acts of translation between cultures?" (Liu 1995: 1). We may edge closer to an answer to questions like these if we imagine an engagement with another culture as a learning experience.

This brings us to what Kwame Anthony Appiah has called 'thick translation' (Appiah 2004). Appiah means by it the academic, heavily footnoted translation of texts from traditions alien to that of the translating language. I will not use the term in Appiah's sense. Instead, I will use it as a label for a self-critical form of cross-cultural translation studies. The transposition seems appropriate if, as I suggested above, we take the study of translation as consisting in translating concepts and practices of translation.

Appiah grafted his term 'thick translation' on Clifford Geertz's characterisation of the ethnographer's work as 'thick description'. This was a notion Geertz introduced in the programmatic essay 'Thick Description: Toward an Interpretive Theory of Culture' which introduced his collection *The Interpretation of Cultures* in 1973. The essay championed detailed and personalised description by a participant observer, and was intended to counter what Geertz saw as the reductiveness of a structuralist anthropology relentlessly squeezing complex lifeworlds into supposedly universal schemas and binary oppositions.

Geertz, in turn, did not invent the term 'thick description'. He borrowed it from two essays by the philosopher Gilbert Ryle, 'Thinking and Reflecting' and 'The Thinking of Thoughts' (Ryle 1971: 465-79, 480-96; Geertz 1973: 6-7). In this latter essay Ryle observes two boys rapidly contracting the eyelids of their right eyes. He asks: is one of them, or are they both, deliberately winking or involuntarily twitching? Could they be parodying either a wink or a twitch, or just rehearsing winks for later use? How can we know what is going on? Establishing which is wink and which is twitch, Ryle argues, requires not only detailed engagement with the phenomenon and its context, but also interpretive effort, because, culturally speaking, the two concepts are interdependent, indeed they are 'parasitic' on each other: a twitch is as much a non-wink as a wink is a non-twitch (Ryle 1971: 474). The way in which winks and twitches mutually define one other in a particular culture is as complex as it is unphotographable. Thick description is the term for this patient engagement and interpretive, contextualising negotiation of meaning. Ryle also stressed that it is the description rather than the reality which is meant to acquire thickness, a point that would not be lost on New Historicists who also discovered Ryle via Geertz and who have revelled in the minute analysis of significant historical detail (Gallagher and Greenblatt 2000: 15ff.).

Applying this line of thought to ethnographic work, Geertz notes several practical points. Firstly, he insists on both the interpretive and constructivist nature of the ethnographer's descriptions (1973: 15-16). The point at issue for him is not whether the ethnographer's thick description presents an accurate account of a particular society – Geertz explicitly subscribes to a Rorty-style pragmatism in this respect – but whether it allows an appreciation both of what is similar and of what is different, and in what ways, from what angles – in what 'respects', as Richards might have said – things appear similar and different.

In addition, such a description will involve a self-conscious moment, as the instruments of the audit are examined together with its outcome. In a footnote to his 'Thick Description' essay of 1973 Geertz lamented the lack of self-consciousness about modes of representation then current in anthropology (1973: 19). Considering the 'Writing Culture' debate and the various experimental practices that accompanied the crisis of representation in anthropology in subsequent decades, there is probably no need to complain of a lack of self-consciousness in anthropology today. Translation studies however have not experienced comparable forms of self-questioning. They are still, comparatively speaking, a thin discipline.

Finally, thick description keeps the universalising urge of theory in check. Preferring the microhistories of particular situations, it prides itself on "the delicacy of its distinctions, not the sweep of its abstractions" (Geertz 1973: 25). As one commentator phrases it, thick description privileges the many over the one (Inglis 2000: 115). It could be an ideal counterweight to balance the hunger for abstraction that characterises social systems theory, for instance.

For all these reasons 'thick translation' seems to me a line worth pursuing if we want to study concepts and practices of translation across languages and cultures. As a form of translation studies, thick translation has the potential to bring about a double dislocation: of the foreign terms and concepts, which are probed by means of a methodology and vocabulary alien to them, and of the describer's own terminology, which must be wrenched out of its familiar shape to accommodate both alterity and similarity. In other words, thick translation is a double-edged technique. It engages with very different ways of conceptualising translation, and it serves as a critique of current translation studies. It ought to be able to counter the flatness and reductiveness of the prevailing jargon of translation studies, and foster instead a more diversified and imaginative vocabulary.

Inasmuch as thick translation revels in the detail of individual cases and histories, it seeks to avoid the imposition of categories deriving from a single paradigm or tradition. It is only a mild exaggeration to claim that thick translation contains within it both the acknowledgement of the impossibility of total translation and an unwillingness to appropriate the other through translation even as translation is taking place.

Such an approach offers a number of advantages. Let me list some for convenience.

1.   It advertises the fact that translation, interpretation and description are played out in the same discursive space; in Lydia Liu's words, the cross-cultural study of translation "enters, rather than sits above, the dynamic history of the relationship between words, concepts, categories and discourses".

2.   It highlights the constructed, contingent, non-essentialist nature of the similarities and differences it establishes, and consequently it remains skeptical as regards that popular and persistent trope in the common understanding of translation, the trope of translating as overcoming barriers and subduing difference.

3.   It relishes what Geertz calls "the delicacy of its distinctions" more than

"the sweep of its abstractions", and therefore seeks out concrete micro-histories and the intricacies of evolving clusters of concepts.

4.   It sets out to disturb the prevailing vocabularies of translation studies by harnessing other conceptualisations and metaphorisations of translation, thus querying the assumptions underpinning Western translation theory and its contemporary avatar, translation studies.

5.   As a highly visible form of translating, it flaunts the translator's subject-position, counteracting the illusion of transparency or neutral description, and instead introducing a narrative voice into the account and supplying it with an explicit viewpoint.

Understood?

It might be possible to imagine a culture whose concepts of translation were so different that our vocabulary would have to be acknowledged to be wholly inadequate to explicate them. Of course, if that were the case we would probably not be able to recognise the relevant activity as translation in the first place. This would be like Quine's clueless field linguist hearing an alien people utter 'gavagai' when a rabbit scurries past (Quine 1959), or like the situation evoked in Wittgenstein's *Remarks on Colour*:

> Imagine a tribe of color-blind people, and there could easily be one. They would not have the same color concepts as we do. For even as-suming they speak, e.g., English, and thus have all the English color words, they would still use them differently than we do and would *learn* their use differently. Or if they have a foreign language, it would be difficult for us to translate their color words into ours. (Wittgenstein in Lyotard 1988: 16)

We can think of a more political variant of this scenario. What if I were writing in English about concepts existing in a community with few English speakers and little access to anglophone academic publishing, and my interpretive and translative efforts, however well-intentioned, left people in this community feeling they had been misrepresented and no redress seemed possible because they did not have access to the language and the outlets that were used to describe them? A situation like this would be what François Lyotard calls a 'differend', a difference that remains irresolvable because any resolution would lead to iniquity in the prevailing linguistic regimes. Here is an example, not from Lyotard himself but from an introduction to his work (Malpas 2003: 57-8). A judge in Australia has to decide between a construction company that has begun building on an island, and a group of Aboriginal women who object on the grounds that the island is sacred. If the women win the case, the company will lose its investment and be bankrupted. But the women have a problem proving their case. According to their beliefs the island remains sacred on condition they do not speak with outsiders about what makes it sacred. The women are trapped: if they fail to provide evidence to the judge, they lose the case; if they do, the island is no longer sacred and they also lose. The judge too faces a dilemma: how to apply the rule of law, whose law will it be and how will justice be done?

It seems safe to assume that with respect to concepts and practices of trans-lation, the differend is a limiting case. Yet this may not be as self-evident as it seems. It depends on how one construes cultural difference. In *The Tao and the Logos,* Zhang Longxi explored similarities between the Chinese concept of *tao* and the Greek *logos*, and between Western and Chinese ideas about the relation between speech and writing (Zhang 1992: 26-7, 29, 32). But in the opening chapter entitled 'The Validity of Cross-Cultural Understanding' in his more recent *Allegoresis*, Zhang felt he had to take a stand against a number of prominent sinologists (including Stephen Owen, François Jullien and Pauline Yu) who stress radical cultural difference between China and the West (Zhang 2005: 1-61).

Zhang takes issue with a relativism that, in his view, makes dichotomies non-negotiable, in the double sense of the word. Instead he opts for a herme-neutic perspective. In yet another book, *Mighty Opposites* (1998) he says he strives for an understanding in which "self and Other meet and join together, in which both are changed and enriched in what Gadamer calls 'the fusion of horizons'" (Zhang 1998: 53), a meeting of minds which he describes in *Al-legoresis* in very similar-sounding terms as "a moment of mutual illumination and enrichment in what Gadamer calls the fusion of horizons" (2005: 10). It is from this position that Zhang criticises the emphasis on radical difference as it appears, for example, in Peter Winch's influential and controversial essay 'Understanding a Primitive Society' of 1964. Winch presented cultures as self-enclosed language-worlds with a meaning and logic of their own. His study of Zande magic held that reality was not independent of language but was constituted by it: "Reality is not what gives language sense. What is real and what is unreal shows itself *in* the sense that language has" (Winch 1964: 308). Zhang sees in this view a sweeping relativism that makes cultures intelligible only to themselves. For him the question is rather how understanding can be achieved beyond and in spite of cultural differences (2005: 9, 10).

The hermeneutic fusion of horizons however requires the development, or more likely the imposition, of a common idiom. This also appears to be the import of Paul Ricoeur's claim that "the aim of all hermeneutics is to struggle against cultural distance and historical alienation. Interpretation brings together, equalises, renders contemporary and similar" (1981: 185). It seems to me, however, that in a postcolonial era, appropriation along these lines can hardly be the point of the exercise.

Interestingly, in his *Hermeneutics Ancient and Modern* (1992), Gerald Bruns draws very different conclusions from Peter Winch's essay. Bruns stresses that modern hermeneutics has come to recognise that understanding involves the historicity and 'situatedness' not only of the object of understanding but of its subjects, including the observer. The self-reflexive element in cross-cultural investigation is what takes him to Winch's work on the Zande. Our helplessness in the face of Zande magic highlights our inability to make sense of the world except in the terms supplied by a particular intellectual context and tradition. The confrontation with the alien brings us up against the contingency and ethnocentricity of our own categories. That is precisely what a discipline can learn from its object. Not only is Zande magic hard to translate into Western terms, but the point of studying it can no longer just be descriptive, let alone evaluative; it must be to prompt a reflective and self-critical reversal (Bruns 1992: 2-7).

Although hermeneutics, the discipline concerned with understanding what is not immediately intelligible, seems the obvious tool for cross-cultural exploration, in the study of concepts and practices of translation across cultures it may have only limited use. I think there are two reasons for this. One is that hermeneutics is focused on authors, not translators. All the expositions of hermeneutic method, from Schleiermacher to Gadamer and Ricoeur, are aimed at understanding the work or works of a writer; they engage with integral and individual texts. Schleiermacher's idea of the hermeneutic circle is predicated on moving from the parts to the whole and back again, and on combining psychological with textual criticism. Even when a modern hermeneuticist like Paul Ricoeur invokes the concept of 'distanciation', which renders a written text autonomous with respect to the intentions of its author and takes into account the de- and recontextualisation of written texts over time (Ricoeur 1981: 131-44), he wants the researcher to address the world of the text but offers little that could help to disentangle the different subject-positions that translators and authors take up in translated discourse. Mikhail Bakhtin's comments on polyphonic writing may provide a more suitable framework to analyse the hybridity of translation.

The other reason why hermeneutics is of limited use only for the cross-cultural study of translation is that the latter deals, to a large extent, with concepts rather than with extended texts. Many of these concepts lie buried in relatively short genres like prefaces and criticism, or they have to be extrapolated from actual translations. This is more the domain of the cognitive sciences or of the history of ideas.

There is however at least one element in modern hermeneutics that cross-cultural translation studies could exploit to make itself thicker. Ricoeur picks it up when he suggests that the object of hermeneutic interpretation is not "to project oneself into the text" but, on the contrary, and perhaps a little too grandly, "to receive an enlarged self from the apprehension of proposed [textual] worlds" (1981: 182-3). In surveying the debate triggered by Peter Winch's account of the Zande and the incompatibility of their idea of magic with Western notions of rationality, Gerald Bruns, too, underlines the view taken by Winch himself and subsequently by the philosopher Charles Taylor that the confrontation of two different modes of thinking compels critical reflection not only on Zande magic but just as much on Western notions of rationality. If ethnocentricity means the imposition of a familiar mode of thought, then, in Taylor's words (in an essay of 1985), "[u]nderstanding other societies ought to wrench us out of this; it ought to alter our self-understanding" (in Bruns 1992: 7).

Not surprisingly, since the insights concerning the understanding of radically different cultures have come mostly from ethnography, this discipline has led the way in this respect. In their *Anthropology as Cultural Critique* George Marcus and Michael Fischer review various ways in which ethnography abroad has been matched with a defamiliarising ethnography at home, and insights gained in fieldwork elsewhere "raise havoc with our settled ways of thinking and conceptualization" (1986: 137ff.). Likewise, in his *Ethnography Through Thick and Thin* (1998) George Marcus champions what he calls the "ideological dimension" of reflexivity (1998: 190), which involves the recognition that working with partial, located, situated knowledges also positions the investigator in an institutionalised cultural practice as well as in an intellectual tradition.

Still, the turn towards self-reflexivity in ethnography chimes with the self-critical moment in hermeneutics, and neither is very far from I.A. Richards's urging the investigator to inspect the instruments of comparison as comparing takes place. This critical self-reflection, it seems to me, is both the main aim of the cross-cultural study of translation and its major prize. Thick translation can act as its primary tool. It will not assume that cultures are incommensurable. No doubt it will produce what A.L. Becker called exuberances and deficiencies, that is, on the one hand, additions and distortions due to the vocabularies and assumptions that researchers bring with them to their projects, and, on the other, blindness to features that seem relevant when seen from another angle (Foley 1997: 176). But the encounter with different kinds of translation can lead translation studies to interrogate its own categories.

In an essay on 'Translation and the Language(s) of Historiography', Alexandra Lianeri (2006) showed how the perception that Western historiography began with the Greeks determined the classification of writers like Thucydides and Herodotus as historians, whereas a Chinese figure like Sima Qian (*c.*145-90 BCE), whose work involved memoirs and annals among other things, received a variety of designations without being called an historian. Of course, similarities and differences can be construed between modern conceptions of history and of historiography on the one hand and, on the other, the modern idea of ancient ideas of history and historiography in both Greece and China; in the same way, transversals from ancient Greece to ancient China will be a function of the perception of continuities and discontinuities between past and present. In all of this, Western historiography is thrown back on the way it has come to conceive its own task and to define is object; it is confronted, that is, with its own historical lineage and boundaries. It must observe itself.

The cross-cultural translation of translation is obliged to move in similar ways. Maria Tymoczko (2006) has indicated some of the presuppositions of Western translation that may need to be rethought as research into translation steps beyond its traditional Western horizon. These received ideas concern such things as the mediating role of translation, the fixed nature of texts, the metaphor of translation as de- and recoding, the notion of professional translating as the model of translation, the idea that translation has been sufficiently defined by now, and the assumption that there is agreement on key achievements of research so far. Among the things to be open to in a study of translation in non-Western contexts, Tymoczko lists the nature of orality, of plurilingual societies, of the notion of text and of a wider range of translation processes and producers. She sees in these explorations the potential to redefine translation as it is currently understood in Western discourses (Tymoczko 2006: 27-30).

This kind of cross-cultural study of translation, then, would not be interested in alien concepts and modes of translation in order to demonstrate the reach and resilience of Western translation studies by subsuming those other concepts and modes. It is not the 'enlarged self' of translation studies in English and related languages that is the object. Nor is the goal the uncovering and description of the alien. Insofar as the study of translation translates disparate cultures neatly and efficiently into its own existing taxonomies, it will only find confirmation of its own preconceptions. To some extent, such confirmation is inevitable, as the prevailing vocabularies and categories are the only ones that are readily available. But just as it follows that the imposition of these vocabularies, with all the history and ideology that are inscribed in them, will not do justice to different notions and kinds of translation across time and space, it must be clear that the aim cannot be to understand these different forms of translation on their own terms or as they really are, since that would either leave the terms untranslated or make of otherness an exotic exhibit. No, the detailed probing that thick translation promotes, turns the investigation back on its own instruments and its own positioning. It is the thickness of the translation of the alien that creates room not only for context and nuance and for exploration and experiment, but also for the critical inspection of the available vocabularies and their lineages.

Thick translation is self-reflexive translation. Like Luhmann's second-order observer it cannot observe itself observing, but it can shift the vantage point. It can rediscover both translation and itself.

Bibliography

Albertsen, Niels and Diken, Bülent (2004) 'Artworks' Networks. Field, System or Mediators?'. *Theory, Culture & Society* 21(3): 35-58.

Anderson, Kristine (1997) 'Karen Blixen's Bilingual Œuvre: the Role of her English Editors'. *Perspectives* 5: 171-91.

Appiah, Kwame Anthony (2004) 'Thick Translation' [1993]. Venuti 2004: 389-401.

Augustine (1972) *Concerning the City of God against the Pagans*. Trans. Henry Bettenson. London: Penguin.

Austin, J.L. (1962) *How to Do Things with Words*. Oxford: Clarendon.

Bachleitner, Norbert (1989) '"Übersetzungsfabriken". Das deutsche Übersetzungs- wesen in der ersten Hälfte des 19. Jahrhunderts'. *Internationales Archiv für Sozialgeschichte der deutschen Literatur* 14(1): 1-49.

Baker, Mona (2000) 'Towards a Methodology for Investigating the Style of a Literary Translator'. *Target* 12: 241-66.

Bakhtin, M.M. (1981) *The Dialogic Imagination. Four Essays*. Trans. Caryl Emer- son and Michael Holquist. Austin: University of Texas Press.

Baraldi, Claudio; Corsi, Giancarlo and Esposito, Elena (1997) *GLU. Glossar zu Niklas Luhmanns Theorie sozialer Systeme*. Frankfurt: Suhrkamp.

Barnes, James and Barnes, Patience (1980) *Hitler's Mein Kampf in Britain and America. A Publishing History 1930-39*. Cambridge: Cambridge University Press.

Bates, Stuart (1936) *Modern Translation*. Oxford and London: Oxford University Press and Humphrey Milford.

Beaujour, Elizabeth Klosty (1989) *Alien Tongues. Bilingual Russian Writers of the 'First' Emigration*. Ithaca and London: Cornell University Press.

------ (1995) 'Translation and Self-Translation', *The Garland Companion to Vladimir Nabokov*, Ed. Vladimir E. Alexandrov. New York and London: Garland, 714-24.

Belgium (1994) Constitution. www.senate.be/doc/const_nl; www.senate.be/doc/ const_fr; www.senate.be/doc/const_de.

Bell, Alan (1984) 'Language Style as Audience Design'. *Language in Society* 13: 145-204.

Berne (1971) Berne Convention for the Protection of Literary and Artistic Works. http://www.law.cornell.edu/treaties/berne/overview.html.

Berthoff, Ann E. (1982) 'I.A. Richards and the Audit of Meaning'. *New Literary History* 14: 63-79.

Bigelow, John (1978) 'Semantics of Thinking, Speaking and Translation.' *Meaning and Translation. Philosophical and Liguistic Approaches*, Ed. F. Guenthner and M. Guethner-Reutter. London: Duckworth, 109-35.

Blix, Hans and Emerson, Jirina (1973) *The Treaty Maker's Handbook*. New York and Stockholm: Oceana and Almqvist and Wiksell.

Bloemen, Henri; Hulst, Jacqueline; De Jong-van den Berg, Nelleke; Koster, Cees; Naaijkens, Ton (1998) Eds. *De kracht van vertaling. Verrijking van taal en cultuur*. Utrecht: Platform Vertalen en Vertaalwetenschap.

Boccaccio, Giovanni (1886) *The Decameron of Giovanni Boccacci (il Boccaccio) now first completely done into English prose and verse by John Payne*. 3 vols. London: printed for the Villon Society by private subscription and for private circulation only.

------ (1893) *The Decameron*. Trans. John Payne. Illustrations Louis Chalon. 2 vols. London: Lawrence and Bullen.

------ (1903) *The Decameron. Faithfully translated by J.M. Rigg with illustrations by Louis Chalon*. 2 vols. London: A.H. Bullen.

Booth, Wayne (1975) *A Rhetoric of Irony*. Chicago and London: University of Chicago Press.

Borges, Jorge Luis (1981) *Labyrinths. Selected Stories and Other Writings*. Ed. D. A. Yates and J.E. Irby. Harmondsworth: Penguin.

------ (2004) 'The Translators of *The Thousand and One Night*s' [1935]. Trans. Esther Allen. Venuti 2004: 94-108.

Botley, Paul (2004) *Latin Translation in the Renaissance. The Theory and Practice of Leonardi Bruni, Giannozzo Manetti and Desiderius Erasmus*. Cambridge: Cambridge University Press.

Bray, Gerald (1994) Ed. *Documents of the English Reformation*. Cambridge: James Clark and Co.

Brodie, Fawn. 1945. *No Man Knows my History. The Life of Joseph Smith the Mormon Prophet*. New York: Alfred Knopf.

Brouckaert, Hugo (1998) 'De Nederlandse rechtstaal in België'. Bloemen *et al.* 1998, 29-39.

Brunot, Ferdinand (1966-) *Histoire de la langue française des origines à nos jours* [1901-]. 23 vols. New ed. Paris: Armand Colin.

Bruns, Gerald L. (1992) *Hermeneutics Ancient and Modern*. New Haven and London: Yale University Press.

Burke, Peter (1993) *Antwerp. A Metropolis in Comparative Perspective*. Antwerp: Martial and Snoeck.

Burton, Richard Francis (1885-88) *A plain and literal translation of the Ariabian Nights entertainments, now entituled The Book of the Thousand Nights and a Night*. 16 vols. London: Printed by the Kamashastra Society for private subscribers only. http://www.gutenberg.org/etext/3435.

Burton, Robert (1994) *The Anatomy of Melancholy* [1621]. Ed. Thomas Faulkner, Nicolas Kiessling and Rhonda Blair. 5 vols. Oxford: Clarendon.

Bushman, Richard (1984) *Joseph Smith and the Beginnings of Mormonism*. Urbana and Chicago: University of Illinois Press.

Butler, S.H. (1907) *The Poetics of Aristotle* [1805]. London: Macmillan..

Bywater, Ingram (1909) *Aristotle on the Art of Poetry*. Oxford: Clarendon.

Calvin, Jean (1957) *Institution de la religion chrestienne* [1541-61]. Ed. Jean-Daniel Benoit. 4 vols (vol. 1). Paris: Vrin.

------ (1970) 'Petit Traicté de la saincte Cene de Nostre Seigneur Jesus Christ' [1542], *Three French Treatises*, Ed. Francis Higman. London: Athlone, 99-130.

Canada (1982) Constitution Act. http://laws.justice.gc.ca/en/const/annex_e.html; http://lois.justice.gc.ca/fr/const/annex_f.html.

Casanova, Pascale (2004) *The World Republic of Letters*. Trans. M.B. DeBevoise. Cambridge (Mass.) and London: Harvard University Press.

Chan, Elsie (2002) 'Translation Principles and the Translator's Agenda: A Systemic Approach to Yan Fu'. *Crosscultural Transgressions*, Ed. T. Hermans. Manchester: St Jerome, 61-75.

Chan, Sin-wai & Pollard, David (1995) Eds. *An Encyclopedia of Translation. Chinese-English, English-Chinese*. Hong Kong: Chinese University Press.

Chartier, Roger (1994) *The Order of Books. Readers, Authors and Libraries in Europe between the Fourteenth and Eighteenth Centuries*. Trans. Lydia Cochrane. London: Polity.

Chesterman, Andrew (1993) 'From "Is" to "Ought": Laws, Norms and Strategies in Translation Studies'. *Target* 5: 1-20.

------ (1997) *Memes of Translation. The Spread of Ideas n Translation Theory*. Amsterdam and Philadelphia: John Benjamins.

China (1908) Imperial Maritime Customs. *Treaties, Conventions, etc. Between China and Foreign States*. 2 vols. Shanghai: Statistical Department of the Inspectorate General of Customs.

Clark, Herbert and Gerrig, Richard (1990) 'Quotations as Demonstrations'. *Language* 66: 764-805.

Clayton, Jay and Rothstein, Eric (1991) Eds. *Influence and Intertextuality in Literary History*. Madison: University of Wisconsin Press.

Colebrook, Claire (2004) *Irony*. London and New York: Routledge.

Conan Doyle, Arthur (1951) 'The Greek Interpreter'. *Sherlock Holmes. Selected Stories by Sir Arthur Conan Doyle*, Ed. S.C. Roberts. Oxford: Oxford University Press, 305-28.

Courtivron, Isabelle de (2003) Ed. *Lives in Translation. Bilingual Writers on Identity and Creativity*. London: Palgrave Macmillan.

Crockett, William R. (1989) *Eucharist: Symbol of Transformation*. New York: Pueblo.

Daniell, David (2003) *The Bible in English. Its History and Influence*. New Haven and London: Yale University Press.

Davies, Bronwyn and Harré, Rom (1990) 'Positioning: The Discursive Production of Selves'. *Journal for the Theory of Social Behaviour* 20: 43-63.

Dear, Peter (1991) 'The Church and the New Philosophy'. *Science, Culture and Popular Belief in Renaissance Europe*, Eds. Stephen Pumfrey, Paolo Rossi and

Maurice Slawinski. Manchester: Manchester University Press, 119-39.

DeLater, James Albert (2002) *Translation Theory in the Age of Louis XIV. The 1683 De optimo genere interpretandi (On the best kind of translating) of Pierre-Daniel Huet (1630-1721)*. Manchester: St Jerome.

Deleuze, Gilles (2001) *The Logic of Sense*. Trans. Mark Lester. London and New York: Continuum.

Deleuze, Gilles and Claire Parnet (1987) *Dialogues*. Trans. Hugh Tomlinson and Barbara Habberjam. London: Athlone.

de Berg, Henk and Prangel, Matthias (1997) Eds. *Systemtheorie und Hermeneutik*. Tübingen: Francke.

------ and Schmidt, Johannes F.K. (2000) Eds. *Rezeption und Reflexion. Zur Resonanz der Systemtheorie Niklas Luhmanns ausserhalb der Soziologie*. Frankfurt: Surhkamp.

de Man, Paul (1983) *Blindness and Insight*. London: Routledge.

de Waal, Cornelis (2001) *On Peirce*. Belmont (CA): Wadsworth.

Derrida, Jacques (1977) 'Signature Event Context'. Trans. Samuel Weber and Jeffrey Mehlman. *Glyph* 1: 172-97.

------ (1977a) 'Limited Inc abc...'. Trans. Samuel Weber. *Glyph* 2: 162-254.

------ (1985) 'Des tours de Babel'. Trans. Joseph Graham. *Difference in Translation*, Ed. Joseph Graham. Ithaca and London: Cornell University Press, 165-207, 209-48.

------ (2004) 'What is a "Relevant" Translation?' [1999]. Trans. Lawrence Venuti. Venuti 2004: 423-46.

------ (1998) *Monolingualism of the Other, or the Prosthesis of Origin*. Trans. Patrick Mensah. Stanford: Stanford University Press.

------ (2004) *Eyes of the University. Right to Philosophy 2*. Trans. Jan Plug *et al.* Stanford: Stanford University Press.

Descartes, René (1984) *The Philosophical Writings of Descartes*. Vols. II and III. Trans. John Cottingham, Robert Stoothoff and Dugald Murdoch. Cambridge: Cambridge University Press.

D'hulst, Lieven (1990) Ed. *Cent ans de théorie française de la traduction. De Batteux à Littré*. Lille: Presses universitaires de Lille.

Dorsch, T.S. (1965) Trans. *Aristotle, Poetics. Classical Literary Criticism*. Harmondsworth: Penguin, 31-75.

Douglas, Mary (1973) *Natural Symbols. Explorations in Cosmology*. New York: Vintage.

Draper, G.I.A.D. (1958) *The Red Cross Conventions*. London: Stevens and Sons.

Eisenstein, Elizabeth (1980) *The Printing Press as an Agent of Change. Communications and Transformations in Early-Modern Europe*. Cambridge: Cambridge University Press.

Ellison, Julie (1990) *Delicate Subjects. Romanticism, Gender, and the Ethics of Understanding*. Ithaca and London: Cornell University Press.

Esposito, Elena (1996) 'Observing Interpretation. A Sociological View of Hermeneutics'. *Modern Language Notes* 111: 593-619.

European Union (2005) Accession Treaty. http://eur-lex.europa.eu/en/treaties/treaties_accession.htm.

Fan Shouyi (1994) 'Translation Studies in China: Retrospect and Prospect'. *Target* 6: 151-76.

Febvre, Lucien and Martin, Henri-Jean (1976) *The Coming of the Book. The Impact of Printing 1450-1800*. Trans. David Gerard. London and New York: Verso. (*L'apparition du livre*, 1958.)

Fenton, Sabine and Moon, Paul (2002) 'The Translation of the Treaty of Waitangi. A Case of Disempowerment'. *Translation and Power*, Eds. Maria Tymoczko and Edwin Gentzler. Amherst and Boston: University of Massachusetts Press, 25-44.

------ (2004) 'Survival by Translation. The Case of Te Tiriti o Waitangi'. *For Better or For Worse. Translation as a Tool for Change in the South Pacific*, Ed. Sabine Fenton. Manchester: St Jerome, 37-61.

Fioretos, Artis (1999) 'Hölderlin and Translation'. *The Solid Letter. Readings of Friedrich Hölderlin*, Ed. Artis Fioretos. Stanford: Stanford University Press, 268-87.

Fitch, Brian (1988) *Beckett and Babel. An Investigation into the Status of the Bilingual Work*. Toronto: University of Toronto Press.

Fleming, Brendan (2001) 'The Frist English Translation of *La Terre* (1888): An Assessment of the Letters from Vizetelly & Co to Emile Zola'. *Publishing History* 50: 47-59.

Folena, Gianfranco (1991) *Volgarizzare e tradurre* [1973]. Torino: Einaudi.

Foley, William A. (1997) *Anthropological Linguistics. An Introduction*. Oxford: Blackwell.

Folkart, Barbara (1991) *Le conflit des énonciations. Traduction et discours rapporté*. Québec: Balzac.

Fong, Gilbert (1995) 'Translated Literature in Pre-Modern China'. Chan and Pollard 1995, 580-90.

Fossa, Lydia (2005) 'Juan de Betanzos, the Man who Boasted being a Translator'. *Meta* 50: 906-33.

Freese, John Henry (2000) *Aristotle, The 'Art' of Rhetoric* [1926]. Cambridge (Mass.) and London: Harvard University Press.

Freud, Sigmund (1963) 'Notes upon a Case of Obsessional Neurosis' [1909]. *Three Case Histories*, Ed. and trans. Philip Rieff. New York: Simon and Schuster, 1-81.

Gadamer, Hans-Georg (1977) *Philosophical Hermeneutics*. Trans. David Linge. Berkeley: University of California Press.

------ (1989) *Truth and Method*. 2nd, revised ed. Trans. Joel Weilsheimer and Donal Marshall. London and New York: Continuum.

Gallagher, Catherine and Greenblatt, Stephen (2000) Eds. *Practicing New Histori-cism*. Chicago and London: University of Chicago Press.

Geertz, Clifford (1973) *The Interpretation of Cultures. Selected Essays*. New York: BasicBooks.

Genette, Gérard (1979) *Introduction à l'architexte*. Paris: Seuil.

------ (1982) *Palimpsestes*. Paris: Seuil.

------ (1997) *The Work of Art. Immanence and Transcendence*. Trans. G.M. Gosh-garian, Cornell University Press. (*L'oeuvre de l'art*, 1994.)

Goffman, Erving (1981) *Forms of Talk*. Oxford: Basil Blackwell.

Gogh, Vincent van (1996) *The Letters of Vincent van Gogh*. Ed. Ronald de Leeuw. Trans. Arnold Pomerans. London: Penguin.

Goodman, Nelson (1978) 'Some Questions concerning Quotation'. *Ways of Worldmaking*, Indianapolis: Hackett, 41-56.

Grayson, Jane (1977) *Nabokov Translated*. Oxford: Oxford University Press.

Greenblatt, Stephen (2000) 'The Wound in the Wall'. Gallagher and Greenblatt 2000, 75-109.

Greenblatt, Stephen (2000a) 'The Mousetrap'. Gallagher and Greenblatt 2000, 136-62.

Gutt, Ernst-August (1991) *Translation and Relevance. Cognition and Context*. Oxford: Blackwell.

Hamilton Fyfe, W. (1940) *Aristotle's Art of Poetry. A Greek View of Poetry and Drama*. Oxford: Clarendon.

Harwoord, Edward (1768) *A Liberal Translation of the New Testament; being An Attempt to translate the Sacred Writings with the Freedom, Spirit, and Elegance, with which other English Translations from the Greek Classics have lately been executed*. 2 vols. London: T. Becket and P.A. De Hondt.

Hatim, Basil and Mason, Ian (1997) *The Translator as Communicator*. London and New York: Routledge.

Hayles, Catherine (1995) 'Making the Cut. The Interplay of Narrative and System, or What Systems Theory Can't See'. *Cultural Critique* 30: 71-100.

Heppe, Heinrich (1950) *Reformed dogmatics: set out and illustrated from the sources* [1861]. Revised and Ed. Ernst Bizer. Trans. G. T. Thomson. London: Allen and Unwin.

Herder, Johann Gottfried (2002) *Philosophical Writings*. Trans. Michael N. Forster. Cambridge: Cambridge University Press.

Hermans, Theo (1996) 'The Translator's Voice in Translated Narrative'. *Target* 8: 23-48.

------ (1997)'The Task of the Translator in the European Renaissance'. *Translating Literature*, Ed. Susan Bassnett. Cambridge: D.S. Brewer, 14-40.

------ (1999) *Translation in Systems. Descriptive and Systemic Approaches Ex-plained*. Manchester: St Jerome.

------ (2006) Ed. *Translating Others*. 2 vols. Manchester: St Jerome.

Heron, Alasdair (1983) *Table and Tradition. Towards an Ecumenical Understanding of the Eucharist*. Edinburgh: Handsell Press.

Hill, Donna (1977) *Joseph Smith, the First Mormon*. Garden City (NY): Doubleday.

Hitler, Adolf (1925-6) *Mein Kampf*. Munich-Berlin: Franz Eher.

------ (1939) *Mein Kampf*. Ed. John Chamberlain, Sidney B. Fay, John Gunther, Carlton Hayes, Graham Hutton Alvin Johnson, William Langer, Walter Millis, Raoul de Soussy de Sales and George Schuster. Trans. Helmut Ripperger. New York: Reynal and Hitchcock.

------ (1939a) *Mijn kamp*. Trans. Steven Barends. Amsterdam: De Amsterdamsche Keurkamer.

------ (1942) *The Speeches of Adolf Hitler, April 1922-August 1939*. Trans. Norman H. Bayes. London, New York and Toronto: Oxford University Press.

------ (1995) *Mein Kampf*. Trans. Ralph Manheim. Intro. D. Cameron Watt. London: Pimlico. First publ. 1943 (USA) and 1969 (UK).

Hofstadter, Douglas (1997) *Le Ton beau de Marot. In Praise of the Music of Language*. New York: BasicBooks.

House, Juliane (1981) *A Model for Translation Quality Assessment*. Tübingen: Gunter Narr.

Hoven, Paul van den (1998) 'Een vertaling die geen vertaling mag zijn. Over artikel 33 van het verdrag van Wenen en andere vreemde zaken'. Bloemen *et al.*1998, 40-47.

Hsiu, C.Y. (1973) Trans. Yan Fu, 'General Remarks on Translation', *Renditions* 1: 1, 4-6.

Huang Yushi (1995) 'Form and Spirit'. Chan and Pollard 1995, 277-87

Hudson, Anne (1985) *Lollards and their Books*. London and Ronceverte: Hambledon Books.

Hung, Eva and Pollard, David (1998) 'Chinese Tradition'. *Routledge Encyclopedia of Translation Studies*, Ed. Mona Baker. London: Routledge, 365-75.

Hutcheon, Linda (1995) *Irony's Edge. The Theory and Politics of Irony*. London and New York: Routledge.

Huydecoper, Balthasar (1726) *Hekeldichten en brieven van Q. Horatius Flaccus. Uit Latynsch Dicht in Nederduitsch Ondicht overgebragt*. Amsterdam: Willem Barents.

Inglis, Fred (2000) *Clifford Geertz. Culture, Custom and Ethics*. Cambridge: Polity

Jakobson, Roman (1959) 'On Linguistic Aspects of Translation'. *On Translation*, Ed. Reuben Brower. Cambridge, Mass.: Harvard University Press, 232-9.

Janko, Richard (1987) Trans. *Aristotle, Poetics*. Indianapolis and Cambridge: Hackett.

Jones, John (1971) *On Aristotle and Greek Tragedy* [1961]. London: Chatto and Windus.

Kartman, Kabi (1999) 'Ideology, Identification and the Construction of the Feminine: *Le journal de Marie Bashkirtseff*. *The Translator* 5(1): 61-82.

Kelly, Gerard (2001) 'The Eucharistic Doctrine of Transubstantiation'. *The Eucharist: Faith and Worship*, Ed. Margaret Press, Sidney: St Pauls, 56-74.

Kinney, Daniel (1986) Ed. *The Complete Works of St. Thomas More*. Vol. 15. New Haven and London: Yale University Press.

Kittel, Harald; Frank, Armin Paul; Greiner, Norbert; Hermans, Theo; Koller, Werner; Lambert, José, and Paul, Fritz (2004) Eds. *Übersetzung. Translation. Traduction. Ein internationales Handbuch zur Übersetzungsforschung. An International Encylcopedia of Translation Studies. Encylopédie internationale de la recherche sur la traduction*. Vol. 1. Berlin and New York : Walter de Gruyter.

Klein-Lataud, Christine (1996) 'Les voix parallèles de Nancy Huston'. *TTR* 9(1): 211-31.

Koester, Olaf (1999) *Painted Illusions. The Art of Cornelius Gijsbrechts*. London: National Gallery Company.

Koller, Werner (1995) 'The Concept of Equivalence and the Object of Translation Studies'. *Target* 7(2): 191-222.

------ (2004) 'Der Begriff der Äquivalenz in der Übersetzungswissenschaft'. Kittel *et al*. 2004, 343-54.

Krawietz, Werner and Welker, Michael (1992) Eds. *Kritik der Theorie sozialer Systeme. Auseinandersetzungen mit Luhmanns Hauptwerk*. Frankfurt: Suhrkamp.

Krog, Antjie (1999) *Country of My Skull*. London: Vintage.

Lakoff, George and Johnson, Mark (1980) *Metaphors We Live By*. Chicago and London: University of Chicago Press.

Lamm, Julia (2000) 'Schleiermacher as Plato Scholar'. *The Journal of Religion* 80: 206-39.

Lane, Edward Wiliam (1839) *The Thousand and One Nights, commonly called, in English, the Arabian Nights' Entertainments. A new translation from the Arabic with copious notes*. 3 vols. London: Charles Knight.

Laplanche, Jean (1992) *Jean Laplanche: Seduction, Translation and the Drives*. Eds. John Fletcher and Martin Stanton. Trans. Martin Stanton. London : Institute of Contemporary Arts.

Lavoie, Judith (2003) 'Le bilinguisme législatif et la place de la traduction'. *TTR* 16(1): 121-39.

Lefevere, André (1977) Ed. *Translating Literature: the German Tradition*. Assen: Van Gorcum.

------ (1992) *Translation, Rewriting and the Manipulation of Literary Fame*. London and New York: Routledge.

Lewis, C.S. (1960) *Studies in Words*. Cambridge: Cambridge University Press.

Lewis, Philip (1985) 'The Measure of Translation Effects'. *Difference in Translation*,

Ed. Joseph Graham. Ithaca and London: Cornell University Press, 31-62.

Lianeri, Alexandra (2002) 'Translation and the Ideology of Culture: Reappraising Schleiermacher's Theory of Translation'. *Current Writing* 14(2): 2-18.

------ (2006) 'Translation and the Language(s) of Historiography. Understanding Ancient Greek and Chinese Ideas of History'. Hermans 2006, 67-86.

Lipsius, Justus (1948) *Twee boecken vande stantvasticheyt* [1584]. Trans. Jan Mourentorf. Ed. H. Van Cromburggen. Antwerp: De Sikkel.

Liu, Lydia (1995) *Translingual Practice*. Stanford: Stanford University Press.

Liu, Miqing (1995a) 'Aesthetics and Translation'. Chan and Pollard 1995, 1-13.

------ (1995b) 'Translation Theory from/into Chinese'. Chan and Pollard 1995, 1029-47.

Lodge, David (1993) *Changing Places. Small World. Nice Work.* Harmondsworth: Penguin.

Lotman, Yuri (1990). *Universe of the Mind. A Semiotic Theory of Culture.* Trans. An Shukman. London and New York: I.B. Tauris.

Louth, Charlie (1998) *Hölderlin and the Dynamics of Translation.* Oxford: Legenda.

Luhmann, Niklas (1986) *Love as Passion. The Codification of Intimacy.* Trans. Jeremy Gaines and Doris Jones. Stanford: Stanford University Press. (*Liebe als Passion*, 1982.)

------ (1986a) 'Das Kunstwerk und die Selbstreproduktion der Kunst'. *Stil. Geschichte und Funktionen eines kulturwissenschaftlichen Diskurselements*, Eds. H.U. Gumpert and K.L. Pfeiffer. Frankfurt: Suhrkamp, 620-72.

------ (1987) *Archimedes und wir. Interviews.* Eds. Dirk Baecker and George Stanitzek. Berlin: Merve.

------ (1989) *Ecological Communication.* Trans. John Bednarz. London: Polity. (*Ökologische Kommunikation*, 1986.)

------ (1990) *Die Wissenschaft der Gesellschaft.* Frankfurt: Suhrkamp.

------ (1990a) 'Weltkunst'. N. Luhmann, F. Bunsen and Dirk Baecker, *Unbeobachtbare Welt. Über Kunst und Architektur.* Bielefeld: Cordula Haux, 7-45.

------ (1995) *Social Systems.* Trans. John Bednarz. Stanford: Stanford University Press. (*Soziale Systeme,* 1984.)

------ (1996) 'A Redescription of "Romantic Art"'. *Modern Language Notes* 111: 506-22.

------ (1997) *Die Gesellschaft der Gesellschaft.* 2 vols. Frankfurt: Suhrkamp.

------ (1998) *Observations on Modernity.* Trans. William Whobrey. Stanford: Stanford University Press.

------ (1999) *Gesellschaftsstruktur und Semantik. Studien zur Wissenssoziologie der modernen Gesellschaft. Band 4.* Frankfurt: Suhrkamp.

------ (1999a) 'The Concept of Society' (Trans. David Roberts). *The Blackwell Reader in Contemporary Social Theory*, Ed. Anthony Elliott. London: Blackwell, 143-55.

------ (2000) *Art as a Social System*. Trans. Eva Knodt. Stanford: Stanford University Press. (*Die Kunst der Gesellschaft,* 1995.)

------ (2000a) *The Reality of the Mass Media*. Trans. Kathleen Cross. Cambridge: Polity. (*Die Realität der Massenmedien,* 1996.)

------ (2002) *Theories of Distinction. Redescribing the Descriptions of Modernity*. Ed. William Rasch. Stanford: Stanford University Press.

------ (2004) *Einführung in die Systemtheorie*. Ed. Dirk Baecker. Heidelberg: Carl-Auer-Systeme.

------ (2005) *Risk. A Sociological Theory*. Trans. Rhodes Barrett. New Brunswick and London: Aldine Transaction. (*Soziologie des Risikos*, 1991.)

Lyotard, Jean-Francois (1988) *The Differend. Phrases in Dispute*. Trans. G. van den Abbeele. Minneapolis: University of Minnesota Press.

Maier, Carol (2006) 'The Translator as *Theoros*. Thoughts on Cogitation, Figuration and Current Creative Writing'. Hermans 2006, 163-80.

Malpas, Simon (2003) *Jean-François Lyotard*. London and New York: Routledge.

Mann, Thomas (1996) *Death in Venice and Other Stories*. Trans. David Luke. London: Minerva.

Manning, John (2002) *The Emblem*. London: Reaktion.

Marcus, George (1998) *Ethnography Through Thick and Thin*. Princeton: Princeton University Press.

------ and Fischer, Michael (1986) *Anthropology as Cultural Critique. An Experimental Moment in the Human Sciences*. Chicago and London: University of Chicago Press.

Mason, Ian (2000) 'Audience Design in Translating'. *The Translator* 6(1): 1-22.

Ma Zuyi (1994) 'History of Translation in China'. Chan and Pollard 1995, 373-87.

McNees, Eleanor (1992) *Eucharistic Poetry. The Search for Presence in the Writings of John Donne, Gerard Manley Hopkins, Dylan Thomas and Geoffrey Hill*. Lewisburg: Bucknell University Press; London and Toronto: Associated University Presses.

McWilliam, G.H. (1972) 'Translator's Introduction'. Giovanni Boccaccio, *The Decameron*. Trans. G.H. McWilliam. London: Penguin, 1972, 21-43.

Mehring, Franz (1966) *Karl Marx. The Story of his Life*. Trans. Edward Fitzgerald. London: George Allen & Unwin.

Montaigne, Michel de (1969) *Essais*. Ed. Alexandre Micha. 3 vols. Paris: Garnier-Flammarion.

------ (1987) *An Apology for Raymond Sebond* [1580-88]. Trans. M. A. Screech. London: Penguin.

Mossop, Brian (1983) 'The Translator as Rapporteur: a Concept for Training and Self-Improvement'. *Meta* 28: 244-78.

------ (1998) 'What is a Translating Translator Doing?'. *Target* 10: 231-66.

Needham, Rodney (1972) *Belief, Language and Experience*. Oxford: Basil Blackwell.

Neubert, Albrecht (2004) 'Equivalence in Translation'. Kittel *et al.* 2004, 329-42.

Noh, Eun-Ju (2000) *Metarepresentation. A Relevance-Theory Approach.* Amsterdam and Philadelphia: John Benjamins.

Noll, Mark (1991) Ed. *Confessions and Catechisms of the Reformation.* Leicester: Apollos.

Nord, Christiane (1997) *Translating as a Purposeful Activity. Functionalist Approaches Explained.* Manchester: St Jerome.

Norton, Glyn (1984) *The Ideology and Language of Translation in Renaissance France and their Humanist Antecedents.* Genève: Droz.

Nussbaum, Laureen (1994) 'Anne Frank'. *Women Writing in Dutch*, Ed. Kristiaan Aercke. New York and London: Garland, 513-75.

Ó Cuilleanáin, Cormac (1998) 'Not in Front of the Servants'. *The Practices of Literary Translation: Constraints and Creativity*, Eds. Jean Boase-Beier and Michael Holman. Manchester: St Jerome, 31-44.

Ornston, Darius Gray (1992) Ed. *Translating Freud.* New Haven and London: Yale University Press.

Ostrower, Alexander (1965) *Language, Law, and Diplomacy. A Study of Linguistic Diversity in Official International Relations and International Law.* 2 vols. Philadelphia: University of Pennsylvania Press.

Padley, G.A. (1985) *Grammatical Theory in Western Europe 1500-1700. Trends in Vernacular Grammar I.* Cambridge: Cambridge University Press.

Payne, John (1882) *The Book of the Thousand Nights and One Night: now first completely done into English prose and verse from the original Arabic.* 9 vols. London: Printed for the Villon Society by private subscription and for private circulation only.

Peirce, C.S. (1991) *Peirce on Signs. Writings on Semiotic by Charles Sanders Peirce.* Ed. James Hoopes. Chapel Hill and London: University of North Carolina Press.

Pelikan, Jaroslav (1984) *Reformation of Church and Dogma (1300-1700)*, vol. 4 of *The Christian Tradition. A History of the Development of Doctrine*, 5 vols. Chicago: University of Chicago Press.

Persuitte, David (1985) *Joseph Smith and the Origins of the Book of Mormon.* Jefferson (NC) and London: McFarland.

Petersen, LaMar (2000) *The Creation of the Book of Mormon. A Historical Inquiry.* Salt Lake City: Freethinker Press.

Petrilli, Susan (2003) 'Translation and Semiosis. Introduction'. *Translation Translation*, Ed. Susan Petrilli. Amsterdam and New York: Rodopi, 17-37.

Phelan, Mary (2001) *The Interpreter's Resource.* Clevedon: Multilingual Matters.

Pickford, Susan (2007) 'Between *version* and *traduction*: Sterne's *Sentimental Journey* in Mid-Nineteenth-Century France". *Translation and Literature* 16: 53-65.

Plett, Heinrich (1979) *Einführung in die rhetorische Textanalyse.* Hamburg:

Helmut Buske.

Plöse, Detlef and Vogler, Günter (1989) Eds. *Buch der Reformation. Eine Auswahl zeitgenössischer Zeugnisse (1476-1555)*. Berlin: Union.

Pohle, J. (2003) 'The Real Presence of Christ in the Eucharist', transcribed by Charles Sweeney. *The Catholic Encyclopedia* [1909], Ed. Kevin Knight. www.newadvent.org/cathen/05573a.htr

Poltermann, Andreas (1992) 'Normen des literarischen Übersetzens im System der Literatur'. *Geschichte, System, Literarische Übersetzung. Histories, Systems, Literary Translations*, Ed. Harald Kittel. Berlin: Erich Schmidt, 5-31.

Pushkin, Aleksandr (1975) *Eugen Onegin. A Novel in Verse* [1964]. Trans. Vladimir Nabokov. 2 vols. Princeton: Princeton University Press.

Pym, Anthony (1992) *Translation and Text Transfer. An Essay on the Principles of Intercultural Communication*. Frankfurt etc.: Peter Lang.

------ (1993) 'On the Market as a Factor in the Training of Translators'. *Koiné* 3: 109-21.

------ (1997) 'European Translation Studies, 'une science qui dérange' and Why Equivalence Needn't be a Dirty Word'. *TTR* 8(1): 153-76.

------ (20004) *The Moving Text. Localization, Translation and Distribution*. Amsterdam and Philadelphia: John Benjamins.

Quine, W.v.O. (1959) 'Meaning and Translation'. *On Translation*, Ed. Reuben Brower. Cambridge: Harvard University Press, 148-72.

Qur'an (1649) *The Alcoran of Mahomet, Translated out of Arabique into French, by the Sieur Du Ryer .... And newly Englished,, for the satisfaction of all that desire to look into the Turkish vanities*. [Trans. Alexander Ross]. London: n.p.

Qvale, Per (2003) *From St Jerome to Hypertext. Translation in Theory and Practice*. Trans. Norman Spencer. Manchester: St Jerome.

Rambelli, Paolo (2006) 'Pseudotranslations, Authorship and Novelists in Eighteenth-Century Italy'. *Translating Others,* Ed. Theo Hermans. Manchester: St Jerome, 181-210.

Rasch, William (2000) *Niklas Luhmann's Modernity. The Paradoxes of Differentiation*. Stanford: Stanford University Press.

Raspergerus, Christophorus (1577) *Ducentae paucorum istorum, et quidem clarissimorum Christi verborum: Hoc est Corpus meum; interpretationes: quibus continentur vocum novitates, depravationes, errores, haereses, contradictiones atque inuentiones istorum Theologorum, qui Euangelico nomine gloriantur, sacrilegae: Exproprijs ipsorum scriptis fideliter collectae*. Ingolstadt: Alexander Weissenhorn.

Reddy, Michael (1993) 'The Conduit Metaphor: A Case of Frame Conflict in our Language about Language' [1979]. *Metaphor and Thought*, Ed. Andrew Ortony. 2nd ed. Cambridge: Cambridge University Press, 164-201.

Reuter, Paul (1995) *Introduction to the Law of Treaties*. Trans. J. Mico and P. Haggermacher. London and New York: Kegan Paul International.

Rice, Eugene F. (1985) *Saint Jerome in the Renaissance*. Baltimore and London: Johns Hopkins University Press.

Richards, I.A. (1932) *Mencius on the Mind*. London: Kegan Paul, Trench, Trubner and Co.

------ (1943) *How to Read a Page*. London: Routledge and Kegan Paul.

------ (1955) *Speculative Instruments*. London: Routledge and Kegan Paul.

Ricoeur, Paul (1981) *Hermeneutics and the Human Sciences*. Trans. John B. Thompson. Cambridge and Paris: Cambridge University Press and Maison des Sciences de l'Homme.

Rigg, J.M. (1903) *The Decameron. Faithfully translated by J.M. Rigg.* London: A.H. Bullen..

Roberts, David (1992) 'The Paradox of Form: Literature and Self-Reference'. *Poetics* 21: 75-91.

Robinson, Douglas (1997) Ed. *Western Translation Theory from Herodotus to Nietzsche*. Manchester: St Jerome.

Rome (1957) Consolidated Version of the Treaty Establishing the European Community. http://eur-lex.europa.eu/en/treaties/treaties_founding.htm.

Rorty, Richard (1989) *Contingency, Irony and Solidarity*. Cambridge: Cambridge University Press.

------ (1999) 'Trotsky and Wild Orchids' [1992] in his *Philosophy and Social Hope*, London: Penguin, 3-20.

Rubin, Miri (1991) *Corpus Christi: The Eucharist in Late Medieval Culture*. Cambridge: Cambridge University Press.

Ryle, Gilbert (1971) *Collected Papers. Vol. II: Collected Essays 1929-1968*. London: Hutchinson.

Santoyo, Julio-César (2004) 'Self-Translation: Translational Competence Revisited (and Performance as well)'. *Translationskompetenz*, Eds. Eberhard Fleischmann, Peter A. Schmitt and Gerd Wotjak. Tübingen: Stauffenburg, 223-36.

Scannell, T.B. (2003) 'Consubstantiation'. *The Catholic Encyclopedia* [1909], Ed. Kevin Knight. www.newadvent.org/cathen/05573a.htr

Schiavi, Giuliana (1996) 'There is always a Teller in a Tale'. *Target* 8: 1-22.

Schillebeeckx, Edward (1968) *The Eucharist*. Trans. N.D. Smith. London and Sydney: Sheed and Ward.

Schleiermacher, Friedrich (1836) *Introductions to the Dialogues of Plato*. Trans. William Dobson. Cambridge: J. and J.J. Deighton.

------ (1978) 'The Hermeneutics: Outline of the 1819 Lectures'. Trans. Jan Wojcik and Roland Haas. *New Literary History* 10: 1-16.

------ (1998) *Hermeneutics and Criticism and Other Writings*. Ed. and trans. Andrew Bowie. Cambridge: Cambridge University Press.

Schmitz-Emans, Monika (2001) 'Sprachphilosophie'. *Die Wende von der Aufklärung zur Romantik 1760-1820*, Ed. Horst Albert Gläser and György

Vajda. Amsterdam and Philadelphia: John Benjamins, 545-66.

Schneider, Wolfgang Ludwig (1992) 'Hermeneutik Sozialer Systeme. Konvergenzen zwischen Systemtheorie und philosophischer Hermeneutik'. *Zeitschrift für Soziologie* 21(6): 420-39.

Schoneveld, C.W. (1992) *'t Word grooter plas, maar niet zoo't was. Nederlandse beschouwingen over vertalen 1670-1760.* The Hague: Bibliographia Neerlandica.

Schroeder, H.J. (1978) *Canons and Decrees of the Council of Trent.* Rockford (Ill.): Tan Books. First publ. 1941.

Schwanitz, Dietrich (1990) *Systemtheorie und Literatur.* Opladen: Westdeutscher Verlag.

------ (1990a) 'Selbstreferentielle Systeme'. *Zeitschrift für Literaturwissenschaft und Linguistik* 77: 100-25.

------ (1995) 'Systems Theory according to Niklas Luhmann. Its Environment and Conceptual Strategies'. *Cultural Critique* 30: 137-70.

------ (1996) 'Systems Theory and the Difference between Communication and Consciousness: An Introduction to a Problem and its Context'. *Modern Language Notes* 111: 488-505.

Schwarz, Werner (1955) *Principles and Problems of Biblical Translation. Some Reformation Controversies and their Background.* Cambridge: Cambridge University Press.

Screech, M.A. (1980) *Erasmus: Ecstasy and the Praise of Folly.* London: Penguin.

Searle, John (1979) *Expression and Meaning. Studies in the Theory of Speech Acts.* Cambridge: Cambridge University Press.

Sevänen, Erkki (2001) 'Art as an Autopoietic Sub-System of Modern Society. A Critical Analysis of the Concepts of Art and Autopoietic Systems in Luhmann's Late Production'. *Theory, Culture & Society* 18(1): 75-103.

Seymour, M.C. (1975) Ed. *On the Properties of Things. John Trevisa's Translation of Bartholomeus Anglicus De Proprietatibus Rerum. A Critical Text.* 3 vols. Oxford: Clarendon.

Sinclair, Ian (1984) *The Vienna Convention on the Law of Treaties.* 2nd ed. Manchester: Manchester University Press.

Sinn, Elisabeth (1995) 'Yan Fu'. Chan and Pollard 1995, 429-47.

Skinner, Quentin (1970) 'Conventions and the Understanding of Speech Acts'. *Philosophical Quarterly* 20: 118-38.

Spencer Brown, George (1969) *Laws of Form.* London: George Allen and Unwin.

Sperber, Dan (1985) 'Interpretive Ethnography and Theoretical Anthropology'. *On Anthropological Knowledge. Three Essays.* Cambridge and Paris: Cambridge University Press and Editions de la Maison des Sciences de l'Homme, 9-34.

------ and Wilson, Deirdre (1981) 'Irony and the Use-Mention Distinction'. *Radical Pragmatics*, Ed. Peter Cole. New York etc.: Academic Press, 295-318.

------ (1986) *Relevance. Communication and Cognition*. Oxford: Blackwell.

------ (1998) 'Irony and Relevance. A reply to Seto, Hamamoto and Yamanashi'. *Relevance Theory. Applications and Implications*, Eds. Robyn Carston and Seiji Uchida. Amsterdam and Philadelphia: John Benjamins, 283-93.

------ (2004) 'Relevance Theory'. *The Handbook of Pragmatics*, Eds. Laurence Horn and Gregory Ward. Oxford: Blackwell, 607-32.

Stegeman, Jelle (1991) *Übersetzung und Leser. Untersuchungen zur Übersetzungs-äquivalenz dargestellt an der Rezeption von Multatulis* Max Havelaar *und seinen deutschen Übersetzungen*. Berlin and New York: De Gruyter.

Steiner, George (1975) *After Babel. Aspects of Language and Translation*. Oxford: Oxford University Press.

Stych, F. S. (1995) *Boccaccio in English. A Bibliography of Editions, Adaptations, and Criticism.* Westport and London: Greenwood.

Sutcliff, E.F. (1948) 'The Council of Trent on the *Authentia* of the Vulgate'. *Journal of Theological Studies* 49: 120-39.

Taivalkoski-Shilov, Kristiina (2006) *La tierce main. Le discours rapporté dans les traductions françaises de Fielding au XVIIIe siècle*. Arras : Artois Presses Université.

Turner, H.E.W. (1972) 'The Eucharistic Presence'. *Thinking about the Eucharist. Essays by members of the Archbishops' Commission on Christian Doctrine,* London: SCM Press, 99-114.

Tymoczko, Maria (2005) 'Trajectories of Research in Translation Studies'. *Meta* 50: 1082-97.

------ (2006) 'Reconceptualising Translation Theory. Integrating Non-Western Thought about Translation'. Hermans 2006, 13-32.

Valerius Maximus (2000) *Memorable Doings and Sayings*. Ed. and trans. D.R. Shackleton Bailey. Cambridge (Mass.) and London: Harvard University Press.

Venuti, Lawrence (1995) *The Translator's Invisibility. A History of Translation*. London and New York: Routledge.

------ (1998) *The Scandals of Translation*. London and New York: Routledge.

------ (2004) Ed. *The Translation Studies Reader*. 2nd ed. London and New York: Routledge.

Vermeer, Hans (2006) *Luhmann's "Social Systems" Theory: Preliminary Fragments for a Theory of Translation*. Berlin: Frank and Timme.

------ (2006a) *Versuch einer Intertheorie der Translation*. Berlin: Frank and Timme.

Vickers, Brian (1988) *In Defence of Rhetoric*. Oxford: Clarendon.

------ (1996) Ed. *Francis Bacon*. Oxford and New York: Oxford University Press.

Wadensjö, Cecilia (1998) *Interpreting as Interaction*. London and New York: Longman.

Wagner, Emma; Bech, Svend and Martínez, Jesús (2002) *Translating for the European Union Institutions*. Manchester: St Jerome.

Waitangi (s.d.) Treaty of Waitangi, with translations and commentary. http://www.treatyofwaitangi.govt.nz/

Wang Nin (1996) 'Towards a Translation Study in the Context of Chinese-Western Comparative Culture Studies'. *Perspectives* 4(1): 43-52.

Wang Zongyan (1995) 'Linguistic Aspects of CE/EC Translation'. Chan and Pollard 1995, 559-67.

Wang Zuoliang. (1995) 'Translation Standards'. Chan and Pollard 1995, 999-1003.

Waquet, Françoise (2001) *Latin, or the Empire of a Sign*. Trans. John Howe. London and New York: Verso.

Waterworth, J. (1848) *The Canons and Decrees of the Sacred and Œcumenical Council of Trent*. London: Burns and Oates; New York: Catholic Publication Society Company.

Wendel, François (1963) *Calvin. Origins and Development of his Religious Thought*. Trans. Philip Maier. Durham (NC): Labyrinth.

Werber, Niels (1992) *Literatur als System. Zur Ausdifferenzierung literarischer Kommunikation*. Opladen: Westdeutscher Verlag.

Wheen, Francis (1999) *Karl Marx*. London: Fourth Estate.

Wilson, Deirdre and Sperber, Dan (1992) 'On Verbal Irony'. *Lingua* 87: 53-76.

Winch, Peter (1964) 'Understanding a Primitive Society'. *American Philosophical Quarterly* 1: 307-24.

Wogan-Brown, Jocelyn; Watson, Nicholas; Taylor, Andrew and Ruth Evans (1999) Eds. *The Idea of the Vernacular. An Anthology of Middle English Literary Theory, 1280-1520*. Exeter: University of Exeter Press.

Wong Wang-chi, Lawrence (1999) 'An Act of Violence. Translation of Western Fiction in the Late Qing and Early Republican Period'. *The Literary Field of Twentieth-Century China*, Ed. Michel Hockx. Surrey: Curzon, 21-42.

------ (1999a) 'Beyond *Xin Da Ya*: Translation Problems in the Late Qing'. Manuscript, University of Göttingen lecture.

Woods, Michelle (2006) *Translating Milan Kundera*. Clevedon. Buffalo and Toronto: Multilingual Matters.

Woudhuysen, Henry (2004) 'The Natural Thing', *Times Literary Supplement*, 2 April 2004: 29.

Wu Jingrong (1995) 'Chinese-English Dictionaries'. Chan and Pollard 1995, 519-32.

Xing Lu (1998) *Rhetoric in Ancient China, Fifth to Third Century BCE. A Comparison with Classical Greek Rhetoric*. Columbia (SC): University of South Carolina Press.

Zhang Longxi (1992) *The Tao and the Logos. Literary Hermeneutics, East and West*. Durham and London: Duke Unversity Press.

------ (1998) *Mighty Opposites. From Dichotomies to Differences in the Comparative Study of China*. Stanford: Stanford University Press.

------ (2005) *Allegoresis. Reading Canonical Literature East and West*. Ithaca and London: Cornell University Press.

Zukofsky, Louis and Celia (1969) *Catullus (Gaii Catulli Veronensis liber)*. London: Cape Goliard; New York: Grossman.

Index